Revel for *Texts and Contexts*

REVEL is Pearson's newest way of delivering our respected content. Fully digital and highly engaging, REVEL offers an immersive learning experience designed for the way today's students read, think, and learn. Enlivening course content with media interactives and assessments, REVEL empowers educators to increase engagement with the course and to connect better with students.

Video and Rich Multimedia Content

Videos, audio recordings, and multimedia instruction provide context that enables students to engage with the text in a more meaningful way.

Interactive Readings and Exercises

Students explore readings through interactive texts. Robust annotation tools allow students to take notes, and post-reading assignments let instructors monitor their students' completion of readings before class begins.

Just-in-Time Context

Just-in-time context—encompassing biographical, historical, and social insights—is incorporated throughout, giving students a deeper understanding of what they read.

Integrated Writing Assignments

Minimal-stakes, low-stakes, and high-stakes writing tasks allow students multiple opportunities to interact with the ideas presented in the reading assignments, ensuring that they come to class better prepared.

TEXTS AND CONTEXTS

Writing About Literature
with Critical Theory

Seventh Edition

STEVEN LYNN

University of South Carolina

PEARSON

Boston Columbus Indianapolis New York San Francisco
Amsterdam Cape Town Dubai London Madrid Milan Munich Paris Montréal Toronto
Delhi Mexico City São Paulo Sydney Hong Kong Seoul Singapore Taipei Tokyo

For Annette and Anna

Senior Editor: Brad Potthoff
Program Manager: Anne Shure
Product Marketing Manager: Nicholas T. Bolt
Field Marketing Manager: Joyce Nilsen
Media Producer: Elizabeth Bravo
Content Producer: Julia Pomann
Media Editor: Christine Stavrou
Project Manager: Donna Campion
Text Design, Project Coordination, and Electronic Page Makeup: Lumina Datamatics, Inc.
Design Lead: Beth Paquin
Cover Designer: Studio Montage
Cover Illustration: Alex Stokes/123RF (puzzle image), Sergey Nivens/Fotolia (tree image)
Senior Manufacturing Buyer: Roy L. Pickering, Jr.
Printer/Binder: RR Donnelley / Crawfordsville
Cover Printer: Phoenix Color/Hagerstown

Acknowledgments of third-party content appear on page[s] 262–263, which constitute an extension of this copyright page.

Library of Congress Cataloging-in-Publication is on file with the Library of Congress.

10 9 8 7 6 5 4 3 2 1—V055—19 18 17 16

Student Edition ISBN 10: 0-321-94562-X
Student Edition ISBN 13: 978-0-321-94562-4
A la Carte Edition ISBN 10: 0-13-411725-5
A la Carte Edition ISBN 13: 978-0-13-411725-6

Brief Contents

Contents

4   Creating the Text: Reader-Response Criticism   73

7 Minding the Work: Psychological Criticism   195

Preface

As teachers, we need to remember what the world looked like before we learned our discipline's way of seeing it. We need to show our students the patient and painstaking processes by which we achieved expertise. Only by making our footsteps visible can we expect students to follow in them.

—Sam Wineburg, Professor, Stanford University
The Chronicle of Higher Education (4/11/03), B20

Literature offers all of us a lifetime of fascinating, mind-expanding experience. This seventh edition aims to help enlightened teachers guide their students to the joys of reading and writing about literature. My strategy involves invigorating literary study by "making our footsteps visible," as Sam Wineburg puts it above—by considering explicitly what adept readers know and assume and how they behave in their engagements with literary texts. There are many fine overviews of literature and how to write about it, of critical theory and literary theory, and you'll find a good sampling of them recommended here as you go along. But I do not think that there is another book so thoroughly committed to showing students, at an introductory level, step by step, how to use different critical strategies to write about literature.

NEW TO THE SEVENTH EDITION

I will say in a moment why this effort is so important, whether you want to be an anthropologist or a zoologist or anything in-between, but I am required by law (no kidding) to begin on the first page of this preface some explanation of what's new in this seventh edition. Like Bill Murray in the 1993 film *Groundhog Day*, I am increasingly aware of how very fortunate I am to have had a chance to re-do this book multiple times. I have benefited from suggestions by both teachers and students (my own and others'). I don't know if this edition will usher in February 3rd (you need to see the movie), but it certainly is an improvement.

SPECIFICALLY:

- Students will find **learning objectives** at the beginning of every chapter reflecting the content that appears in that chapter.

- I have made **stylistic improvements** throughout, tightening some sentences, deleting some, adding examples, clarifying possible obscurities. I've been occasionally thrilled to discover students who have read more than they were assigned, who read some part of the book by their own free will. My goal with every sentence has been to try for a reading experience that is pleasurable, clear, useful, and makes you want to pick up a literary work to see how all this plays out.

- I've **updated the references to other works and to the various approaches**. Literary criticism, like any human endeavor, is dynamic. New books, new ideas, new editions of other books—I've tried to capture these and reflect the evolution of the field of literary study.

- I give a lot more attention to the value of literary study in this edition, including my **Top Ten Reasons to Study Literature** in Chapter One. We have in recent years had an epidemic of Chicken Littles forecasting the decline of literary studies and the inevitable demise of the English department; observing that we are returning to an oral culture, and therefore writing and what has been written are going to fade from importance; and stressing the critical importance of turning our resources toward science and engineering. It's important to remind ourselves why literary study powerfully prepares us for useful and enjoyable lives.

  I am acutely aware of the student who feels the pressure to earn a living, to prepare to get a job, and who wonders how poetry and fiction can possibly be helpful. Understanding other people and their motivations, reading carefully and critically, speaking and writing clearly and persuasively—these are important abilities in just about every endeavor, and they are nurtured by literary study, as I explain in some detail.

- **Film and other genres get more attention**, underscoring the idea that critical theories can be usefully applied to any "text." Given the porous boundaries of literary study, film and other genres are increasingly being included in literature courses.

- The **addition of ecocriticism and digital humanities**: I've added some notice of ecocriticism, a particularly exciting kind of political stance, in the survey of critical theories in Chapter Two. I've also added some consideration of digital humanities, which is (I think) more of a tool for the variety of approaches rather than a distinctive approach in itself. It is possible, however, that this rapidly expanding tool may alter our ends as well as our means.

- I have continued to find sentences and references to trim down or delete or rephrase. I appreciate the help of my own students, who, sometimes with greater enthusiasm than I expected, have identified weak or boring or confusing sentences and ideas in the book. Many newer resources appear in the suggested readings at the end of every chapter. These are some terrific resources, and you really should check them out.

- An **updated Instructor's Manual** will provide, among other things, a discussion of possible answers to the questions in the "Practicing" sections, including the new works. The Instructor's Manual also considers how to build a syllabus around this book, and it offers guidance on how to assign enough writing to make a difference without sinking under the paper load. Sample student papers and ideas for in-class activities are also featured.

- Some earlier editions of this text offered in the final chapter a step-by-step explanation of how to write a research paper. Over the years, that chapter seemed increasingly unnecessary, and so it has been moved aside. If you miss that chapter, or just want to see what's in it, email me and I'll be happy to send it to you (stevenwlynn@gmail.com). The current edition of the *MLA Handbook for Writers of Research Papers* offers a thorough explanation of all things related to writing a research paper.

- *Texts and Contexts* is available in REVEL™, "a fully digital and immersive learning experience designed for the way today's students read, think, and learn," as my publisher describes it. I expect that this new digital platform will provide students with even more ideas about how to incorporate critical theories into their writing.

WHAT'S HERE, AND WHY IT MATTERS

So, why is it so important to explain in such detail the variety of critical approaches available, and the process to apply them? Reading and writing about anything can be difficult, even frustrating, especially if you do not have a clear understanding of what you are trying to accomplish and how to go about your task. Literature poses some particular challenges because it embodies our most thoughtful, imaginative, stimulating writing—and thus also offers some unique rewards. The endeavor to understand literature is important because you are important. If you can read and write about literature more effectively and satisfyingly, then you can read and write about anything more effectively and satisfyingly. Every discipline and field of study depends upon various assumptions about language, meaning, and knowledge; and every discipline involves reading and writing, interpreting data, and constructing arguments. Critical theory and literary study are thus vitally important. Every educated person can and should understand the fundamentals involved.

When the first edition of this book came out, in 1994, critical theory had pretty much already moved beyond its most controversial and intoxicating phase. I remember vividly getting into an elevator in 1981 at the Modern Language Association convention, the meeting for college teachers in English and

foreign language departments, and overhearing an argument between two professors—one insisting that he would not allow his department to hire someone
who was a fan of absurd French critical fads, and the other saying that he was
embarrassed to be in the same department with someone so backward and pre-
historic. By 1994, even the most conservative faculty had to admit that theory
did not appear to be going away anytime soon, and the most progressive faculty were surfing on a wave of theoretical excitement. What was happening in
the study of literature was, many people felt, relevant to every field, including
even the sciences. Today however, in part because of those intrepid theorists,
undermining assumptions, dismantling foundations, the value of the humanities seems much more uncertain. The world problems that we were going to
solve by reading French theorists or Emily Dickinson seem to have persisted,
mutated, and multiplied. The need remains, however, to understand how we
make sense, and especially how we make sense of literary texts. It is in fact even
more important today that we understand how our assumptions and strategies
may create meaning—as the rest of this book will argue.

The first two chapters prepare students for the in-depth tour of the world
of critical theory in Chapters 3 through 8. The first chapter addresses some
fundamental questions: "Is there one correct interpretation of a literary work?"
"Are all opinions equally valid?" "Does theory distract from literary study?"
"Is theory too difficult for an introductory-level course?" The answers to these
deceptively simple questions underscore both the necessity and the feasibility of
working with theory in introductory courses. The second chapter then offers a
survey of the theories covered here, illustrating a variety of approaches by explaining how each one might be applied to the same text.

Each particular theoretical orientation is in a sense like a different place,
a different culture that inhabits its own set of values and practices. The maps
at the beginnings of these chapters are intended as playful reminders of this
insight: each theory involves a different way of seeing. The first section in each
chapter is an orientation: the basic principles of a particular theoretical orientation are explored and articulated as clearly as possible. In "The Purpose of
New Criticism," for instance, which is the first part of Chapter 3, an analysis of an Archibald MacLeish poem reveals the assumptions of what is called
New Criticism. The second section of each theory chapter explains the process
of applying these assumptions. In Chapter 3 for example, the section entitled
"How to Do New Criticism" takes students step by step through the process of
"doing" a New Critical reading.

The third section of these chapters illustrates the construction of an essay,
from start to finish, using that chapter's theory. The sample essay in Chapter 3
traces the evolution of an essay on Gwendolyn Brooks's masterful poem, "The
Mother." The fourth and final section provides some materials to practice
upon—works that will resonate in some way with the other works in the chapter. In "Practicing New Criticism," for instance, three works about fatherhood
are offered to complement in some sense Brooks's "The Mother." The tour of
each theory includes recommendations for "Further Reading."

ACKNOWLEDGMENTS

To those people who have adopted a previous edition, I am especially grateful. Students may not have chosen this book, but I do deeply appreciate their use of it, and I cherish every bit of feedback I've gotten from them. Many of my friends and colleagues have helped me, sometimes when I was walking across campus or losing golf balls, and I want to thank them all. I'm especially indebted to Bill Rivers, Ed Madden, and Lee Bauknight, my fellow teacher-trainers years ago, and to the many dozens of graduate students who have taken English 701B with me, and who helped to establish that this pedagogy works.

I also want to thank the following reviewers, who have made useful suggestions for this or previous editions: Jon Adams, Western Michigan University; Patricia Angley, University of Central Florida; Stephen Barber, University of Rhode Island; M. Bracher, Kent State University; Suzanne Bunkers, Minnesota State University; Maria Carrig, Carthage College; Bryon Lee Grigsby, Centenary College; Harold Hellwig, Idaho State University; Catherine Lewis, Louisiana State University; Leslie Lockett, Ohio State University; Judith K. Moore, University of Alaska; Warren Moore, Ball State University; Jessica O'Hara, Pennsylvania State University; B. Orton, Truman State University; Kandy Robertson, Washington State University; Sally Bishop Shigley, Weber State University, Jack Fisher Solomon, California State University Northridge; and Don Ulin, University of Pittsburgh at Bradford.

I celebrate the existence of Erika Berg, who helped me develop this book. Anne Shure has been an extremely patient and helpful manuscript developer, and Joseph Terry, who has been the editor-in-chief for my recent editions, continues to be much appreciated by me. My brothers and sisters, congenital and acquired, have provided comfort, counsel, and comic relief at various opportune moments. Gregory Jay and David Miller got me interested in critical theory, and I appreciate their patience so long ago. Karl Beason, Todd Stebbins, and Ken Autry helped me develop these ideas as we worked with Advanced Placement high school teachers. My colleagues in the English Department and in the South Carolina Honors College are an inspiration to me, and I am fortunate to have been able to work at the University of South Carolina for over thirty years now.

Everything depends upon and is made real by my wife and daughter, Annette and Anna, to whom this book is dedicated.

STEVEN LYNN
COLUMBIA, SC
MAY 2015

TEXTS AND CONTEXTS

CHAPTER ▮

An Introduction, Theoretically

We should study literary criticism and the theories of literature for the same reasons we read literature—to forever alter our perspectives, to escape our own vanities, and to extend the horizons of our limitations.

—Lynn Jordan Stidom

What you'll learn in this chapter:

- To explain the relationship of literary study to intellectual and personal development.
- To explain the relationship of critical theories to interpretation.
- To use this book effectively.

TEXTUAL TOURS

Why should we read literature? Why should we talk and write about it? With so many problems in the world—from drug-resistant microbes to global climate change, from outrageous acts of terrorism to violently repressive regimes—do we really have the luxury to ponder literary art? You'd be surprised, wouldn't you, if I said, "No, I suppose not," and the rest of this book contained my thoughts on bluegrass music and extraterrestrials. We do, in fact, know that literary study, in uniquely powerful ways, helps to prepare us for rewarding and meaningful lives. We know this from thousands of years of educational and cultural history; from research in linguistics, cognitive psychology, brain imaging, and neuroscience; and from personal testimonies and common sense.[1] No other reading experience or learning activity duplicates this foundation.

It is, to be sure, entirely possible to be dull, mean, boring, even evil, and read great gobs of literature. You may know someone who goes to the gym regularly and still is in lousy shape, or someone who's had months of violin lessons and can't play a decent scale (um, this might be me), or someone who has traveled to exotic lands and failed to notice much of anything different from home. There are no guarantees. It is theoretically possible that not all English professors, including the ones who read a lot of literature, are entirely charming and happy. Sometimes people are remarkably impervious to their experiences. But you certainly increase your chances of getting into shape, playing an instrument skillfully, or experiencing another culture if you go to the gym, take lessons, or travel. And you increase your chances of being the most insightful, persuasive, engaged, and productive person possible if, among other things, you have meaningfully rich experiences with literature throughout your life.

A large claim, yes: But reading and writing about literature does something especially valuable for your mind.

1. **Imagination:** "Literature" in the sense of fiction, poetry, and drama cultivates the imagination by asking us to envision what isn't, to create another reality, to think otherwise. That's one reason despots and dictators hate literature and free expression, banning or strictly controlling verbal freedoms. From the ancient Greeks to the present day, cultures steeped in literary study have flourished because of their creativity and innovation.

2. **Communication:** Although "literature" can refer to any body of writing, as in "the literature on measles and vaccines" or "the literature on Egyptian embalming," the term usually indicates some kind of value judgment, implicitly claiming "this is an example of our best writing, the most interesting, most deserving of careful attention." By studying those uses of language that our culture values most, which we tend to call "literature," our own ability to use language effectively is likely to be enhanced.

3. **Analysis:** Literary works—whether fiction, poetry, drama, creative nonfiction—invite readers to make connections, to weigh evidence, to question, to notice details, to see *this* and infer *that*: to make sense. Students may sometimes wonder, "If that's what the author meant, why didn't he or she just *say that*?" The answer in part is that literature is suggestive, opening up a role for the reader. The analytical abilities called for in our reading, which are fundamental life skills, almost certainly improve with practice. Reading literature offers that practice in a way that is often stimulating, entertaining, and moving.

4. **Empathy:** Literature leads us to inhabit different perspectives, which may be similar to our own, or vastly different, or something in between. Reading literature, we can explore how other people see the world. We may come to accept or even agree with others, or we may disagree vigorously with them, but in any event literature offers a pathway to empathy and dialogue.

5. **Story-making:** We think in terms of stories: A longtime bachelor inherits a schnoodle puppy, and several months later he is proposing marriage to his new girlfriend. We naturally try to see some link between these events, and we also naturally try to anticipate what is going to happen next. People who've experienced more stories tend to be better able to construct narratives and think about possible actions and consequences.

6. **Agility:** Literary works often ask us to think in complex ways, to hold contradictory or apparently conflicting ideas in our minds. Our tendency is to classify people and events, but perhaps a particular character is both a villain and a hero; perhaps a thoughtless gesture is also a brilliant insight. We need to be able to resist closure, to un-decide things sometimes and look again. As brain imaging has shown, this kind of complex processing helps us to be more mentally flexible and nimble—more open to new ideas. It's uncomfortable sometimes, but also invigorating. When we can't change our minds, when we know everything important (in our own estimation at least), then in some sense we're intellectually dead.

7. **Knowledge:** Literature can vividly give us access to places, times, and cultures that we could not experience otherwise—the antebellum South, the nineteenth-century whaling industry, tenant farmers during the Great Depression. Works of fiction can convey facts and truths in powerful ways, and works of nonfiction (histories, biographies, travel narratives, autobiographies, and more) may be so well-written that we consider them to be "literature," worthy of our careful attention.

8. **Wisdom:** Literature often encourages us to examine and question our values, to think about the purpose of life, about the significance and meaning of what we are trying to do. We may value literary works for the way that they are written, or for the ideas that they convey—and sometimes for both.

9. **Inspiration:** Writers that we value use words in ways that move us. Readers throughout the ages have found reasons to live, and ways to live, in literature.

10. **Fun:** If you don't find literature to be a whole lot of fun, you are almost certainly reading the wrong things (too difficult, too removed

from your interests; unskilled, uninsightful) and/or you are almost certainly not reading enough. Sometimes just the *requirement* to read something is enough to make it unappealing. But great literature wasn't originally assigned reading. The ordinary people in Elizabethan England weren't required to attend Shakespeare's plays. This may be mind-boggling to students who aren't quite ready to appreciate Shakespeare, but many of his contemporaries apparently loved his work. They paid good money *to stand outside* (usually) and experience his plays. When you do discover the fun of literature, if you haven't already, you'll want to read and experience more and more, vaulting forward in verbal skills and reasoning abilities, and becoming a better reader of other kinds of texts (scientific articles, memos, legal briefs, political speeches, love letters, etc.).

As Lynn Jordan Stidom put it on an exam when she was a student (quoted in my epigraph), we study literature and literary criticism "to forever alter our perspectives, to escape our own vanities, and to extend the horizons of our limitations." These reasons to read and write about literature sound a lot like the reasons we should travel, and I'd like to elaborate for a moment on the idea that literary works are, in a way, like places we can visit. Some are foreign, mysterious, puzzling; others make us feel right at home. Some call us back again and again; others we feel obliged to experience, knowing they'll do us good even though we may never fully enjoy them. We can just go places, seeking distraction and enjoyment, but travel is most likely to enrich our lives when we express our thoughts about what we've experienced. And we ought to write about literature and other cultural experiences for some of the same reasons that we like to write and think about where we've been. Indeed, we send postcards and letters back home, we make pictures and even movies (for sometimes captive audiences), in part because we want to share our experiences with others, but also because we want to capture and reconsider and ponder and make sense of our travels for ourselves. Life is the journey, it's often said, but reflecting on where you've been can be the most meaningful part of that journey.

Although wandering around is always an option, travelers who know what they're looking for and have a plan for getting there are often more likely to have satisfying, interesting excursions. Literary criticism aims to bring such order and organization to our experience of literary works, focusing our attention, putting various parts together, helping us comprehend what we see. When you write about literature, you serve as a kind of tour guide, leading your reader (and yourself) through the work. Readers and travelers usually can see what's in front of them, but they don't necessarily know what to make of it without some persuasive commentary or explanation. Plus, different readers have different interests and backgrounds, and they necessarily bring different insights and desires to a work. Some travelers, with lots of miles, keen eyes, and fertile imaginations, may tend to provide especially wonderful guides and reports, but even inexperienced travelers may come upon marvels, and notice things that no one else has seen in quite the same way. Even if you are an unseasoned traveler in the literary world, you just can't substitute someone else's experience for your own: Don't believe that anyone's "Notes," whether by Clifford or Sparkie or your best friend, will expand your horizons or deepen your awareness in the same way as a firsthand encounter. Even the people who sell these literary guides do not expect them to be substitutes for the real thing. And absolutely don't believe that you have nothing of importance to say. To be sure, we all can benefit from the advice and guidance of genuine experts, of scholars who publish in academic journals and with university presses. Your teachers and reference librarians can help you locate this kind of reliable and helpful commentary. But you have to see the (literary) world for yourself first and foremost. It would seem silly to pay someone else to go to an exotic place and then come back and tell you about it.

Critical theories are like the different travel agencies through which the various tour guides generally work. Different agencies feature different kinds of tours, just as different theories generate different kinds of readings: One specializes in cultural immersion, another in artistic appreciation, another in historical recollection, another in personal indulgence. The agencies provide the frameworks, the general guidelines for the performances of the tour guides. "The Museums of London," "Shakespeare's London," "Supernatural London," and "The Pubs of London" are all tours of the same city, but they start from very different assumptions about what the travelers are there for. A theory is a set of assumptions, a context for assigning value, making meaning, and guiding behavior. If you are familiar with a variety of theories, then you're able to draw upon a wider range of assumptions and strategies as a reader; you're better able to see how other readers are motivated. If an assignment asks you to focus on the formal features of a literary work, you're less likely, given some familiarity with various critical theories, to concentrate on how the work affects you personally, or on how it reflects its author's psychological state, or its racial and ethnic implications.

Just as no one who is living in any significant sense can avoid having a personality, it is impossible to read (meaningfully) without some theoretical orientation. Even the belief that one should just experience a text without saying anything about it, without any self-consciousness,

without considering one's own purposes or suppositions, without exploring other ways of reading—even this effort to evade a theoretical stance
is itself theoretical. It stands to reason, then, that some understanding of
the kinds of tours available, and how they might be combined or adapted,
will be valuable and reassuring. The goal of this book is to give you a
working understanding of a variety of critical theories and practices.
You won't find every theory covered here, and I freely affirm that many
complexities and controversies and ambiguities have been passed over in
the pursuit of clarity and usefulness. This is, after all, an introduction, a
starting point, for people who have some familiarity with required literary study but who aren't familiar with different strategies for talking and
writing about literature. If you've ever read a literary work or a writing
assignment in a literature class and wondered "now what?"—then this is
the book for you.

CHECKING SOME BAGGAGE

Before we launch, let's consider some basic questions often asked by
embarking students, and then map out the purpose and plan of this book.

"Is There One Correct Interpretation of a Literary Work?"

Perhaps there are English teachers somewhere who truly believe that they
have the correct interpretation of a literary work—the only reading of, say,
Hamlet that their students will ever need, and their job is simply to pass it
along to students. But most teachers (and certainly your own if this book has
been assigned) cherish variety and difference in literary criticism, encouraging students to think for themselves when they write about literature. Just as
there is no one best place to view the Blue Ridge Mountains, so there is no
one best reading of *Hamlet* or any work (although it might be fun to argue
about such things). Shift your vantage point a little, change your interests,
or just let some time pass, and you'll see something new.

"So, Are All Opinions About Literature Equally Valid?"

Still, surely some opinions seem more convincing or satisfying than others.
Endorsing variety doesn't necessarily mean that all opinions are equal, that
any piece of literary criticism is just as good as any other. Just because we

appreciate various views of the mountains, we need not also agree that all vantage points are equally satisfying to all people at all times. A geologist, a botanist, an artist, and a civil engineer might see the mountains in very different ways. If you construct a reading of *Hamlet* this week and a different interpretation next week, it's unlikely that you or your readers will value both of them equally or even that everyone will agree on which one is superior. Some readings are arguably better than others, but to make such a determination, we need first to ask: Better for what? Better for whom? This book aims to address such questions, attempting not only to explain clearly and explicitly how to use various critical approaches but also to assess what purposes different approaches are likely to serve (better for what), as well as what sort of audience is likely to be influenced and even created by different critical strategies (better for whom).

Consider, for instance, the photograph below: What does it mean?

- Are these men standing so close together because they're close friends? Are they from some other culture, in which men stand this close? Are they, in fact, standing unusually close, or am I revealing something about myself in asking this question?

© AP Images

- Are they father and son, perhaps—genetically disposed to superior beards? Is that the wife/mother in between and behind them? What is the expression on her face?
- Are they trying to kiss, and laughing because their caps are getting in the way? The younger man's attire does have sort of a Village People look. Is it possible these men are gay?
- Does this scene seem somehow staged or unreal? Are they actors or politicians? Don't they seem a little too jovial?
- Is it possible these men never actually met? Perhaps the picture has an air of unreality about it because it is a computer-generated fake? Perhaps these are wax models?

Some of these suggestions no doubt seem less plausible than others, but it would be difficult to exclude totally even the wackiest of readings on the basis of the picture alone, wouldn't it?

So let's see what happens when we bring different contexts to this image. The photograph, as you may know, famously captures Ernest Hemingway, the great American writer (on the left), talking in May 1960 with Fidel Castro, Cuba's legendary leader. One of many possible frames for "reading" this photograph would be President Obama's call in December 2014 for the United States to normalize relations with Cuba. Fifty years of isolation, Obama noted, have not worked, and "It's time for a new approach," he said. Once upon a time, the photograph might suggest, Hemingway and Castro seem to have been getting along very well. Why shouldn't their countries be friendly again?

This interpretive move involves seeing Hemingway and Castro in symbolic terms, as standing for in some sense the United States and Cuba. Both men certainly are mythic figures, larger than life. As a brilliant writer, able to express his dreams and desires, Hemingway, we might say, embodies the openness, creativity, and accomplishment of the United States. His casual shirt and comfortable cap contrast sharply with Castro's militaristic hat and stiffly starched uniform, just as the freedom and democracy of America contrast with the oppressive state control of communist Cuba. Even the backdrop of the photo supports this reading, with a window and vegetation behind Hemingway (American prosperity and openness), and a starkly blank wall behind Castro (poverty and repression).

But a supporter of Castro's Cuba might say that my own context as an American is skewing my interpretation and offer an alternative: The aging Hemingway, in his floppy cap and rumpled shirt, partially unbuttoned, is not a symbol of creativity and freedom; instead, a fan of Castro might say, Hemingway represents America's moral and social bankruptcy, its weak self-indulgence. A few months after this photograph was taken, Hemingway left Cuba, never to return, and slightly more than a year afterward, in mental and physical distress, he used his favorite shotgun to commit suicide in Idaho. Despite the appearance of health in the photograph, a Cuban nationalist might remind us that Hemingway was married to his fourth wife at that time, drinking heavily, and behaving erratically. America, like Hemingway, one might argue from this communist Cuban context, is headed toward its own inevitable decline and self-annihilation, while Castro's Cuba, based on his disciplined vigor, will continue to live on and on.

Many other contexts are possible. For a third, consider that in September 1994 this image appeared in Michael Elliott's *Newsweek* article on President Clinton's Cuban policies, where it was captioned "Tangled up in Myths: Hemingway with the Cuban leader in 1960" (p. 26). Elliott's point in his article was that U.S. attitudes toward Cuba are clouded by fantasies and misperceptions. When we think of Cuba, we tend to think of "romance, casinos, and marlin," of Hemingway, Jimmy Buffett, and relaxing in the island sun. We think, Elliott says, of Cuba as an extension of the United States—our playground, our tropical resort. Hemingway lived off and on in Cuba from 1939 until 1960, writing, fishing, breeding cats (his famous polydactyl cats were in Key West, but he also had Cuban cats), enjoying visits from his three sons, drinking, and partying. According to Jacobo Timerman, who toured Cuba years later, in 1987, "no worship is promoted more in Cuba than that of Ernest Hemingway," with the exception, of course, of their revolutionary founders, Castro and Che Guevara (68). The tourist, Timerman writes, "gets the impression that Hemingway supported Fidel Castro, that the writer is part of the Revolution" (68). Indeed, in 1982 Cuba issued a peso coin with Hemingway's face, another coin featuring his yacht, and a third coin depicting his small fishing boat (in honor of *The Old Man and the Sea*, published in 1952). And in 2010 Cuba issued a "*50 Aniversario*" one peso coin depicting Castro and Hemingway in a pose very nearly the same as this photograph, which is one of a series of photos taken that day.[2]

A more in-depth historical context suggests yet another way of reading the photograph. Researchers believe that Hemingway and Castro in fact likely met only once, as Timerman notes (68), when this photograph was taken at a fishing tournament in Hemingway's honor, which Castro surprisingly enough won. In this context, the photograph works beautifully with Elliott's article, illustrating our misunderstanding of Cuba, which is intertwined with myths about Hemingway. Although it is possible that Castro did actually win the fishing tournament (without a scuba diver putting a fish on his hook, or someone leaning on the scales), even though he was a "novice" at fishing by his own admission ("a lucky novice" Hemingway said),[3] just about everything else we might assume from the photograph certainly seems to be an illusion. In May of 1960 Castro had not admitted publicly that he was a socialist, but he was without doubt an enemy of the United States; he and Hemingway were not close friends; Hemingway was not part of the revolution or a supporter. And in this context, we might make some sense of a minor detail in the photograph—the face just visible between Castro and Hemingway's shoulders. The significance of this woman, who might appear to be an admiring onlooker, becomes in this reading of the photograph's illusions easy to flip: We can see her as representing the common people of Cuba, who are being squeezed out of the picture in Castro's one-man rule, which will purportedly be all about the working class, but in truth obscured, diminished, and ultimately eliminated their power and visibility.

The point I'm emphasizing here is that our understanding of a "text" is shaped by the context in which we see it. This point is not limited to literature or even to written texts, as we are naturally inclined to make meaning out of anything from cloud formations to slight facial movements. If this insight isn't surprising to you, its implications are nonetheless profound— and often overlooked. Although a picture sometimes might, as we say, be worth a thousand words, even a picture can be read in many different ways, including opposing ways. When we think about how to take, or to create, the meaning of anything—a poem, a story, a photograph, a life— we cannot avoid this interplay of texts and contexts. The territory in which we think explicitly about how meaning is made is called "critical theory" or simply "theory."

The modifier "critical" in this context doesn't mean theory that is "inclined to find fault or judge severely"—just as "literary *criticism*" is not devoted to making harsh or negative judgments. "Critical" also means "involving skillful judgment" and "of essential importance" (*Webster's* definitions). Critical theory is thus concerned with those ideas that are essential to the process of making skillful judgments about literature.

ANYTHING TO DECLARE?

Theory Enables Practice

The focus in this text on the assumptions, strategies, and purposes shaping literary criticism—on critical theories in other words—is not a step away from literature or writing about literature; rather, such assumptions, strategies, and purposes make a deeply rewarding engagement with literature possible. Even the simplest acts of literary response, such as "This is boring," depend on a certain theoretical stance, which in this case would include the assumptions that the purpose of literature includes entertaining the reader, and the critic's job includes identifying works that fail this test.

You Already Have a Theoretical Stance

Even if you're unaware of them, some kind of principles guide you in determining what you expect a literary work to do, how you evaluate its performance, what you decide to say about it. (Even the absence of principles constitutes a theoretical position, as does the presence of contradictory principles.) The "elements" of literature, such as plot, character, point of view, are relatively easy to understand, and most students have been through these terms and concepts many times, perhaps without noticing much help from them in interpreting literature. What is harder, and where more guidance is needed, is knowing what to say about such elements—how to approach them and how to use them. In the explanations and illustrations of the various critical approaches presented here, you'll get to see the "elements" in action. You'll see, for instance, how New Criticism, psychological criticism, and deconstruction provide very different views of "character," or "plot," or "theme," giving you a wider range of purposes and strategies in writing about literature.

To begin enhancing your awareness of literary criticism, take an inventory of what you already assume, asking yourself the following questions:

- What do I suppose is the function of literature? What do I look for in a literary work?
- What do I think is the function of writing about literature? What should literary criticism do?
- How do I believe the task of criticism is carried out? What strategies, routines, procedures, and activities do literary critics engage in?

As you try out the various approaches discussed here, you'll be able to compare your own starting assumptions with some of the various options available. At the least, you'll have a better understanding of the critical possibilities, allowing you to understand published criticism more readily; more likely, you'll find yourself incorporating new strategies or stances into your writing about literature, enriching and deepening your insights.

This is an Introduction

Such theoretical work is challenging at times, but it isn't beyond your abilities if you've read this far. There are, to be sure, many controversies, variations, complexities, exceptions, and qualifications that are not treated here. Critical theory can be astonishingly difficult (and often just astonishing). After working through this book, you may find the work of Jacques Derrida or Annette Kolodny more accessible, but they certainly won't be easy to understand—just as an introduction to physics wouldn't make the scientific papers of Steven Hawking or John Wheeler a breeze to comprehend. But there's no reason you shouldn't be told about black holes or deconstruction simply because the theories, in all their specifics and intricacies, are difficult. Few people, if pressed, could read Isaac Newton's foundational works with complete understanding, but just about anyone can understand in a useful way how momentum and gravity work.

This text offers a basic, working understanding of critical theory and practice, freely acknowledging that a more advanced understanding is possible. Is this book's treatment simplified and formulaic? Yes, absolutely. I have tried hard to clarify without distorting, but some matters have no doubt been represented to be simpler than they are. This book aims to be a guided tour suitable for just about anyone. My hope is that it will whet your appetite for more detailed and adventurous critical travel.

Here's the Plan

Unfortunately, there's no way a reasonably sized textbook (one without wheels and a handle) can cover adequately all the different kinds of criticism that can be identified today—even if I understood them all. Nor, as I say, can any one particular theory in all its mutations, combinations, and complexities be presented here. What I can do is provide a practical introduction to a sampling of some of the most influential theories. My goal is simply to put you in a position to develop and refine your understanding, to move into other critical arenas, to evolve your own readings and even theories.

The plan is simple. The second chapter briefly visits all the approaches discussed here by applying them to a single passage. Then, each of the next six chapters inhabits a theory or a cluster of related theories in some detail, again applying the theory or theories to various passages. Essays are evolved step by step from each of the various critical stances, not to provide you with a formula that will work for every text, but rather to give you a sense of how theories are applied. At the end of each chapter you'll find a very select list of suggested further readings. Where it seemed useful, I've annotated these items to give you a better sense of what's out there and where you might want to go from here. Bon voyage!

Notes

1. For a sampling of the research on reading's effects, see, for instance, Maryanne Wolf's *Proust and the Squid: The Story and Science of the Reading Brain*, Alberto Manguel's *A History of Reading*, Gregory Berns and others' "Short- and Long-Term Effects of a Novel on Connectivity in the Brain," and Annie Murphy Paul's "Your Brain on Fiction."

2. For more on these coins, see Dolan and Cuhaj. Images are available at www.coincraft.com, www.ngccoin.com, and other sites for collectors and investors.

3. The encounter between Hemingway and Castro is imagined in a 1960 poem by John Updike, "Meditation on a News Item." The meeting, Timerman's article, and a portion of Updike's poem are discussed in Jon Michaud's "Hemingway, Castro, and Cuba," *New Yorker*, May 24, 2012. Michaud cites *Life* magazine, without a specific reference, as the source for Hemingway's "lucky novice" comment, but I could not locate this quotation in *Life*. It does appear in the 30 May 1960 issue of *Sports Illustrated*. Ron McFarland notes that he was unable to find in *Life* magazine the photograph of Castro and Hemingway that Updike describes, but he points to a similar photograph in Fuentes (facing page 97).

Works Cited and Recommended Further Reading

Adler, Mortimer, and Charles Van Doren. *How to Read a Book*. New York: Simon, 1972. Print. Originally published in 1940, this book still offers valuable advice on "How to Be a Demanding Reader," "How to Use a Dictionary," and much else. Chapter 15 deals with "Suggestions for Reading Stories, Plays, and Poems."

Berns, Gregory, et al. "Short- and Long-Term Effects of a Novel on Connectivity in the Brain." *Brain Connectivity* 3.6 (2013): 590–600. Print.

Bloom, Harold. *How to Read and Why*. New York: Simon, 2000. Print. Offers dozens of dazzling examples of careful and imaginative reading, proceeding from the assumption that by reading great literature we "strengthen the self."

Bressler, Charles. *Literary Criticism: An Introduction to Theory and Practices*. Upper Saddle River, NJ: Prentice, 2003. Print. A thorough overview including a valuable historical survey.

Cuhaj, George S., ed. *2014 Standard Catalogue of World Coins, 2001–*. Blue Ash, OH: F + W Media, Inc., 2013. 316. Print.

Culler, Jonathan. *Literary Theory: A Very Short Introduction*. Oxford: Oxford UP, 2000. Print. Sophisticated yet extremely lucid.

Denby, David. *Great Books: My Adventures with Homer, Rousseau, Woolf, and Other Indestructible Writers of the Western World*. New York: Simon, 1996. Print. An inspiring book for anyone embarking on serious literary studies. Denby, a movie critic, tells the story of his decision at age 48 to return to Columbia University and read great literature.

Dolan, Yossi. *Watercraft on World Coins: America and Asian, 1800-2008*. Sussex: Sussex Academic, 2010. 117, 142–43.

Eagleton, Terry. *How to Read a Poem*. Oxford: Blackwell, 2007. Print. "Like thatching or clog dancing," Eagleton says, "literary criticism seems to be something of a dying art." This book delightfully illustrates how to revive it.

Elliott, Michael. "How Do We Get to the Endgame?" *Newsweek* 5 Sept 1994: 26–27. Print.

Fuentes, Norberto. *Hemingway in Cuba*. Secaucus, NJ: Lyle Stewart, 1984.

Harmon, William, and C. Hugh Holman. *A Handbook to Literature*. 11th ed. Upper Saddle River, NJ: Prentice, 2008. Print. If you want to know what the "Spasmodic School" was, or what a Spoonerism is, or the meaning of just about any other word related to literature, here's a handy place to look. There are many good handbooks, but this one is especially lucid and thorough.

Hirsch, Edward. *How to Read a Poem: And Fall in Love with Poetry*. New York: Harcourt, 2000. Print. As the title suggests, this is a book about the joy, the pleasure, the "ecstatic response" even that constitute perceptive and committed reading.

Lentricchia, Frank, and Thomas McLaughlin. *Critical Terms for Literary Study*. 2nd ed. Chicago: U of Chicago P, 1995. Print. Somewhat challenging but richly rewarding essays by leading scholars on various topics: "Representation," "Structure," "Writing," "Narrative," and so forth.

Manguel, Alberto. *A History of Reading*. New York: Penguin, 1997. Print.

McFarland, Ron. "Hemingway and the Poets." *Hemingway Review* 20.2 (2001): 37–58. Print.

Michaud, Jon. "Hemingway, Castro, and Cuba." *New Yorker* 24 May 2012. Web. 30 Aug. 2015.

Paul, Annie Murphy. "Your Brain on Fiction." *New York Times* 18 Mar. 2012: Page SR6.

"Lucky Novice." *Sports Illustrated* The Vault 30 May 1960. Web. 30 Aug. 2015.

Timerman, Jacobo. Trans. by Toby Talbot. "A Summer in the Revolution: 1987." *New Yorker* 13 Aug. 1990: 62–81. Print.

Trimble, John. *Writing with Style: Conversations on the Art of Writing.* 2nd ed. Upper Saddle River, NJ: Prentice, 2000. Print. The best little book on writing I know. Many times I've assigned the first chapter to first-year English students, and they show up for the next class having read the whole book. If you're at all weak as a writer, or if you just want to get stronger, get this book. It's lively, fun, useful, and the examples are mostly drawn from writing about literature.

Wolf, Maryanne. *Proust and the Squid: The Story and Science of the Reading Brain.* London: Icon, 2008.

Critical Worlds

A Selective Tour

*"The question is," said Alice, "whether you can make words
mean so many things."*
*"The question is," said Humpty Dumpty, "which is to be
master—that's all."*

—Lewis Carroll

What you'll learn in this chapter:

- To distinguish the basic principles of various theories.
- To apply the basic principles of New Criticism; reader-response criticism; structuralist and deconstructive Criticism; historical, postcolonial, and cultural studies; psychological criticism; political criticism; and other related theories.
- To generate ideas about texts, inventing ideas and arguments.

It is wonderful for us to argue about what words mean. When we stop arguing, and we're sure that our interpretation is the only possible correct one, the lights of civilization begin to go out.

This chapter begins to show you how arguments are made and received. Specifically, we're concerned here with arguments about literary texts, but the process is in crucial ways the same in any realm. When you finish reading this chapter, you should have a pretty good idea of the basic assumptions and strategies of the various approaches treated in more detail in the rest of this book. The emphasis throughout will be on what is practical—on how you can use critical theories.

It's entirely possible that you are encountering some or all of these critical strategies for the first time. Your prior experience with literature also

may be limited. Don't be dismayed if some of the terms and ideas presented
in this chapter are unfamiliar and a bit challenging. In subsequent chapters,
each approach and its use in the process of writing about literature will be
explained in more detail. You may well want to use this chapter as a review
also, returning to it after you've read the other chapters. As you may have
noticed, there are brief summaries of these theories inside the front cover
for handy reference. Also, an appendix includes a very brief consideration
of how different theories relate to one another.

But why, we might ask at this point, are there so many different strategies? Why not just show you the best way to write about literature? Because,
as we saw in the previous chapter, there isn't any way that everyone would
agree is the best way for writing about any given work for any given purpose. As we noted, there is no single "correct" reading of a particular text.
Some interpretations are no doubt more sophisticated, insightful, stimulating, or useful than others. Some interpretations no doubt will seem to many
people implausible, unbelievable, strained, driven by prejudice, obtuse. But
for different readers at different times and places, what is best will be a
matter of opinion. This claim about readers and interpretations applies, of
course, to just about everything, from music to enchiladas—we have different opinions at different times. That is not a bad thing, and lively discussion
of our differing interpretations is invigorating and enlightening.

To allow you to compare and contrast different theories, I illustrate
how each one might be applied to the same passage, an excerpt from Brendan
Gill's *Here at "The New Yorker."* It's a wonderful passage, and since it will be
used for all the theories presented here, you'll want to read it carefully:

> When I started at *The New Yorker*, I felt an unshakable confidence in
> my talent and intelligence. I revelled in them openly, like a dolphin diving
> skyward out of the sea. After almost forty years, my assurance is less than
> it was; the revellings, such as they are, take place in becoming seclusion.
> This steady progress downward in the amount of one's confidence is a
> commonplace at the magazine—one might almost call it a tradition. Again
> and again, some writer who has made a name for himself in the world will
> begin to write for us and will discover as if for the first time how difficult
> writing is. The machinery of benign skepticism that surrounds and besets
> him in the form of editors, copy editors, and checkers, to say nothing of
> fellow-writers, digs a yawning pit an inch or so beyond his desk. He hears
> it repeated as gospel that there are not three people in all America who
> can set down a simple declarative sentence correctly; what are the odds
> against his being one of this tiny elect?
>
> In some cases, the pressure of all those doubting eyes upon his copy
> is more than the writer can bear. When the galleys of a piece are placed
> in front of him, covered with scores, perhaps hundreds, of pencilled
> hen-tracks of inquiry, suggestion, and correction, he may sense not the

glory of creation but the threat of being stung to death by an army of gnats. Upon which he may think of nothing better to do than lower his head onto his blotter and burst into tears. Thanks to the hen-tracks and their consequences, the piece will be much improved, but the author of it will be pitched into a state of graver self-doubt than ever. Poor devil, he will type out his name on a sheet of paper and stare at it long and long, with dumb uncertainty. It looks—oh, Christ!—his name looks as if it could stand some working on.

As I was writing the above, Gardner Botsford, the editor who, among other duties, handles the copy for "Theatre," came into my office with the galleys of my latest play review in his hand. Wearing an expression of solemnity, he said, "I am obliged to inform you that Miss Gould has found a buried dangling modifier in one of your sentences." Miss Gould is our head copy editor and unquestionably knows as much about English grammar as anyone alive. Gerunds, predicate nominatives, and passive periphrastic conjugations are mother's milk to her, as they are not to me. Nevertheless, I boldly challenged her allegation. My prose was surely correct in every way. Botsford placed the galleys before me and indicated the offending sentence, which ran, "I am told that in her ninth decade this beautiful woman's only complaint in respect to her role is that she doesn't have enough work to do."

I glared blankly at the galleys. Humiliating enough to have buried a dangling modifier unawares; still more humiliating not to be able to disinter it. Botsford came to my rescue. "Miss Gould points out that as the sentence is written, the meaning is that the complaint is in its ninth decade and has, moreover, suddenly and unaccountably assumed the female gender." I said that in my opinion the sentence could only be made worse by being corrected—it was plain that "The only complaint of this beautiful woman in her ninth decade. . ." would hang on the page as heavy as a sashweight. "Quite so," said Botsford. "There are times when to be right is wrong, and this is one of them. The sentence stands." (7–8)

What can you say about this passage? I'd encourage you to take a few moments and write down a reaction to it or an analysis of it. I think you'll find it interesting to see how an understanding of different critical strategies can give you more options, more material to work with. We begin with New Criticism, the critical approach that transformed the study of literature in the modern age. It's no longer "new," but it's still a pervasively influential way of reading.

NEW CRITICISM

New Criticism focuses attention on the work itself, not the reader or the author or anything else. New Critics are not allergic to talking about the responses of readers or the intentions of authors, but they believe that the work itself ultimately must stand on its own as an artistic object. This commitment to the work itself is what made the New Critics' strategies distinctive and "new." And what are the New Critics looking for as they read so carefully and closely the work itself?

New Critics especially value artistic works that have both complexity and unity.

In terms of "complexity," they value richness, tension, paradox, striking language, and insights. Significant art, New Critics believe, brings order and harmony to the multifarious flow of experience. In an artistic work that has unity, every element works together toward a purpose, a theme. Every element is essential. New Critics popularized what they called "close reading," the careful analysis of a literary work to reveal its complex unity. Great literature, New Critics assume, contains oppositions, ambiguities, ironies, tensions, and these are unified by the work—if it is successful by the standards of New Criticism. New Critics, in other words, are looking for qualities that would seem to be in opposition: complexity and unity.

So how does one do New Criticism? Begin by reading closely. Everything should contribute to the work's unity—figures of speech, point of view, diction, imagery, recurrent ideas or events, and so forth. Therefore, careful analysis of any aspect of the work should be revealing. Look for oppositions, tensions, ambiguities. A mediocre work might be unified but have little complexity, or it might be complex but never really come together. The New Critic, ultimately, shows how the various elements of a great work unify it.

My New Critical reading of Gill's passage was developed by reading carefully, marking up the text, asking myself questions, drafting answers to the questions, brainstorming and freewriting, and then putting my ideas together. Although this reading didn't just pop out of my head, it wasn't a frustrating struggle because I knew what I was trying to do, and I was confident that my assumptions and strategies would eventually produce something interesting. Specifically, I knew that a New Critical reading would identify some tension (or irony, or opposition) in the text, and I immediately saw that some tensions in the story are pretty clear:

> editor vs. writer
> the world vs. *The New Yorker*
> grammar vs. style
> confidence vs. doubt
> right vs. wrong

I also knew that such tensions or oppositions must somehow be resolved if the text succeeds (by New Critical standards). Therefore, how the text ends is especially important from a New Critical perspective.

New Critics might have some trouble with the idea of an "ending" in this case, because the "work" I've chosen is not really a work, but rather an excerpt from a work. But for the purposes of demonstration, let's imagine this passage stands alone, entitled "Writing a Wrong." This title, as is often the case, points toward the unifying idea that I am finding in the work, a paradox (being right is wrong) that my punning title points toward. Endings are crucial, especially for New Critics, and this reading does focus on the reconciliation at the end, when Botsford pronounces "right is wrong." As a New Critic, I had to consider, "How does this idea—'right is wrong'—unify or resolve the work in a complex or ambiguous way?" In other words, what conflicting ideas are at work in the passage that are brought into balance and harmony by this theme? So, New Criticism invites you to do three things: focus on the text's details and read closely; look for oppositions, ironies, and tensions; and show how the work's complexity is artistically unified (how these oppositions come together).

This may well sound obscure and difficult, but an example will help to clarify, I think, and keep in mind that there will be a much fuller explanation in the next chapter. You'll benefit most, I think, if you try to sketch out your own New Critical reading before (and perhaps again after) you read mine.

The Paradoxical Unity of "Writing a Wrong"

In Brendan Gill's story of a dangling modifier, "Writing a Wrong," the editor Botsford solves the conflict between Miss Gould's rules and Gill's taste. He does so by offering a paradox that unifies Gill's story: sometimes "right is wrong," Botsford says. It turns out that Miss Gould was right to spot the error, but Gill was right to have written the sentence as he did. The irony of this solution is reinforced by various paradoxical images in the story.

For example, the dolphin in the second sentence is "diving skyward." This action simultaneously suggests a downward movement ("diving") and an upward motion ("skyward"). The description thus embodies the same sort of logic as a wrong rightness. Likewise, the "progress downward" of the writer and even his "becoming seclusion" ("becoming"—attractive and appealing to others; "seclusion"—unknown to others) convey the same kind of image. In larger terms, the writer's "unshakable confidence" quickly becomes a "dumb uncertainty"—which again suggests the kind of reversal that resolves the story.

In such an upside-down world we would expect to find imagery of struggle and violence, and we do encounter a "yawning pit" and an "army of gnats." Such tension is harmonized by Gill's brilliant conclusion: in writing, conducted properly, the demands of correctness and style are unified by the writer's poetic instincts. Similarly, the story itself is resolved by the notion of a correct error.

READER-RESPONSE CRITICISM

Reader-response criticism starts from the idea that the critic's interest ultimately ought to be focused on the reader rather than the text itself or the author. Without readers, it seems safe to say, there would be little reason to talk about literature; it is the reader who brings the text to life, who gives it meaning. Otherwise, it's just black marks on a white page.

If you want to use the techniques of reader-response criticism, you'll want to focus on the reader's activity in one of two ways: by describing how readers should respond to the text, or by giving your own personal response. That is, the reader-response critic either is claiming to be describing what is "normal," or conventional, or ideal, or implied by the text. Or, in the other variety of reader-response, the critic is expressing a reaction that is personal, subjective, perhaps even eccentric. One could argue that readers are always engaging in a subjective response, even when they think they're objectively describing "the" response. Obviously, the goal of this kind of reading is entirely different from a New Critical reading. On the one hand, you're describing a response; on the other, you're describing the qualities of a text. Reading from a New Critical perspective, you would naturally tend to value works that can be shown to have a complexity that is artistically unified. Reading from the perspective of reader-response criticism, you would naturally value works that elicit some sort of interesting, or valuable, or revealing response.

So how does one do reader-response criticism? If the goal is to offer a personal, subjective response, one simply reads the text and responds. As you can imagine, such a strategy has been especially popular with students and teachers because it really liberates the reader. It's difficult to see how any response could be wrong: Who could say, "No, that isn't your response"? Some responses may seem richer than others; some responses may seem to deal more fully with the text; some responses may seem more authentic and honest than others. But any particular response may well help another reader to a more interesting or satisfying experience of the work.

If the idea, however, is to describe how a reader ought to respond, which might better be called "reader-reception" criticism, then you'll need to try to suppress whatever is personal in your response and offer instead an "ideal" response, one that is (or rather ought to be) shared by other attentive and informed readers. Describing in careful detail the slow-motion progress of a hypothetical reader through the text, such "objective" or receptive reader-response criticism may consider these kinds of questions: What expectations does the text create? What happens to those expectations as one reads? (Are they met, undermined, exploited, transformed, denied?) What literary conventions does the text employ to affect the reader? How, in other words, does the text shape the reader's response?

Although I'm presenting these two versions of reader-response criticism as oppositions, flip sides of a single coin, it may be more accurate and helpful to see them in terms of a progression. Reader-response critics unavoidably must use their own personal responses as a starting point for talking about how the ideal, or implied, or "common" reader responds; but the close examination of such "ideal" responses would seem inevitably to reveal some personal and subjective features. (No one, I would suggest, not even the author, can be the ideal, ultimate reader, saying everything that should be said about a work, once and for all.)

The following essay tries to present a record of my movement through this passage. It was fairly easy and fun to write because I simply read through the passage slowly and asked myself, "Okay, how am I responding now? What does this make me think? What am I expecting next?" Although I decided that the passage was continually surprising me, I would not argue that surprise is the only or the correct way to describe one's response: I might have focused on the passage's humor, on a pervading sense of doom, or something else. That's the beauty of reader-response criticism: different responses. As a piece of reader-response criticism, the little essay that follows strives to be neither rabidly subjective nor dogmatically objective. I focus on my personal response, but I also try to play the reader's role that I believe Gill has imagined. I quote the text repeatedly, trying to show my reader exactly what I'm responding to.

The Reader's Surprise in an Excerpt from *Here at "The New Yorker"*

Beginning with its first sentence, the story of the buried dangling modifier in Brendan Gill's *Here at "The New Yorker"* is continually surprising, setting up expectations and then knocking them down. Gill begins the first sentence with "When I started at *The New Yorker*," and I naturally expect him to talk about how nervous and insecure he was starting off at one of the largest and most famous magazines in the world. Instead, Gill refers to his "unshakable confidence." The third sentence begins with "After almost forty years," leading me to expect some explanation of how his joy at the magazine has grown. But 40 years of experience, it turns out, have not developed Gill's confidence and happiness. Instead, his "assurance is less than it was." How, I must wonder, has he managed to work there for 40 years and yet grow less confident?

Expecting Gill to explain the oddity of his deteriorating confidence, I find, surprisingly, that such an effect "is a commonplace at the magazine," a "tradition" even. Since the loss of confidence occurs for everyone, we might then expect that the *New Yorker* staff sticks together, sharing insecurities and supporting each other. Such is hardly the case, as Gill continues to surprise me by tracing one imaginary writer's loss of confidence to the point of what appears to be a nervous breakdown. The writer, who is said to have "made a name for himself in the world," is reduced to weeping on his blotter and trying to revise his name. Such is not what I expect from a famous writer.

Given this tradition of disaster, it seems clear to me that Gardner Botsford is appearing in the third paragraph to star in the story of Gill's own downfall. Botsford points to a major error Gill has made, and Gill's assertion that he "boldly challenged" the allegation seems to set him up for a major humiliation. "Unshakable" confidence and bold challenges certainly seem unwarranted in the atmosphere of *The New Yorker*. But, once more, Gill crosses me up and provides a story of triumph. Rather than undermining his confidence, which is what everything in the story suggests will happen, Botsford becomes Gill's champion. "The sentence stands," he says, as the last reversal provides a happy ending.

STRUCTURALIST AND DECONSTRUCTIVE CRITICISM

Language makes meaning by oppositions: we know what "good" means because it is the opposite of "bad"; "tired" means something to us because it is the opposite of "rested." So, words make sense because of their relationship *to other words*, not because of any "natural" grounding in reality. Although we may like to think "bad" and "rested" refer to something solid and real, they don't. "Bad" has come to mean "good" in certain contexts. It could come to mean "blue," or "hungry," or anything. "Rested" with regard to a fighter pilot during combat may mean "having had three hours' sleep in the last twenty-four." Meaning is relative and relational, based on language's structure. So, a structuralist reading of a text exposes the system of meaning that is at work in that text. Structuralism is thus a bit like New Criticism, except that structuralists are interested in an individual text not so much as an artistic object, but as an example of a system of meaning.

Deconstructive criticism, we might say, takes the insights of structuralism (meaning is made by a binary structure) or New Criticism (literary works unify oppositions) and reverses or inverts or explodes them. Whereas New Criticism aims to reveal the coherence and unity of the work, deconstruction aims to expose the gaps, the incoherences, the contradictions of the text. Whereas a structuralist reading of a text reveals its underlying system of meaning, a deconstructive reading shows how the system falls apart. Deconstructive critics assume that gaps are present in texts because of what they assume about the arbitrary and unstable nature of language. By taking texts apart—undoing them until we see how a text inevitably contradicts itself, containing traces of its opposite or "other"—deconstructive critics are able to call into question many of our settled and comfortable assumptions.

Depending on how you feel about these assumptions (are they truths or prejudices?), deconstruction may seem scandalously offensive or delightfully inventive.

One of the many ironies of deconstruction, it appears, is that any effort to explain deconstruction is doomed according to the theory itself. Any effort to say *anything*, in fact, must go astray. Such an assumption could be dismaying, but many deconstructive critics have chosen to adopt a comic and even shocking stance, practicing a critical strategy that by its own definition cannot be defined. Although deconstructive criticism can be very difficult to read (perhaps as an illustration of how language eventually fails?), it can also be very amusing and engaging—and a lot of fun to try.

Thus, deconstructing a text calls for careful reading and a bit of creativity. One way to think of your goal as a deconstructive critic is that you're trying to turn the text against itself. For instance, Botsford's concluding decision, "The sentence stands," may appear to be reassuring. Here is a case where a writer makes a mistake, but the mistake turns out to be okay. If we were to press this reading, however, asking if the text might say something other than what it appears to say, we may begin to move into the realm of deconstruction. If you are a student in a writing-about-literature class, I suspect that Gill's passage is only superficially comforting. If a writer at *The New Yorker* can't always tell whether a sentence is right or wrong—if, in fact, the rules of writing are so complex that not even three people in America "can set down a simple declarative sentence correctly"—then how is a college student to feel? If a grown man and an established writer is weeping onto his desk blotter and considering revising his name, then how can the ordinary student hope to write an error-free paper—especially when the rules seem to apply in one case and not in another, and the rules for determining such exceptions don't seem to exist but are instead invented and applied by those who happen to be in charge? Writing becomes a nightmare.

In fact, looking very closely, one might observe that Botsford's "reassuring" vindication is deceptive, for he does not actually say that sometimes right is wrong and wrong is right. He only says that sometimes "right is wrong." Botsford's apparent reversal of the dismantling of authors at *The New Yorker* is finally ambiguous, since we never know if the writer is ever correct, no matter what he does. Maybe he is always wrong. "The sentence stands" indeed, but it stands with its error intact, a monument to Gill's inability to correct it and to the inevitable errors of writing—a monument to the way language masters us.

Although deconstructive critics may well deal with obviously major features of a text, such as its ending, they may also choose some marginal element of the text to focus upon and vigorously explore its oppositions, reversals, and ambiguities. In fact, for some critics, deconstruction is simply a name for "close reading" of an especially rigorous kind. The deconstructive critic, for example, might well decide to concentrate on the assertion that because of the editors' merciless correction, "the piece will be much improved." A New Critic, I think, would not be very likely to consider this assertion central, the key to the passage. But a deconstructive critic might. Here is what happened when I turned around the idea that "the piece will be much improved" and questioned it.

"The Sentence Stands" Triumphant: A Deconstructive Reading

In *Here at "The New Yorker,"* Brendan Gill offers an anecdote that clearly sets the world's writers against the editors, and the latter control the game. Gill has written an essay, but the editors and their accomplices, the checkers and copy editors, get to say what is wrong with it. They get to dig the "yawning pit" in front of the helpless writer's desk; they determine the "tiny elect" who can write correctly; they make the scores and hundreds of "hen-tracks" on the writer's manuscript, which serve as testimony to the incompetence of writers, the near-impossibility of writing, and the arbitrary power of the editor.

To be sure, it is acknowledged that these editorial assaults upon the writer serve their purpose, for "thanks to the hen-tracks and their consequences, the piece will be much improved." But the cost is terrible. Not only is the writer unable to write his own name with any confidence; he has also become a "poor devil," outside "the elect." In delivering his writing over to the editors, conceding their dominance, the writer inevitably places his own identity, perhaps even his very soul, in jeopardy. Thus, the cry "oh, Christ!" comes to be an invocation to the only power who can save the writer from the devil and the editor's destructive forces.

But this story of the hopelessness of writers also reveals that the kingdom of editors is based upon a lie: It simply is not true, despite the beleaguered writer's admission under torture, that "the piece will be much improved" by editorial intervention. In this instance, Miss Gould's enormous grammatical lore does not, in fact, improve the piece at all; her effort nearly made it "worse." And Botsford's contribution as editor involves simply leaving the piece as it was written—a strange method of improvement! So who is in charge—writers or editors?

In the end, Gill can never again become like the gill-less dolphin of the first paragraph, confidently "diving skyward," because the dangling modifier defiantly remains: it is a part of the sea of language the author cannot leave. In the end, both writer and editor are defeated by their inability to control their language. The status of the writer at *The New Yorker* becomes a paradigm for the alarming status of writing itself: deceptive, mute, and intractable, "The sentence stands," neither improved nor made worse, standing really for nothing that is under the writer's or editor's rule.

HISTORICAL, POSTCOLONIAL, AND CULTURAL STUDIES

One way to think about literature is to consider the people who wrote it and have read it. Not the text itself (New Criticism), not the reader's reactions (reader-response), not the system of language at work in the text (structuralism), not how the text falls apart (deconstruction), but rather the life and times of the author and the readers. It is a fascinating approach, appealing to our natural curiosity: Inquiring minds want to know how great works of art came into being, and whether great writers are ordinary people, or eccentrics, or something else, and whether other readers see things the way we do. Writers must live and write in particular places and particular times, and so biographical research is intertwined with historical research. "History" includes the history of literature, and so the effort to enrich our understanding of a work by examining the conditions of its production can usefully include studying the literary tradition. Also, literature, which can both reflect and influence history powerfully, has proved in recent decades to be an especially revealing resource for thinking about the relationships between and among cultures—and about colonial and postcolonial cultures in particular. Is the writer part of a dominant culture? A minority? Does the work shape our understanding of power and influence in a particular historical situation?

In theory, this approach to criticism is simple: Just find out the biographical and historical facts and see how they illuminate the literature. If you are reading a novel set in the Vietnam War, wouldn't you like to know if the author perhaps fought in that war, or protested against it, or both? Are there letters from that period of the author's life? Wouldn't it also be helpful to know the history of the Vietnam War? And be familiar with other novels written about this war? And even literary works about other wars?

Of course, we cannot know everything, and we don't always know what we don't know, as Yogi Berra might have said. And so the discovery of new historical or biographical facts may substantially or entirely alter our perception. What if a work that we thought was written by a combat veteran turns out actually to be written by a journalist who never saw a battle? Or by a soldier's mother, who never even visited Vietnam? One reasonable response to these questions would be that such information doesn't matter at all. The text of the work isn't altered by this information. If one accepts this response, then the value of historical criticism is arguably diminished. It may be interesting to learn about the author's biography and the relevant history, but if the text is all we need, then this information is perhaps extraneous to the work, nonessential.

The validity and importance of biographical and historical criticism can, however, be defended. For starters, some readers have larger purposes than simply appreciating a literary work. If readers want to understand the insights and expressions of a brilliant mind, or of an age, then the work itself is just the visible part of a much larger picture. Further, a writer's audience inevitably has knowledge and suppositions that are not immediately available to a later audience, removed in time and space. In other words, even if the reader's interest is limited to the literary work, biographical and historical research is still valuable, arguably crucial, to an understanding of the work itself. It would be, however, a naïve mistake to equate writers with their works: If we learn that a writer protested against the Vietnam War, we should not therefore assume that his novel is a political statement against the war. It might be, but he might also have changed his mind, or grown tired of that issue and be working on some other problem in the novel. Or the work, read carefully, might actually support an unintended point of view. Biographical and historical research can highlight certain aspects of a work for us, calling our attention to one thing or another, suggesting ways of reading, but the work itself must still somehow support the argument.

In the last half-century or so, even more fundamental problems have been raised regarding our traditional views of history and biography. New ways of thinking about language and meaning, coming out of structuralism and poststructuralism, led to a movement called "New Historicism" (often called "cultural materialism" in Great Britain), which emphasizes that it is no longer possible to assume that there are stable "facts" objectively out there, waiting to be discovered; instead, all we really have access to is an indeterminate number of texts waiting on a process of interpretation. Hence, new historicists shift their attention away from trying to determine what "really" happened, and toward exploring how different versions of history are made. Since history is unavoidably motivated by the interests and values of the historian, it cannot be objective. Literature, biography, and history from this perspective all participate in creating a "discourse," which embodies a set of values and assumptions. As a result, literary critics who embrace new historicism end up reading all sorts of texts—literary works, newspapers, advertisements, graffiti, anything that can be used to expose the discourse that is at work.

But how is this approach "new"? Or for that matter, "historical"? Haven't good historians always doubted the objectivity of their "facts," and haven't they always looked for coherent systems for making meaning? Perhaps the key distinction of New Historicism is that history itself becomes textual. The point is not that New Historicists deny Shakespeare's existence, for instance; it is rather that "Shakespeare" for us is unavoidably a text—or rather a whole range of texts that construct the constantly evolving meaning of that name. In a sense, "Shakespeare" is a name that marks the site of our efforts to imagine Shakespeare. This observation may strike you as obvious ("Of course, 'Shakespeare' is a textual phenomenon; I didn't think he was still walking around in London"), or stimulating, opening up all sorts of possibilities for connecting all sorts of texts, extending far beyond literary texts, to build an understanding of the web of culture at a particular time. New Historicism shifts the focus from the quest to find particular causes for historical events, and attempts instead to identify an ideology—or ideologies—at work in a particular time and place. To put this another way, rather than moving through time, from an origin which leads to an effect, which leads to another event, a New Historical perspective moves in a sense through space, reading poems, advertisements, music, novels, law textbooks, children's stories, graffiti, anything, in the same way that an intellectual archaeologist might sift through the layers of a culture, examining all sorts of things going on at the same time period.

Postcolonial criticism is in some ways similar to New Historicism: Postcolonial criticism examines the shaping of ideas and values in a particular kind of culture. That kind of culture is one that has been colonized—subjected to the rule of another, or an "other." Literature is often an important part of the way a ruling power thinks about and influences its subjects, and also an important feature of the way the "native" people both absorb and resist the colonizing power. Like New Historicism, postcolonial criticism is not restricted to the analysis of literary texts, but rather seeks to connect any grouping of texts that may help us to understand the complex relationships of a dominant to a dominated culture. The goal here is to intervene: to expose the way that one culture represents and therefore controls another, and thereby to undermine that power. Thus, the excluded, repressed, "savage," "primitive" culture can be rewritten in other terms.

The idea of writing about culture as a way of intervening in culture is also at the heart of cultural studies. Cultural studies, like New Historicism and postcolonial criticism, assumes that meaning is constructed. That means, for instance, that we cannot assume European culture, with its technological and industrial achievements, is superior to some other culture; we cannot assume that *House of Cards* is inferior to *Hamlet*. It depends on what we are looking for, what we are valuing. The popularity of cultural studies derives in part from this dizzyingly liberating erasure of our assumptions, which may be no more than our prejudices. If we recognize that cultural values are invented, then cultural studies seeks to expose the systems of meaning-making that create the worlds of culture that human beings inhabit. Cultural studies is indeed so open in terms of what it studies and the methods that are employed, that even its adherents are not entirely clear or united regarding what cultural studies is. But people who say they are "doing" cultural studies do appear to share, it seems, a commitment to a radical or alternative political stance. That is, they seem to be exposing how culture works from an outsider or antagonistic or at least questioning perspective. This stance is not surprising, given cultural studies' roots in poststructuralism (emphasizing the arbitrariness of meaning) and Marxism (emphasizing the shaping power of economics and class).

Because New Historical, postcolonial, and cultural studies require readers not only to control a literary text, but also to assemble diverse historical materials into coherent systems of meaning, these strategies are likely to seem more appropriate for advanced students. Biography and history, however, are intrinsically interesting, as the success of *People* magazine and the *History Channel* arguably suggests, and students at almost any level will benefit from efforts to link the work to its world. The following passage illustrates briefly how even a little biographical and historical research can be applied to a text, drawing on both traditional and new historical strategies.

"To Take a Favorable View": Brendan Gill and the Writer's Depression

Brendan Gill began working at *The New Yorker* in 1936—"almost forty years ago," as he says in *Here at "The New Yorker,"* published in 1975. Thus, the "unshakable" confidence that Gill mentions in the first sentence of the excerpt quoted above is particularly remarkable for having arisen in the midst of the Great Depression, with failure and fear of failure presumably rampant all around him. It appears that the confidence is extraordinarily fragile, however, as the writer who is reveling in his talent and intelligence as the passage begins is bursting into tears, his head on his blotter, before many more sentences pass by. Does the skepticism and correction really account for this collapse? Did real writers typically experience emotional collapses at the magazine? Does Gill really believe that at any time between 1935 and 1975 fewer than three people "in all America" could "set down a simple declarative sentence correctly"?

Although Gill's book is presented as a memoir, an autobiography, the reality of his life, along with what he "really" believes, begins to seem a bit elusive as one reads through it. Elsewhere in *Here at "The New Yorker,"* for instance, Gill writes, "I am always so ready to take a favorable view of my powers that even when I am caught out and made a fool of, I manage to twist this circumstance about until it becomes a proof of how exceptional I am" (62). Obviously, this sentiment is not consistent with the reality of a weeping writer, his confidence shattered. In another passage, Gill writes, "I started out at the place where I wanted most to be and with much pleasure and very little labor have remained here since" (24). This comment also does not sound at all like the experience of the sobbing writer with "hundreds" of "hen-tracks of inquiry," endlessly revising even his name. In fact, the writer whose confidence has been broken, who cannot bear "all those doubting eyes upon his copy," is not, strictly speaking, Gill. It is "some writer who has made a name for himself in the world," an imaginary generic writer, who is crushed into a state of "dumb uncertainty" by his service at The New Yorker—not Gill himself. Gill says only that after "almost forty years, my assurance is less than · it was." Why does Gill mention this typical writer, suggesting—despite contrary evidence elsewhere—that his own career follows this same structural path?

The reason, I would argue, is that Gill is creating a "Gill" character who fits into a recurring narrative. He is making himself into an example, in other words. The structure of the passage, which is the story of the dangling modifier, involves three movements: First, the writer exudes mastery and confidence; then, the writer falls into doubt and uncertainty; finally, the writer is vindicated, his confidence restored. It is this structure that shapes the autobiography Gill presents: "unshakable confidence," "progress downward," "rescue," and vindication. Thus, the anecdote becomes an illustration of his experience at the magazine, which is one instance of everyone's experience at the magazine. This structure is, of course, a pervasive one, easily relevant to both the mid-1930s (the passage's starting point) and the mid-1970s (where it ends). Both the mid-1930s and mid-1970s followed periods of exuberant assurance, and represented times of doubt and crisis, as Americans struggled to rise above the depression in 1935 and the Vietnam War in 1975. Like many other narratives, Gill's life as he presents it here fits the national paradigm. This narrative structure suggests a positive view of history: Although writers lose their confidence, it can be restored, just as a depression or war can be surmounted. This plot structure is thus reassuring, giving shape to biography and history.

PSYCHOLOGICAL CRITICISM

Anyone whose writing is evaluated will be intrigued, I think, by what Gill's passage implies about the psychological effects of criticism. You too may have felt at some point the discomfort of "pencilled hen-tracks of inquiry, suggestion, and correction." The passage provides a good opportunity to consider how such feelings arise and what purpose, if any, they serve. You don't, in other words, have to be a psychologist in order to do psychological criticism. Common sense and an interest in human thinking and behavior are the only essentials.

Still, psychological concepts can be valuable and stimulating in writing about literature. Take, for instance, the idea put forward by Sigmund

Freud that creative writing is like dreaming: Both allow wishes or fears to be fulfilled that would otherwise be suppressed. A desire or a fear too powerful to be confronted directly can be disguised by the unconscious and expressed by the author or dreamer, Freud said. One possible task of the psychological critic, then, like the psychologist, would be to decode what is being disguised. The critic may make educated guesses about what has been repressed and transformed by the author, or by characters, or even by other readers. Why is this worth doing, other than for its intrinsic interest? For one thing, we may gain insight into underlying or hidden desires or fears, our own or others'. We may refine our ability to make sense of what is below the surface, unseen but influential.

Another useful psychological concept is the idea that there are basic patterns of human development, even though everyone's formative history is different in particulars. One of the most famous and controversial of these developmental concepts is Freud's idea of the Oedipus complex. In Greek myth, as you may know, Oedipus was the man who unknowingly murdered his father and married his mother. For Freud, this myth depicted the infantile desire experienced by all little boys, who want (Freud said) to see the mother as the principal object of their affections, and who resent sharing her with the father. The Oedipus complex comes about when this sensual desire for the mother is not suppressed. And the vehicle for this suppression, Freud argued, is the young boy's recognition that the father is more powerful. Rather than lose his capability for pleasure, the boy pulls back from his focus on the mother and eventually turns his desires elsewhere. At its most instinctual level, Freud maintained, the threat to the boy's sexuality is perceived as a threat to that which determines his sex: It is ultimately a fear of castration that motivates the boy's withdrawal.

Although many of Freud's ideas, including the Oedipus complex, have been vigorously challenged or revised, especially by poststructuralist and feminist thinkers, his work has formed the basis for modern psychology. Many of his ideas are so well known that any educated person can be expected to be familiar with them. It would be difficult to go very far toward understanding psychology or psychological criticism today without some awareness of Freud, who relied heavily on literature in developing his ideas. By no means, however, should you infer that psychological criticism means Freudian criticism. Other approaches are welcome. But since an introduction to the field of psychology isn't practical here, I've elected to indicate simply how psychological concepts can be applied by using Freud, who is arguably the most important single figure. If you can apply Freud, you can apply Abraham Maslow, Carl Rogers, Luce Irigaray, or whomever.

The following essay, as I hope you'll see, was developed primarily by applying Freud's central theory of the Oedipus complex to Gill's passage.

A Psychological Reading of Gill's Passage

Writers are brought into the world by editors, and Brendan Gill is thus in a sense the product of Miss Gould and Gardner Botsford's union. Gardner Botsford imposes the grammatical law in a fatherly enough way, but his counterpart, Miss Gould, functions only as a kind of uncreating antimother: she is a "Miss," and her notion of "mother's milk" is truly indigestible—"gerunds, predicate nominatives, and passive periphrastic conjugations." She nurtures neither writing nor writer.

But, at the same time, the well-being of the writers at *The New Yorker* depends on her approval because, like Gill, they have accepted the criterion of correctness as the law of the father. Miss Gould imposes that law to the letter, undermining the writer's self-esteem until finally his very identity is threatened, plunging him into such "self-doubt" that his name is called into question. He may then become an orphan; his work may be abandoned.

In fact, the source of the writer's neurotic breakdown seems to be the linking of self to writing. Although the many corrections are imprinted upon the paper, Gill shifts them to the writer and transforms them from "pencilled hen-tracks" into stings. It is not, as we might suppose, the particular work that may be attacked so much that it dies, but rather the writer who may be "stung to death by an army of gnats." Gnats do not, so far as I know anyway, have stingers; they bite. The displacement here, one might argue, is the result of the writer's sense of personal vulnerability, making the threat more plausible since being bitten to death by gnats sounds absurd, while being stung is more ominous.

The more serious threat to Gill's identity is posed by Botsford, his editor and symbolic father. Botsford enters the scene with Gill's review "in his hand." Part of the review has been illegally "buried" and may subsequently be removed. This threat to Gill's writing is a disguised fear of castration because the writer identifies with his writing. The writer's identity, his name, is crucial to his potency. His name is the key to his ability to reproduce and promulgate himself. Yet, his name "looks as if it could stand some working on."

Gill recognizes then that his editorial parent may correct and improve his "piece," but the cost may be terrible, for the piece may be taken over by the authorities who control the emissions of his pen. Gill's image for what he has lost, the dolphin, thus becomes a rather blatant phallic symbol, reemerging as the pen (the grammatical penis) that the "dumb" writer loses. In other words, the writer must give up his "piece" to be published, to survive as a writer, but he is no longer intact as the writer.

We now may see the psychological fittingness of the error Miss Gould finds: It is a structure that is "dangling." The writer may see his own fate in the sentence that sticks out, for it has suddenly "assumed the female gender." The writer's castration anxiety emerges here: He has desired to please Miss Gould, but focusing on grammar and correctness will render him impotent and emasculated. Thus, Gill's story works to resolve his Oedipus complex by pointing out the advantages of accepting the values of the father (Botsford) and shifting his desire from Miss Gould to a more appropriate object: the reader. Gill evades symbolic castration. "The sentence stands," the father says, saving the writer's pen(is).

POLITICAL CRITICISM

Political criticism starts from the idea that the study of literature is not part of some ivory tower of learning, withdrawn from the real world. Rather, literary criticism is inevitably involved in politics—in shaping our understanding of the culture we inhabit, and the role that literature (including all sorts of texts) plays in altering or reinforcing values and beliefs. Even when literary critics argue that literary study should avoid political issues, focusing instead on the literature itself, they are taking a political position, as politically alert critics would say.

Political criticism can proceed from any number of positions— liberal, conservative, moderate; free-market capitalist, socialist, communist. The idea is simply that the reader brings a certain political stance to the text. Perhaps it can be argued that the text supports or opposes this political stance, or there is evidence that the author supported or opposed this stance, or the text somehow illuminates or obscures or otherwise influences our understanding of this political stance. The most successful avowedly political criticism, I think most people would agree, has been feminist criticism, which has transformed the study of literature in the modern era by bringing attention to how gender and sexuality are represented. Feminist criticism has led to masculine studies, queer theory, gay and lesbian criticism, and a striking number of influential studies. But Marxist criticism, African American studies, Chicano studies, and Native American studies have also made significant contributions by foregrounding political concerns.

Any political orientation can drive a reading. Let's say, for instance, that you are concerned about the environment, and you want to consider how various works of literature have portrayed the natural world, or you want to use literary analysis to make a point about the environment. Such a critical stance has been called a variety of things, but since the 1990s it has increasingly been called "ecocriticism." How we think about natural resources, about human impact on the environment, about "nature," about pollution, about the importance of humanity versus the natural world, or humanity's place within the natural world—all these and many more ideas are certainly shaped by and reflected in literature.

Since everyone has some political stance (including being apolitical or uninterested in politics), one could argue that we are all practicing political criticism in a sense, no matter what we say we are doing. Imagine, for instance, that you are concerned about being left-handed in a mostly right-handed world. Although the idea of left-handed criticism may seem silly, many cultures do stigmatize left-handedness. We might note that "right" means "correct" as well as the opposite of "left." In Latin, the word for "left" is "*sinestra*," the origin of the English word "sinister," which has come to mean "evil." The Irish word "*ciotag*," which refers to left-handed people, also means "a very strange person." The Portuguese word for a left-handed person, "*canhoto*," also referred to the devil at one time, and "*canhestro*" means "clumsy." In Mandarin, the word for "left" also means "improper." In Norwegian, saying that something is left-handed work means that it was done poorly. These examples could be multiplied many times over with a few minutes of Internet searching. Left-handed criticism, so far as I know, doesn't exist, but it could, given the pervasive social and political implications of "left-ness." Readers using this stance might identify representations of left-handedness in literature, or explore other textual evidence that would illuminate how we see people who use the "other" hand.

In this text, I've elected to focus primarily on feminist criticism to illustrate political approaches, while glancing at a few other political strategies. If you understand how to use feminist criticism, then you can easily make use of other political stances, whether Marxist or Native American or ecocriticism—if you understand the politics. Feminist criticism generally assumes, like reader-response criticism, that a literary work is shaped by our reading of it, and this reading is influenced by our own status, which includes gender, or our attitude toward gender. But, as feminists point out, since the production and reception of literature historically have been controlled largely by men, the role of gender in reading and writing has historically been slighted. The interests and achievements of half of the human race have been neglected—or appreciated largely from only one sex's point of view.

Thus, you don't have to consider yourself a feminist to benefit from feminist criticism. Simply taking gender into account, regardless of your social and political views, is likely to open your eyes to important works, authors, and issues you would have missed otherwise.

Although it is difficult to generalize, given the diversity and development of feminist criticism in recent decades, particularly as the developments of postfeminism and queer theory have challenged the very terms of gender and sexuality, there are still some basic strategies you can adopt. You'll want to consider the significance of the gender of the author and the characters. You'll want to observe how sexual stereotypes might be reinforced or undermined in the work. How does the work reflect or alter or complicate the place (or the construction) of women (and men) in society? Perhaps the most powerful strategy is to imagine yourself reading the work as a woman. If you happen to be female, this last suggestion may seem easy enough; but feminist critics point out that women have long been taught to read like men or to ignore their own gender. And postfeminist critics have challenged the idea that there is some particular thing that "as a woman" refers to. So, reading as a woman, even if you are a woman, may be unexpectedly challenging and illuminating.

I developed the following feminist reading of Gill's passage simply by noticing references to gender and paying attention to any potential stereotypes.

A Feminist Reading of the Gill Passage

We know not all the writers at The New Yorker were men, even during the period Brendan Gill discusses in this passage from Here at "The New Yorker." When he speaks of "some writer who has made a name for himself in the world," and about the editorial "machinery" that besets "him," Gill is, of course, referring to writers in the generic sense. It is clear, however, that "himself" and "him" in this passage do not include "herself" and "her."

The idea that one sexual marker includes its opposite, although the grammatical norm for many years, seems absurd today—as if "white" included "black" or "communist" included "democratic." But the motivations for such a claim are suggested even in this brief passage, for Gill's story not only contains this obvious bias in pronouns, still accepted even today by some editors and writers, but his story also conveys more subtle messages about sexuality and sexual roles. For example, Miss Gould functions as a familiar stereotype: the finicky spinster, a Grammar Granny, who has devoted her life to "English grammar" and its enforcement. She is a copy editor, subservient to the male (standard) editor and male writer, and her lack of imagination and taste, as Gill presents it, seems to testify to the wisdom of this power structure.

This division of labor—male/creative, female/menial—is subtly reinforced by the reference to the "hen-tracks" that cover the writer's galley. Petty correction is the realm of the hen, the feminine. But these "hen-tracks" (they could not be rooster tracks) are more than aggravating correction; they come to threaten the writer's very identity. In attempting to produce "his copy," the writer is in a sense attempting to reproduce himself. The "glory of creation" is his literary procreation, and thus Miss Gould's effort to remove a particular sentence is a symbolic threat to cut off some more essential part of the writer. It is, after all, a "dangling modifier" that she has located; and this dangling structure is in danger of being fed to the "yawning pit," symbolic of the feminine editing and its excising dangers. Thus, men should fear women, the passage suggests. Do not give women power.

Because Gill's initial image for the writer starting out at the magazine, the dolphin in the sea, derives some of its power from the well-established association of the ocean and the womb, the images of the "yawning pit," not to mention the poisonous "mother's milk," become more telling. Even the error itself is subtly connected to the feminine, for the problem with the sentence is that part of it has "assumed the female gender." That part, in the context of nagging copy editors who chop up one's prose, can only be a "complaint." The nonagenarian's complaint itself seems significant: In the mode of feminine busybodies like Miss Gould, she laments not having "enough work to do." Miss Gould, similarly overzealous, has herself done more work than is reasonable, and Botsford's masculine, phallic pronouncement that "The sentence stands" returns her to her place, negating her feminine fussiness.

OTHER APPROACHES

The feminist reading above does include some interest in money, class, and power, but these features could conceivably be brought to the forefront. Criticism that focuses on the economic and class structures involved in literature is sometimes called "Marxist" criticism even if the critic does not endorse Marxism. Typically, feminist and Marxist approaches have pushed against a dominant ideology, exposing injustice and oppression, but attention to issues of gender or economy could be focused from any political position. Historical criticism might be particularly attuned to representations of gender, or class and power, or attitudes toward the environment. The critic may have a case to make, and use the literary work as a tool, or the critic may approach the literary work to see what can be learned from it—or perhaps both. It would be naïve to think that readers don't use literature for their own purposes, but it would be depressing to think that literature doesn't alter and enrich readers' perspectives.

As tools for inventing ideas, critical approaches may work singularly or in concert. And how do you know which approach or combination of approaches to invoke? It depends, of course, on what you're trying to do, which may depend upon what you've been asked to do. An understanding of different strategies will help you to understand your task and your options. A particular strategy, by itself or blended, may appear at first to offer little promise in a particular case. Ecocriticism, for instance, might seem unpromising in the case of Gill's passage, which is surely not at all concerned with the environment. But literary criticism, especially in the wake of psychological and deconstructive approaches, has made us more sensitive to what is being excluded or obscured, and it is oftentimes surprising what a particular approach will spark with a little focus and creativity.

There are, we might note, references to the natural world in Gill's passage, with its deadly biting gnats and painful hen-tracks. Nature, to the extent that it is portrayed, appears in an amusing but negatively threatening light. These are not real gnats and hens; they are metaphorical, linguistic devices. The crisis that the passage turns upon, the existence or not of a grammatical error, illustrates (one could argue from an ecocritical perspective) how insulated from the natural world the writers and editors at *The New Yorker* are. For a dangling modifier to be "humiliating," one would have to think that language and its correct use are extremely important. Such an exaggerated focus on human language, an environmentalist might argue, has helped us to devalue other species of life on our planet. If animals don't have language, or rather don't have our language, then they don't have the kind of consciousness that we have—one might assume. Not only have humans viewed animals as inferior to us, but we have tended to act as if animals have no value except as they are valued by us. The question of whether animals can feel pain is still an issue for many people—although for anyone who has spent any time in the presence of a very wide range of animals, it's ridiculously obvious that they do. The question really is whether their pain has any meaning or value to us.

Gill's passage certainly does not encourage us to trash the environment or use animals recklessly in scientific experiments, but an ecocritical stance does suggest how the passage reflects our larger cultural ecosystem. Humans are animals who have language, which has created the illusion for some that we are not animals, as well as the equally delusive ideas that other animals do not communicate, and that communicating in a way that we can understand is the correct marker of significance and value. The dolphin in the passage appears to be a figure of joy, but turns out to convey only blissful ignorance, as Gill is disillusioned. What the passage tells us, ultimately, is that getting our language correct is crucially important. If you think that policing our language is not important, and does not require your constant vigilance, then you are like the not-fish out of water that is the dolphin incarnation of Gill. What we choose to worry about shapes our fate. Gill, Miss Gould, and Botsford, because they are consumed with language, are concerned with "a complaint" that has "unaccountably assumed the female gender." Perhaps today, an ecocritic might observe, we should focus more on how frogs change their gender when exposed to the most commonly used pesticide in the world, atrazine. Over 200 species, in fact, are affected by a variety of endocrine disruptors that pollution has released into the environment.[1] We are the language animals, but perfect grammar won't protect us from pervasively toxic substances.

My point here is that ecocriticism and many other approaches might have been given more extended treatments in this book. I would have liked, for instance, to focus on ethical and religious criticism. These interests are arguably not prominent at the moment in literary studies, or they are embedded in other approaches, and so I have resisted enlarging what is supposed to be a brief introduction. But a critic interested in religious issues might wonder if the reference to "this tiny elect" in Gill's passage signals the importance of religious values or their trivialization. Likewise, what does the reference to "oh, Christ!" tell us? Is Botsford a Christ figure, forgiving Gill for his sins? Indeed, is there a religious backdrop that makes this passage meaningful? Certainly an entire chapter could be devoted to African American criticism. Using that stance to think about this passage might start from the question of the role that race plays in it and indeed at *The New Yorker* of the time. One might observe that race plays no discernible part in the passage. And that might be, in fact, quite to the point. Do any *New Yorker* advertisements from the 1970s feature African Americans? Do we assume that any of the characters in Gill's tale are or even might be black? What difference does our assumption make? In this respect, one might suggest, the passage reads us, perhaps showing us some of our racially motivated assumptions. If you were to do a reader-response criticism of the passage, would your racial or ethnic status play any part in your reading?

In an ideal world, an introduction to writing about literature would include every identifiable approach. The goal of this introduction is necessarily more limited: Using a sampling of the most visible approaches, it aims to show you how theory shapes practice—how assumptions stimulate and guide the process of developing critical essays. This goal is still an ambitious one but well worth your effort, providing a powerful passport to the various ways meaning is made, preparing you for these and other kinds of literary excursions. For the goal here is not an understanding of the maps and the travel guides and the stories that other travelers have told. It is, of course, your own rich and stimulating engagement with literature.

Note

1. See, for instance, James Owen, "Animals' Sexual Changes Linked to Waste, Chemicals," *National Geographic News*, March 1, 2004, Web, March 4, 2015, and Robert Sanders, "Pesticide Atrazine Can Turn Male Frogs into Females," *UC Berkeley News Center*, March 1, 2010, Web, accessed March 5, 2015.

Works Cited and Recommended Further Reading

Barry, Peter. *Beginning Theory: An Introduction to Literary and Cultural Theory*. 3rd ed. Manchester: Manchester UP, 2009. Print. A lively and genuinely useful introduction, including good questions and exercises for students.

Bertens, Hans. *Literary Theory: The Basics*. 3rd ed. New York: Routledge, 2013. Print. This fairly sophisticated introduction includes a nice chapter on ecocriticism and a generous historical perspective on the various theories.

Bressler, Charles. *Literary Criticism: An Introduction to Theory and Practice*. 5th ed. New York: Longman, 2011. Print. An excellent advanced introduction, including a nice historical survey of criticism, a chapter on "Cultural Studies," information on websites, and sample essays and excerpts from students and professionals.

Carpenter, Scott. *Reading Lessons: An Introduction to Theory*. Upper Saddle River, NJ: Prentice, 2000. Print. This is "not a how-to manual," Carpenter says, refusing to "present recipes for producing" different kinds of criticism. He does, however, provide an often entertaining overview that includes website resources and films.

Eagleton, Terry. *Literary Theory: An Introduction*. 3rd ed. Minneapolis: U of Minnesota P, 2008. Print. Witty and opinionated, Eagleton's introduction to theory had a huge impact on the popularization of theory. For advanced students.

Eagleton, Terry. *How to Read Literature*. New Haven, CT: Yale UP, 2014. Print. An amusing and provocative introduction to concepts like "character," "narrative," and "openings."

Gill, Brendan. *Here at "The New Yorker."* New York: Random, 1975. Print.
———. *A New York Life*. New York: Poseidon, 1990. Print.

Liu, Alan, ed. *Voice of the Shuttle*. Web. This website, maintained at the U of California, Santa Barbara, by Liu, graduate students, and others, contains pages introducing various topics—hypertext fiction, cyberculture, gender studies, deconstruction, etc. It's also a good portal to other electronic resources. Accessed March 7, 2015.

Remnick, David. "Miss Gould." *The New Yorker*. Feb. 28, 2005. Print. A lovely elegy for Miss Gould, who died the week before this issue at the age of 87. This essay can be accessed on *The New Yorker*'s website.

Selden, Raman, Peter Widdowson, and Peter Brocker. *A Reader's Guide to Contemporary Literary Theory*. 5th ed. New York: Routledge, 2005. Print. Detailed and authoritative introductions to "Russian Formalism," "Marxist theories," "postcolonialist theories," "gay, lesbian and queer theories," and others.

Sim, Stuart, and Borin Van Loon. *Introducing Critical Theory: A Graphic Guide*. Cambridge: Icon Books, 2009. Print. This advanced introduction is especially user-friendly, employing a comic-book style and an irreverent sense of humor.

Unifying the Work

New Criticism

The study of literature means the study of literature,
not of biography nor of literary history (incidentally of
vast importance), not of grammar, not of etymology,
not of anything except the works themselves, viewed
as their creators wrote them, viewed as art, as transcripts
of humanity—not as logic, not as psychology, not as ethics.

—Martin W. Sampson[1]

What you'll learn in this chapter:

- To identify opportunities to use New Critical principles.
- To develop ideas about texts using New Criticism.
- To write and revise essays, step by step, about literary texts, using New Criticism.
- To apply New Criticism in a variety of contexts.

THE PURPOSE OF NEW CRITICISM

Martin Sampson's point in the epigraph to this chapter may seem so obvious that you wonder why he felt compelled to say it: Well, yes, the study of literature means studying literature, just as the study of mollusks does not mean the study of monkeys or dust mites or meerkats. But Sampson is writing at the end of the nineteenth century, when the idea of an English department and the academic study of literature is a relatively new invention (the first professorship devoted to literature was created in 1876 at Harvard). To study literature itself for its own sake, and not for what it can tell us about biography, history, grammar, logic, psychology, or ethics, was a remarkable and exciting notion. And it was an idea that quickly caught traction in colleges and universities: By the 1920s, the English department at Harvard was drawing twice as many students as Economics, the runner-up.

For much of the twentieth century, much of this study of literature itself was primarily based on principles that became known as the "New Criticism." The name came from John Crowe Ransom's 1941 book entitled *The New Criticism*, even though the point of Ransom's book, ironically, was that *the* New Critic had not yet appeared. The effects of this way of reading literature continue even to the present day, when it might better be called "the old New Criticism." Although those who have been called "New Critics" have not agreed in every respect, and some have even rejected the title, it is possible to identify a number of fundamental assumptions shared by an enormous number of critics and teachers and their students over the past century or so. The odds, in fact, are excellent that some of your English teachers were trained in the methods of New Criticism, even if they never heard the term; and in surprisingly many classrooms today, even in the midst of a cornucopia of critical options, New Criticism is often essentially the only approach on the menu, its principles so pervasive that they seem natural and obvious—and therefore remain, often enough, unarticulated. Let's have a close look at close reading.

Basic Principles Reflected

One way to begin to see why New Criticism has been so appealing and enduring is to look at a famous poem written about the time that this way of reading was really emerging as a critical force. This poem is of particular interest because it is about poetry, attempting to define it, advising us how to view it. Thus, it seeks to provide a kind of guide for criticism: "Here is what poetry ought to be," the poem says; "read it with these standards in mind." Widely anthologized in introduction-to-literature texts since its appearance, Archibald MacLeish's "Ars Poetica" (Latin for "The Art of Poetry") not only reflects the ideas of a nascent New Criticism, but it also probably helped to promote those ideas over several generations.

Ars Poetica
Archibald MacLeish

A poem should be palpable and mute
As a globed fruit,

Dumb
As old medallions to the thumb,

Silent as the sleeve-worn stone   5
Of casement ledges where the moss has grown—

A poem should be wordless
As the flight of birds.

A poem should be motionless in time
As the moon climbs,   10

Leaving, as the moon releases
Twig by twig the night-entangled trees,

Leaving, as the moon behind the winter leaves,
Memory by memory the mind—

A poem should be motionless in time   15
As the moon climbs.

A poem should be equal to:
Not true.

For all the history of grief
An empty doorway and a maple leaf.   20

For love
The leaning grasses and two lights above the sea—

A poem should not mean
But be.

                                                                    (1926)

    This poem is startling from its opening lines, asserting that a poem should be "palpable and mute." How can a poem possibly be "palpable," or "capable of being handled, touched, or felt" (*American Heritage Dictionary*)? Whether we think of a poem as an idea, or a group of ideas, or the writing on a piece of paper, or a group of spoken words, none of these seems to be the sort of thing we can handle. And how can a poem be "mute"? Isn't a poem made of words? Don't we at least imagine a voice speaking the words? Suggesting that a poem be mute seems a bit like suggesting that a movie be invisible, or a song be inaudible, or a sculpture be without shape.

    But MacLeish reiterates these ideas in subsequent lines, saying explicitly that a poem should be "Dumb," "Silent," and (most amazingly) "wordless" (lines 3, 5, and 7). He uses comparisons that reinforce particularly the idea of being "palpable." In comparing the poem to a "fruit," for instance, MacLeish suggests that the poem should be a real thing, having substance. The idea that it should be "globed" (a "globed fruit") emphasizes the three-dimensionality that MacLeish desires: like a globe, the poem should have more extension in time and space than a map or a picture. Not just a depiction of a fruit, it should somehow *be* a *globed* fruit. Likewise, "old medallions to the thumb" and "the sleeve-worn stone / Of casement ledges where the moss has grown" are both not only "silent" or "dumb," but they also have

an enduring solidity, a tangible reality. These images of fruit, old medallions, and worn ledges may also seem a bit mysterious, like "the flight of
birds" (line 8), which in some "wordless," seemingly magical way is organized and orchestrated—as anyone knows who's ever seen a flock of birds
rise together and move as one, silently.

From lines 1 to 8, then, we draw our first principle of New Criticism:

☞ 1. A poem should be seen as an object—an object of an extraordinary
    and somewhat mysterious kind, a silent object that is not equal to
    the words printed on a page, but has some reality that transcends the
    page.

Lines 9–16 articulate another idea: "A poem should be motionless in time." What does this mean? Most obviously, MacLeish is saying that poems shouldn't change. Aren't Shakespeare's sonnets the same
today as they were when he wrote them? ("So long as men can breathe
or eyes can see, / So long lives this, and this gives life to thee," as Sonnet 18 says.) But MacLeish's comparison, "As the moon climbs," is not
so easy to grasp: how can the moon be "climbing" through the sky, yet
"motionless in time"? Perhaps the answer lies in the repeated idea that
the moon, like the poem, should be "Leaving, as the moon releases /
Twig by twig the night-entangled trees" (11–12); it should be "Leaving,
as the moon behind the winter leaves / Memory by memory the mind"
(13–14). Something that is "leaving" is neither fully here nor fully gone;
it is caught in time and space, in an in-between contradictory timespace.
We do not notice a memory deteriorating: it is there, unchanging; then
it is only partly there; then it may be gone. The moon climbing in the
sky does seem like this: it appears to sit there, motionless in time, yet it is,
paradoxically, leaving and will "release" the trees. MacLeish repeats lines
9–10 in lines 15–16, as if his own poem is motionless, continuing on but
remaining in the same place it was.

This paradox adds to the mystery of the earlier lines and also suggests
a second principle:

☞ 2. The poem as silent object is unchanging, existing somehow both
    within and outside of time, "leaving" yet "motionless."

Lines 17–18 offer a third surprising idea: "A poem should be equal
to: / not true." It's difficult to believe that MacLeish is saying that poems
should lie. But what is he saying? Lines 19–22 appear to explain his point,
but these lines seem particularly difficult. What can these lines possibly
mean—ignoring for the moment the concluding assertion of lines 23–24,
which seems to be that poems ought not have meanings? The lines are
obscure basically because the verbs are missing, so our task of making sense

must include imagining what has been left out. MacLeish, in other words, is forcing us to create the poem in our minds, beyond the page.

First MacLeish says, "For all the history of grief / An empty doorway and a maple leaf" (19–20). If we look closely at this statement, its form is familiar and clear enough: "For X, Y." Or, adding a verb, "For X, substitute Y." Thus, I take these lines to mean simply that instead of recounting "all the history of grief," the poet should present instead "An empty doorway and a maple leaf." An empty doorway can speak to us of someone departed, conveying an emptiness and an absence that may be more compressed and intense than an entire history of grief. A maple leaf, perhaps lying on the ground, bursting with fall colors inevitably turning to brown and crumbling, may tell us something about loss more directly and powerfully and concisely than any history book.

The next two lines are similarly structured: "For love / The leaning grasses and two lights above the sea." That is, "For love," an abstraction, impossible to grasp, the poet should present something concrete: "The leaning grasses and two lights above the sea." Although I can't say precisely how the grasses and lights here stand for love, somehow as images they do seem romantic, mysterious, moving. This principle of selecting something concrete to stand for an abstraction had already been advocated by T. S. Eliot in 1919 in what turned out to be an extremely influential opinion for the formation of New Criticism: "The only way of expressing emotion in the form of art," Eliot said, "is by finding an 'objective correlative'; in other words, a set of objects, a situation, a chain of events which shall be the formula of that *particular* emotion" (124–125). Not surprisingly, throughout its history New Criticism has been especially concerned with analyzing the imagery of particular works, noticing how a poem's "objective correlatives" structure its ideas.

It is not then that the poem should lie, but rather that it does not strive to tell the truth in any literal or historical or prosaic way. Poetry, MacLeish is saying, should speak metaphorically, substituting evocative images for the description of emotions, or historical details, or vague ideas. Instead of telling us about an idea or emotion, literature confronts us with *something* that may spark emotions or ideas. A poem is an experience, not a discussion of an experience.

The final two lines summarize this point in a startling way: "A poem should not mean / But be." Ordinarily we assume that words are supposed to convey a particular meaning, transferring ideas from an author to a reader. But the images that MacLeish's poem has given us—the globed fruit, the old medallions, the casement ledges, the flight of birds, the moon climbing, the empty doorway and the maple leaf, the leaning grasses and the two lights—these do not "mean" anything in a literal, historical, scientific way. What is the meaning, for example, of a flight of birds? Of a casement ledge where some moss has grown? These things just *are*. They are suggestive and even moving, but their meaning is something we impose on them; they simply exist, and we experience their being more powerfully than any abstract idea. It would be a mistake to think an empty doorway is somehow a *translation* of all the history of grief.

In much the same way, poems (MacLeish is asserting) do not mean, but rather have an existence—which takes us to the third principle:

☞ 3. Poems as unchanging objects represent an organized entity, not a meaning. In this way, poems are therefore fundamentally different from prose: Prose strives to convey meaning; but poems cannot be perfectly translated or summarized, for they offer a being, an existence, an experience perhaps—not a meaning.

Radicals in Tweed Jackets

What was the appeal of these principles? Why did New Criticism, a drastically new way of reading, become so popular on college campuses?

In the landmark study that did much to solidify the academic prestige of New Criticism, Wellek and Warren's *Theory of Literature* (1949), René Wellek declares, "The work of art is an object of knowledge" (156). Because the literary work has an "objective" status, Wellek says, critical statements about a work are not merely opinions of taste. "It will always be possible," he maintains, "to determine which point of view grasps the subject most thoroughly and deeply." Thus, "all relativism is ultimately defeated" (156).

Although this assumption that the poem exists like an object, like fruit, like medallions, allows New Critics to think of literary criticism as a discipline just as rigorous and prestigious as a science, it is clear that for New Critics poems are in an important way also not like the objects studied by science. Poems, as MacLeish puts it, are "motionless in time"; they embody, as Marianne Moore says in a poem entitled "Poetry," "imaginary gardens with real toads in them." Thus, a poem is an entity somehow transcending time, existing in a realm different from that of science, the realm of the literary, of the imagination. (Curiously, as if to refute the ideas her poem seems to embrace, Moore repeatedly revised "Poetry," drastically cutting the poem in one version—the worst one, many of her admirers have thought—from over fifty lines down to three. So much for "motionless in time.")[2]

The implications of this second crucial assumption, that poems exist outside of time, can already be seen in the criticism of T. S. Eliot, whose ideas (as we've just seen) influenced the New Critics. In "Tradition and the Individual Talent," Eliot's famous essay of 1919, poetry is said to be "not the expression of personality, but an escape from personality" (10). The New Critics are aware, of course, that poems have authors, and they will sometimes refer to biographical information, but it is not the focus of their attention. Close reading of the work itself should reveal what the reader needs to know. Historical and biographical information, to be sure, may sometimes be helpful, but it should not be essential.

This exclusion of authors and their contexts is taken to what might appear to be its logical extreme in Wimsatt and Beardsley's influential essay on "The Intentional Fallacy in *The Verbal Icon*." Even when biographical and historical information is meticulously and voluminously gathered, Wimsatt and Beardsley question its value for reading the work. Even Coleridge's own account of how "Kubla Kahn" came to him (in a dream, supposedly), does not tell us anything about how to read the poem itself, Wimsatt and Beardsley say—even if we could be sure Coleridge is telling the truth. Only the poem can tell us how to read the poem, according to the New Critics.

In other words, the person who bought the eighteen-page manuscript of Don MacLean's massively popular "American Pie" for $1.2 million on April 7, 2015, no doubt hoping to discover what the heck the song's much-discussed lyrics really mean, acquired a document of biographical and historical interest, but not anything that should affect how we understand the song, or that would reveal the identity of the jester, of the king and queen, or any other mysteries.[3] In interviews related to the auction, MacLean observed that the 1971 song, which proceeds from "the day the music died" (in 1959 when Buddy Holly's plane crashed, it seems), is about the decline and decay of American music and culture.[4] As New Critics would point out, we should not take MacLean's word for this—he may be kidding us, or have forgotten his intentions, or failed to realize his aims, or have created something that surpasses his own appreciation. This general meaning, to be sure, does seem to fit the song itself, but it is hardly a revelation. When the singer tells us he drove his "Chevy to the levee but the levee was dry," for instance, the song clearly conveys a sense of loss and disappointment. The chorus's refrain of "Bye, bye, Miss American Pie" seems to combine a farewell to the idealism of Miss America pageants and to the vanishing patriotism suggested by the saying "American as apple pie."

To press this point: The manuscript reveals that MacLean drafted a verse in which the music that has died is being revived. Does the discovery of this draft affect the way we should interpret the song? New Critics would say, "No, of course not; it's not in the song. The study of the song means studying the song." It's worth noting that although newspapers worldwide featured headlines the day after the auction announcing "Don McLean Explains Enigmatic Lyrics to American Pie," as the *Newcastle Herald* put it, he, in fact, "declined to run through all the cultural references," as the accompanying article noted. The reporter went on to observe that "the catalogue said it was probably safe to conclude that references to the king meant Elvis Presley, Helter Skelter referred to the Charles Manson murders, and 'the jester on the sidelines in a cast' was Bob Dylan. But that still leaves plenty of other details up for debate."

The problem with drawing these conclusions—as much as many people would like to have these correspondences settled—is that there may be other and arguably better interpretations. The song says that "The jester sang for the king and queen / In a coat he borrowed from James Dean," and there is a striking resemblance between the coat Bob Dylan is wearing and the way he is posed on an album cover from this era, and a coat worn by James Dean in a famous publicity shot. But if the Jester is Bob Dylan, then who are "the king and queen"? We know that Dylan in August 1963 sang at a Martin Luther King rally, and that President John F. Kennedy and his wife, Jacqueline, watched him on television. I'm not aware in the voluminous analyses of this song (and I admittedly may have missed it) of anyone noting a time when Dylan sang for Elvis and someone else who would fit nicely as his "queen." The king and queen might be Elvis and Priscilla Presley, or Pete Seeger and Joan Baez, or someone else, but it hardly "seems safe" to declare this case closed.

Perhaps you have wondered "Why doesn't the author just tell me what he or she meant to say? Why is literature so obscure and ambiguous?" MacLean's answer, which the New Critics would thoroughly approve of, can be inferred from this preauction observation: "People ask me if I left the lyrics open to ambiguity. Of course I did. I wanted to make a whole series of complex statements."[5] If he were to explain the song now, line by line, detail by detail, he'd be diminishing and limiting the rich responses that listeners have had to the song for over forty years.

If the author's life, manuscripts, and culture are the wrong place to focus our study of literature, according to the New Critics, then what about the reader's individual and personal response? In "The Affective Fallacy," also in *The Verbal Icon*, their complementary essay to "The Intentional Fallacy," Wimsatt and Beardsley undermine the importance of the individual reader's reaction. The groundwork for their position had already been worked out in the 1920s by I. A. Richards, who conducted a series of close-reading experiments with his students at Cambridge. He began with the assumption that students should be able to read poems richly by applying careful scrutiny to the work itself. To focus students' attention on the work itself, Richards would often remove the distraction of authors' names, dates, even titles. In 1929, when he reported his results in *Practical Criticism*, two things appeared to be clear.

First, his students seemed not to be very good at reading texts carefully. Richards thought, and many people agreed, that students obviously needed much more training in "close reading." They needed to learn how to look carefully at a text, suppressing their own variable and subjective responses, as Wimsatt and Beardsley would later persuasively argue. How a work affects a particular reader, Wimsatt and Beardsley assert, is not critically significant. Whereas "the Intentional Fallacy," they say, "is a confusion between the poem and its origins," the "Affective Fallacy is a confusion between the poem and its *results*" (21). Biographers may want to speculate on the poet's intention, and psychologists may want to theorize about a poem's effects, but literary critics should study the poem itself.

The second thing made evident by Richards' "experiments" was that such close reading was not only possible but very rewarding, as Richards himself was able to read these isolated works in revealing and stimulating ways, exposing unsuspected complexities and subtleties in the works he examined. Even in the following description of the creative process of poets, taken from Cleanth Brooks and Robert Penn Warren's New Criticism textbook, *Understanding Poetry* (1938), the author's intention is of little enduring interest:

> At the same time that he [the poet] is trying to envisage the poem as a whole, he is trying to relate the individual items to that whole. He cannot assemble them in a merely arbitrary fashion; they must bear some relation to each other. So he develops his sense of the whole, the anticipation of the finished poem, as he works with the parts, and moves from one part to another. Then as the sense of the whole develops, it modifies the process by which the poet selects and relates the parts, the words, images, rhythms, local ideas, events, etc.... It is an infinitely complicated process of establishing interrelations. (527)

Implicit in this description of how a poet works are the directions for what a critic should do: Most obviously, the critic will want to recover the idea, or principle, or theme, that holds the poem's parts together and thereby reveal how the parts relate to each other and to the whole. (Such a careful unfolding of the poem's parts and their relationships is often called an "explication.") Although speculation about the poet's actual process of creating the poem may be entertaining, it is finally irrelevant, for the critic's real interest is in the finished poem, not how it was finished. We can tell what the poet was working toward—the poem as a whole, the "interrelations" of its parts—simply by looking carefully at the shape and structure of the poem: at its form, in other words.

This emphasis on a work's form has led some people to think of New Criticism as a kind of "formalism" and also to link New Criticism to another movement, Russian formalism, which originated with the work of Viktor Shklovsky in 1917—about the same time that New Criticism's ideas first began to emerge in Western Europe and North America. The Russian formalists do seem to prefigure the New Critics when they assume that a writer should be evaluated as a craftsman who fashions an artistic object. The writer should *not* be evaluated, New Critics and Russian formalists would agree, on the basis of the work's message. *Paradise Lost* is a great poem (or it isn't) because of Milton's artistic performance, not because of the validity of its theological or political message. Russian formalism (not too surprisingly) was rather short-lived, fading away by the late 1920s, discouraged by the Russian authorities, who no doubt noted that focusing on style and technique would tend to let all sorts of ideas float around.

Although New Criticism has been criticized at times for its lack of political commitment, one could argue (especially in light of Russian formalism's fate) that an attention to form (not message) is, in fact, a subtly powerful commitment to openness and freedom: You can say whatever you like, New Criticism implicitly suggests, as long as you say it well. Admittedly, in celebrating a certain kind of form (unified complexity, or organic unity), New Criticism has perhaps not been so entirely open in its actual practice, as feminist critics have persuasively argued, noticing the predominance of white males in the canon of works valued by New Critics. Is the relative absence of women in the traditional canon of New Criticism really a consequence of its principles? One could argue that women have tended to write in genres that may resist New Criticism's particular kind of close reading (in journals and letters, for instance), but certainly some women (Jane Austen, George Eliot, Emily Dickinson, Virginia Woolf) have produced works celebrated by New Critical readings.

It is clear enough that New Criticism's kind of formalism, which turns away from politics, must take place within some (unacknowledged, invisible) political context, but at the same time it does not seem clear to me that any particular political stance is inherently more or less suited to New Critical strategies. New Criticism discriminates against works that are "poorly made" by its definition—works that are simplistic, single-sided, shallow, inarticulate, lacking in irony and self-consciousness. New Criticism champions works that repay our careful and imaginative attention, works that seem to challenge us to look again, to look more deeply, to find a more complex unity. It might even be said that New Criticism makes it both possible and necessary for other kinds of approaches to arise. At the least, many critics would agree that New Criticism remains a kind of "norm" against which other approaches can be delineated. At its best, it remains an exciting and revealing strategy for unfolding literary works.

How to Do New Criticism

To make sure the process is clear in your mind, let's think of it in three steps:

1. What complexities (or tensions, ironies, paradoxes, oppositions, ambiguities) can you find in the work?
2. What idea unifies the work, resolving these ambiguities?
3. What details or images support this resolution (that is, connect the parts to the whole)?

1. The first step assumes that great works are complex, even when they appear to be simple. Literature does not imitate life in any literal way, according to the New Critics; instead, poems (and other works) create realities of their own, transforming and ordering our experience. A poem, as Coleridge says, in a quotation often cited by New Critics, is an act of the imagination, "that synthetic and magical power"—an act that "reveals itself in the balance or reconciliation of opposites or discordant qualities" (11). Poems have the power, Coleridge says, "of reducing multitude into unity of effect." And, for the New Critics, the richer and more compelling the "multitude" of ideas or "discordant qualities," the greater the poem's power. The sort of complexity that New Critics particularly value is captured in Keats' concept of "negative capability," which is also often cited by New Critics: It is the capability "of being in uncertainties, mysteries, doubts, without any irritable reaching after fact and reason" (1:193).

When New Critics identify a poem's complexities (the first step here), they use a number of closely related terms, especially "irony," "ambiguity," "paradox," and "tension." Although these terms mean slightly different things, they all point to the idea of complexity—that the poem says one thing and means another, or says two things at once, or seems to say opposing things, or strains against its apparent meaning. For instance, in "The Language of Paradox," a celebrated essay from *The Well-Wrought Urn* (1947), Cleanth Brooks shows how Donne's famous poem "The Canonization" (included here in Appendix I) sets up a dilemma:

> Either: Donne does not take love seriously; here he is merely sharpening his wit as a sort of mechanical exercise. Or: Donne does not take sainthood seriously; here he is merely indulging in a cynical and bawdy parody. (11)

2. The second step assumes that great works do have a unifying idea, a theme. It's much more useful to think of this theme in terms of a complete thought or a sentence rather than a phrase. For instance, to say that the theme of Donne's "Canonization" is "love and religion" really doesn't tell

us much about how Donne solves the dilemma of sainthood versus love. Here's what Brooks tells his readers:

> Neither account [that Donne doesn't take love seriously, or that he doesn't take religion seriously] is true; a reading of the poem will show that Donne takes both love and religion seriously; it will show, further, that the paradox is here his inevitable instrument. (11)

A cynical reader might observe (with some justification) that paradox is Donne's "inevitable" instrument because the New Critics inevitably find something like paradox in every great poem. But Brooks' point, of course, is that paradox is inevitable because Donne, with the imagination of a great poet, sets up the problem in such a way that only paradox will resolve it.

3. The third step unfolds or explicates the poem, indicating how the parts work together. This description of the poem is no substitute for the poem itself, but it should enrich our experience of it. Oftentimes, as in the case of Brooks' essay on "The Canonization," the critic will move through the work carefully from beginning to end, dividing the work into parts, and then suggesting how every aspect of the parts relates to our sense of the whole. Following Aristotle's ancient ideas, New Critics have talked about the "organic unity" of works, as if the poem were a creature, a living being, with every part playing an essential role.

Here is a sample of Brooks' explication:

> In this last stanza, the theme receives a final complication. The lovers in rejecting life actually win the most intense life. This paradox has been hinted at earlier in the phoenix metaphor. Here it receives a powerful dramatization. (15)

In this passage, notice how Brooks identifies a paradox related to the theme and then connects that paradox to an earlier image. These are both characteristic moves for New Critics.

Film and Other Genres

These steps won't read a poem for you; they won't supply the sort of imagination, creativity, and attention you'll need to read literature closely. But they will help to structure your process of reading and writing, and they can, in fact, be used to help you analyze any kind of literary work or artistic object, or perhaps anything. Consider, for example, this concluding paragraph from Michael Atkinson's review of *Napoleon Dynamite*, a bizarre, award-winning film released in 2004 (to understand the paragraph, you should know that Jared Hess is the film's director, and Jon Heder plays

Napoleon; also, Atkinson refers in this passage to a Todd Solondz film, *Welcome to the Dollhouse*, that offers a darker view of teen-age angst):

> But the center of Hess's cyclone is Heder and his tetherball-playing monster teen, who is both the film's forbidding hero and its great object of derision. Unlike the Solondz film, *Napoleon Dynamite* exudes little sense of social horror; it struggles to maintain a sunny disposition despite the traumatic social meltdown we witness and the apparent fact that Napoleon is headed not for a tech college but for a long, dire career in food service. He's all too emblematic of too many Americans, and if Hess's movie weren't so funny, it'd be a tragedy.

Even without seeing this movie, or reading the rest of the review, you can see the assumptions that are driving Atkinson's analysis. In the first sentence, Napoleon, played by Heder, is paradoxically both "hero" and "object of derision." The adjective that modifies "hero" is "forbidding," while the adjective that modifies "object of derision" is "great," and this pulling in opposite directions also occurs in the description of Napoleon as a "tetherball-playing monster teen": Tetherball is an elementary school game, played by children during recess—not at all what one associates with a "monster teen." The second sentence also celebrates the film's balancing of oppositions, maintaining "a sunny disposition despite the traumatic social meltdown we witness" and Napoleon's apparently dim future. The third and final sentence continues to see the film in paradoxical terms, as Napoleon's weirdness is somehow also "all too emblematic of too many Americans." As an earlier sentence puts it, Napoleon "is such a fantastic creation you can't help seeing him as both a catastrophically extreme case and the common flailing nerd we all still shelter in our deepest memory banks." This kind of both/and vision, unifying oppositions, extends even to the genre of the film, as Atkinson's conclusion asserts that the film is a comedy that would have been a tragedy, if it "weren't so funny."

Clearly Atkinson, like a New Critic, is noticing and valuing paradoxes, ironies, and tensions. Moreover, Atkinson sees how these oppositions are held together: The movie is dismal yet ultimately "sunny," a tragedy that is really a comedy; Napoleon is both heroic and ridiculous, "catastrophically extreme" and everyman. This idea, in fact, is arguably what unifies the film for Atkinson—that at some deeper level, we are like Napoleon. His absurdity is what sets him apart, and at the same time what makes him part of us. We laugh at Napoleon, but he is constructed in such a way that we are also laughing at some core aspect of ourselves. Although Atkinson is obviously interested in how audiences respond to the film, he tends to view the movie as an artistic object, rather than an

© Photofest, Inc.

experience. He sees the character of Napoleon, for instance, as a coherent thing, "a perfectly conceived and executed battery of melodramatic
harrumphs, bruised exhalations, defensive squints, clueless pronounce-
ments, and explosively irate retorts." And the movie as a whole succeeds
because its complex ironies and paradoxes are held together in a satisfying unity. Although I seriously doubt that Atkinson considers himself to
be a card-carrying New Critic, his assumptions and values are in line with
New Criticism—which isn't surprising, when we consider its pervasive
popularity over the past century.

This brief look at a movie review suggests how we might reason backward from a finished essay to the strategies employed. To give you a better
idea of how to use these principles, let's work through the process of writing
a sample New Critical essay in the next section.

THE WRITING PROCESS: A SAMPLE ESSAY

Literary works are often charming, uplifting, amusing; but they are also
often troubling and challenging, confronting difficult and disturbing issues,
stimulating our thought. The following poem will probably haunt you. It is

a powerful and moving engagement with one of the most controversial and emotional topics of our day. Read it carefully, writing down any questions or comments that occur, looking particularly for tensions or oppositions or ambiguities.

The Mother
Gwendolyn Brooks

Abortions will not let you forget.
You remember the children you got that you did not get,
The damp small pulps with a little or no hair,
The singers and workers that never handled the air.
You will never neglect or beat   5
Them, or silence or buy with a sweet.
You will never wind up the sucking-thumb
Or scuttle off ghosts that come.
You will never leave them, controlling your luscious sigh,
Return for a snack of them, with gobbling mother-eye.   10

I have heard in the voices of the wind the voices of my dim
    killed children.
I have contracted. I have eased
My dim dears at the breasts they could never suck.
I have said, Sweets, if I sinned, if I seized
Your luck   15
And your lives from your unfinished reach,
If I stole your births and your names,
Your straight baby tears and your games,
Your stilted or lovely loves, your tumults, your marriages,
    aches and your deaths,
If I poisoned the beginnings of your breaths,   20
Believe that even in my deliberateness I was not deliberate.
Though why should I whine,
Whine that the crime was other than mine?—
Since anyhow you are dead.
Or rather, or instead,   25
You were never made.
But that too, I am afraid,
Is faulty: of, what shall I say, how is the truth to be said?
You were born, you had body, you died.
It is just that you never giggled or planned or cried.   30

Believe me, I loved you all.
Believe me, I knew you, though faintly, and I loved, I loved you
All.   (1945)

Preparing to Write

Compare what you've written in your brainstorming to the following list of observations:

(a) The speaker says, "Abortions will not let you for-get," as if abortions could actively do something. But an abortion is a medical procedure; it can't make *"you"* remem-ber or keep *"you"* from forgetting. Why doesn't the speaker just say, "You can't forget about your abortion"? And why does the speaker say "you" rather than "me," especially since the second section reveals that she has had abortions?

(b) The second line is contradictory, referring to chil-dren "you got that you did not get." Either you got them or you didn't, it would seem.

(c) Why is the poem called "The Mother" if she has had abortions? Does this refer to her other children or to the abortions? This is probably an important tension: It is, after all, the title.

(d) Lines 3–4 offer conflicting views. In line 3, "the chil-dren" are simply "damp small pulps with a little or with no hair." A "pulp" isn't alive, isn't a person, so removing a hair-less (or nearly hairless) pulp isn't a big deal. But line 4 refers to the abortions in a strikingly different way, as "singers and workers that never handled the air." As singers and work-ers, the children are real, and their loss is tragic: They did not even get a chance to handle the air—which is a wonder-ful and surprising description of living. We are all, as singers and workers, handling the air.

(e) Another opposition shapes the next few lines. Lines 5–6 suggest that the abortions were in some respects a good thing: "You will never neglect or beat / Them." The next image, never "silence or buy with a sweet," is perhaps faintly negative or even neutral: It doesn't sound good to think of silencing or buying chil-dren, and giving them "a sweet" probably isn't the greatest thing to do, but every parent resorts to such strategies. And the next image moves into the realm of tenderness: to "wind up the sucking-thumb" or "scuttle off ghosts that come"—these are acts of kindness. So the lines move from abuse, which places the abortions in a more positive light, to parental care, which makes the abortions seem more tragic.

(f) I notice that the speaker seems to be talking about more than one abortion. But the pain revealed in the poem won't let us easily conclude that the speaker is callous, readily aborting babies without a thought.

(g) The idea of eating up the children in line 10 is strange ("a snack of them, with gobbling mother-eye").

It's fine if your ideas aren't similar to those above. In fact, it's great because we'd certainly be bored if everyone thought the same things. But you may find it useful to notice the level of detail involved above and the kind of attention being paid. This kind of preparation will make writing about the poem much easier.

You might reasonably wonder how much you need to know about 1945, when the poem was published; about the history of the debate over abortion; about Gwendolyn Brooks' life; about her career as a poet and about her other poems; and on and on. All these things would be good to know, but in adopting a New Critical stance, you will assume that the poem itself will reveal whatever it is essential for you to know. So, remind yourself specifically what a New Critical reading attempts to expose: unity and complexity. Great works confront us with a unified ambiguity; second-rate works see things simply or fragmentarily.

Shaping

What would you say is the unifying idea of "The Mother"? What holds it together? Those questions are crucial to a New Critical reading because they lead to your thesis, which will shape and control the development of your essay. Even in the few notes I've reproduced above, it seems clear that the title points us toward the poem's complexity: The speaker, as the title identifies her, is "The Mother," and yet she speaks only of the children she does not have, the children who have been aborted. So how can she be a mother without any children? How can she love her children, or have destroyed them, if they don't exist? That, it seems to me, is one way of saying what the poem struggles through. The theme or unifying idea, holding together the ambiguous status of the speaker, can be stated in any number of ways, and you might try out your own way of expressing it. Here's one way to put it:

Although her children do not exist, and may have never existed, the speaker is a mother because she loves her "children."

In articulating this theme, I've given emphasis to the way the poem ends. Generally that's where the oppositions are resolved. In this case, I would argue, the ambiguity between the speaker as mother and nonmother is resolved at the end of the poem with her declaration of love. She could not love the children if they did not have some kind of existence, and if they exist in some way, then she is some kind of "mother." But her status is by no means simple. Likewise, she "knew" them, she says, even if it was "faintly"; and, again, it would seem she could not know them if they did not exist, if they were not her children.

The strategy of a New Critical reading, then, would involve showing how the details of the poem support and elaborate this complex or ironic unity. Your structure involves arranging this evidence in a coherent way, grouping kinds of details perhaps or moving logically through the poem. That is, throughout the poem, a New Critical reading would find oppositions reinforcing and support- ing in some way the poem's central ambiguity. For instance, line 21 would be seen as a reflection of the central opposition. The speaker says, "even in my deliberateness I was not deliberate." Just as the children who are aborted are not children; just as the woman who gives up her motherhood by having an abortion nonetheless retains her claim to the name of "mother"; by the same token, the speaker's "deliberateness is not deliberate."

In other words, her decision to have the abortion was made with "deliberateness," and for such decisions we are more accountable, by some measures anyway, than for impulsive decisions. Premeditated murder, for instance, is in theory a more serious crime than a spontaneous crime of passion. But the mother's culpability is qualified by the rest of the sen- tence, which says that the deliberateness was not "deliberate." She carefully decided something she did not carefully decide, so it seems.

Drafting

After you've worked your way through the poem, noting oppositions, ten- sions, ambiguities, paradoxes, and considering how these relate to the poem's unity, then it's time for a draft. Here is a draft developed out of the annotations above; it's been polished up a bit, and there are annotations in the margin to help you see what is going on.

The Mother Without Children: A Reading of Gwendolyn Brooks' "The Mother"

From the notes: see (c).	Gwendolyn Brooks' "The Mother" points to a paradox with its first word, "Abortions." Although the speaker is called "the mother" in the title, she quickly
Setting up the essay's form: mother vs. not-mother.	reveals that "the children" have actually been aborted. How can she be a mother if her children never existed? Her opening line asserts that "Abortions will not let you forget," but what is there for her to remember? The rest

of the poem shows the "mother's" struggle with this problem: how to remember "the children that you did not get" (2).

On the one hand, the speaker realizes the children are nothing more than "damp small pulps with a little or with no hair" (3), but the rest of this sentence sees them as "singers and workers that never handled the air" (4). If they can be called "singers and workers," then they must have some existence. But if they never "handled the air," they did not work and sing, and so their status as workers and singers is problematic, to say the least. This question is what is distressing the "mother," because if these fetuses were children, then her statement in line 17 is accurate: "I stole your births and your names." But the line begins with an "If," and it is this uncertainty that provides the speaker with some comfort.

The comfort takes two forms. The mother first eases her pain by pointing to the uncertainty of her decision to have the abortions: "even in my deliberations I was not deliberate" (21). Since she is uncertain about the status of what is being aborted, she decided without knowing what she was deciding. In truth, she still does not know what her decision means: No one can say with authority when life begins, or when fetuses become persons and when they are still unviable tissue masses, or "pulps" (3).

More importantly, the speaker is also comforted in the end by declaring her love, even though this expression paradoxically sustains her pain and mourning. She clings to the idea of her "dim killed children" (11), refusing to let them become "pulps," because she can love them only if they actually existed. So she must say that she "knew" them, even while admitting it was only "faintly" (32). She does claim her status as "the mother," as the title says, even though it causes her pain. As she says in the opening line, "Abortions will not let you forget," but perhaps only if you continue to see yourself as a mother, even though you have no children. Thus, the poem balances the speaker's two visions of herself, as murderer and as mother; and it resolves this conflict in the final lines, as the mother is able to atone for her decision, in some measure, by suffering with her memory always, saying, "I loved you, I loved you / All" (32–33).

This paragraph elaborates on the two possibilities: children or not.

The two possibilities come together in the uncertainty.

This explains how the uncertainty comforts the mother.

This point began to emerge in (f): the mother's pain suggests her love, which is explicitly declared later on.

Still relying on the opposition: mother/not; children/not.

From (a) above.

Resolving the problem set up in the intro.

In this essay I obviously didn't explicate every detail that supports my thesis. Rather, I tried to bring forth enough evidence to be persuasive. How much evidence you need to present to make a close reading convincing will vary depending on the work and your thesis. Follow your common sense and the guidance of your teacher.

Finally, as you apply New Criticism on your own, notice how two factors helped the sample essay develop smoothly.

1. Thorough preparation. The essay, for the most part, arranges and connects the extensive notes on the poem. When I came to write my essay, I had already written a great deal. I had much more material than I could use in my essay, and so I was able to pick and choose which ideas to use. This process, of selecting from an abundance of ideas, is a whole lot more pleasant than struggling for something to say.

2. Theoretical awareness. Since I knew what kind of approach I wanted to take, I knew to look for certain things in the poem: ideas or images in opposition; complexity or ambiguity; the unifying idea or theme. Likewise, I knew what my essay was going to set out to do. I didn't have to worry about whether Brooks might have intended to say this or that, nor did I have to worry about my own attitude toward abortion or even my own reaction to the poem. My job was to focus on the text itself, exposing its complexity and unity. By being aware of the theoretical stance you are evolving or adopting, you clarify for yourself what you're doing and how to do it.

PRACTICING NEW CRITICISM

It's highly unlikely that one example will make New Criticism crystal clear for you. You'll need to practice it for yourself, see other examples, and (ideally) discuss its workings with your teacher and classmates.

To get you started, I offer here two poems and a parable, along with guiding questions for each.

My Father's Martial Art
Stephen Shu-ning Liu

When he came home Mother said he looked
like a monk and stank of green fungus.
At the fireside he told us about life
at the monastery: his rock pillow,
his cold bath, his steel-bar lifting   5
and his wood-chopping. He didn't see
a woman for three winters, on Mountain O Mei.

"My Master was both light and heavy.
He skipped over treetops like a squirrel.
Once he stood on a chair, one foot tied   10
to a rope. We four pulled; we couldn't
move him a bit. His kicks could split
a cedar's trunk."

I saw Father break into a pumpkin
with his fingers. I saw him drop a hawk   15
with bamboo arrows. He rose before dawn, filled
our backyard with a harsh sound *hah, hah, hah:*
there was his Black Dragon Sweep, his Crane Stand,
his Mantis Walk, his Tiger Leap, his Cobra Coil...
Infrequently he taught me tricks and made me   20
fight the best of all the village boys.

From a busy street I brood over high cliffs
on O Mei, where my father and his Master sit:
shadows spread across their faces as the smog
between us deepens into a funeral pyre.   25

But don't retreat into night, my father.
Come down from the cliffs. Come

with a single Black Dragon Sweep and hush
this oncoming traffic with your *hah, hah, hah.*

                                                                 (1982)

Questions

1. Where is the poem's speaker located? How does this location relate to what he remembers?
2. What has happened to his father? What does line 25 suggest? Why does it seem especially appropriate that the "smog" comes between them?
3. What do you make of the name of the mountain? What might the oncoming traffic symbolize?
4. In each of the following pairs, which quality is embodied in the poem?
   Closeness, distance
   Presence, absence
   Power, impotence
   Light, heavy
   Spiritual, mundane

5. Do you think the word "Infrequently" in line 20 is significant? How does it contribute to the poem? (Does it simplify things? Make them more complex?)

6. What is the speaker struggling against in the poem? How is the struggle resolved? How is the resolution ambiguous and complex?   ■

On My First Son
Ben Jonson

Farewell, thou child of my right hand, and joy;
My sin was too much hope of thee, lov'd boy.
Seven years thou wert lent to me, and I thee pay,
Exacted by thy fate, on the just day.

Oh, could I lose all father now! For why   5
Will man lament the state he should envy?
To have so soon 'scaped world's and flesh's rage,
And if no other misery, yet age!

Rest in soft peace, and, asked, say, Here doth lie
Ben. Jonson his best piece of poetry.   10
For whose sake henceforth all his vows be such
As what he loves may never like too much.

(1616)

[escaped]

Questions

1. Ben Jonson's son was named "Benjamin," a Hebrew name that translates into English as the "child of the right hand." How does this fact help you to make sense of the poem? What does the first line tell us about the person who is being addressed in the poem? And what do you think New Critics mean when they say that we should focus upon the poem itself? (Is the significance of the child's name "in" this poem?)

2. What is the role of Jonson's religious faith in this poem? How is it a source of both comfort and tension?

3. In two places in the poem, Jonson points to "too much" of an emotion, creating an opposition between hope and love in the second line, and between loving and liking in the final line. How does this opposition contribute to the poem's unifying idea? (What, in other words, is the poem's unifying idea? Hint: What is the problem that Jonson is trying to solve in this poem? See lines 5–6.)

4. Explain how our understanding of lines 9–10 changes as we continue to read. That is, what do we think when we read "Here doth lie /

Ben. Johnson"? And what do we think as we finish this sentence? What does this shift in reference contribute to the poem? Does New Criticism value this kind of complexity?

5. In the sciences, ambiguity is usually considered undesirable. New Criticism, emerging as part of an alternate culture to the sciences, generally celebrates ambiguity and multiplicity of meaning. In line 11, "For whose sake" seems to have at least three possible references: Benjamin Jonson (the son), Ben Jonson, Jonson's poetry. Is this ambiguity fruitful? Can it be convincingly resolved? ∎

The Parable of the Prodigal Son[a] (c. 90 CE)

And he [Jesus] said, A certain man had two sons:

And the younger of them said to *his* father, Father, give me the portion of goods that falleth to me. And he divided unto them *his* living.[b]

And not many days after the younger son gathered all together, and took his journey into a far country,[c] and there wasted his substance with riotous living.

And when he had spent all, there arose a mighty famine in that land; and he began to be in want.

And he went and joined himself to a citizen of that country; and he sent him into his fields to feed swine.[d]

And he would fain have filled his belly with the husks[e] that the swine did eat: and no man gave unto him.

And when he came to himself, he said, How many hired servants of my father's have bread enough and to spare, and I perish with hunger!

I will arise and go to my father, and will say unto him, Father, I have sinned against heaven, and before thee,

And am no more worthy to be called thy son: make me as one of thy hired servants. And he arose, and came to his father. But when he was yet a great way off, his father saw him, and had compassion, and ran, and fell on his neck, and kissed him.

And the son said unto him, Father, I have sinned against heaven, and in thy sight, and am no more worthy to be called thy son.

But the father said to his servants, Bring forth the best robe, and put *it* on him; and put a ring on his hand, and shoes on *his* feet:

---

[a]Luke 15:11–32

[b]*divided ... his living:* one-third of the father's estate; the son had to renounce all further claim.

[c]*far country:* countries of the Jewish dispersal, or diaspora, in the areas bordering the Mediterranean Sea.

[d]*feed swine:* in Jewish custom, pigs were unclean.

[e]*husks:* pods of the carob tree, the eating of which was thought to be penitential.

And bring hither the fatted calf,[f] and kill *it*; and let us eat, and be merry:
For this my son was dead, and is alive again; he was lost, and is found. And
   they began to be merry.
Now his elder son was in the field: and as he came and drew nigh to the
   house, he heard music and dancing.
And he called one of the servants, and asked what these things meant.
And he said unto him, Thy brother is come; and thy father hath killed the
   fatted calf, because he hath received him safe and sound.
And he was angry, and would not go in: therefore came his father out, and
   intreated him.
And he answering said to *his* father, Lo, these many years do I serve thee,
   neither transgressed I at any time thy commandment: and yet thou
   never gavest me a kid, that I might make merry with my friends:
But as soon as this thy son was come, which hath devoured thy living with
   harlots, thou hast killed for him the fatted calf.
And he said unto him, Son, thou art ever with me, and all that I have is thine.
It was meet[g] that we should make merry, and be glad: for this thy brother
   was dead, and is alive again; and was lost, and is found.

Questions

1. The speaker of this story (or parable) is of course Jesus, as reported in
   The Gospel of Luke, and the context is that Jesus has been accused by
   "the Pharisees and scribes" of "welcoming sinners" and even eating
   with them. The parable apparently answers this charge—that Jesus
   spends time in the company of sinners. Does an awareness of that
   context affect your reading of the parable? How?
2. What irony do you find in the story?
3. How does a phrase like "the fatted calf" (in this translation) affect the
   tone of this parable? What other words and phrases do you find that
   contribute to the voice here?
4. What is the unifying idea of this parable?   ■

USEFUL TERMS FOR NEW CRITICISM

Here are some essential terms that are useful in literary analysis, including
New Criticism:

   Voice: The voice is what we don't actually hear, but must imagine that
   we hear in order to read the work itself effectively. In fiction, we are

---

[f]*fatted calf:* grain-fed calf.
[g]*meet:* appropriate.

usually given information about who is speaking. In drama, when it is performed anyway, we can actually see and hear the characters speaking. But in poetry, the reader often has to invent the voice out of clues in the work. Oftentimes, readers of poetry are not told directly who is speaking, to whom, from where, on what occasion. We have to figure that out, and that effort helps us to imagine the voices we should hear in the poem.

Speaker: The person speaking in the poem is not equivalent to the author. Even if the poem's speaker has the same name as the author, we should not assume that this speaker is the author. The speaker within the poem is a presentation, a kind of character.

Tone: Tone means pretty much the same thing in critical circles that it means in everyday life. It's the way something is said. What is interesting about texts, again, is that they have no tone until we supply it, and we do so based upon the clues of the text, as we read them. This invention is often not easy, necessitating careful attention. Many readers find it helpful to read a poem aloud, to hear the tone of the work. But note that you cannot simply read the poem aloud in order to create an interpretation of it; you really need an interpretation in order to read it aloud appropriately. Finding the right tone for a speaker in a poem is a process of trial and error. As you read the work, evolve your understanding of the way something is being said. Tone is sometimes part of the work's complexity—since the literal meaning may be altered by the tone.

Point of View: Everyone has to be somewhere, and point of view is simply that place from which a voice is speaking. Stories may be told by a *first-person narrator*, an "I" who tells us what happened. This "I" may be a participant in what happened, or not. The **narrator** (or speaker, if there doesn't seem to be a story to narrate) can also be a voice standing outside the story. Instead of saying, "I thought John was going" (first person), the narrator could say, "Sam thought John was going" (*third-person narrator*). If the third-person narrator seems to know everything, then we say the narrator is *omniscient*; if the third-person narrator knows more than any person or other entity could (for instance, what other characters are thinking), but not everything, then we have a "*limited omniscient narrator.*"

Irony: Irony calls for the reader to create, in a sense, a certain kind of mask for the speaker. When the reader identifies irony, the reader says, in effect, "I see two of you: a false you who's saying something that I'm supposed to see through; and another more true you who is really saying something different from what you appear on the surface to be saying." The mask may be serious; the face underneath may be kidding.

For New Critics, irony is a key term, pointing to the multiple meanings of a single assertion. A text with irony is complex, meaning potentially more than one thing. "Paradox," "oxymoron," "tension," and other terms are also used by New Critics to point to unified complexity.

✔ Checklist for New Criticism

1. Read closely, identifying the work's oppositions, tensions, paradoxes, ironies.

2. Read closely, assuming that everything in the work—figures of speech, point of view, diction, recurrent ideas or images, every-thing—is carefully calculated to contribute to the work's unity.

3. Read closely, determining how the poem's various elements create unity.

Notes

1. The epigraph for this chapter comes from *English in American Universities*, edited by William Payne (Boston: Heath, 1895), p. 96.
2. See Robert Pinsky's "Marianne Moore's 'Poetry': Why Did She Keep Revising It?" *Slate*, June 30, 2009, Web, accessed May 17, 2015.
3. The manuscript was auctioned by Christie's, which offered brief discussions of the song by music experts. Over a dozen websites feature analyses of the song's lyrics, and several offer moving and entertaining montages of images to accompany the song. For an especially good live performance of the song, solo, search for MacLean's 1972 BBC appearance.
4. "Basically in 'American Pie,' things are heading in the wrong direction," McLean said in Christie's auction catalogue. "It is becoming less idyllic. I don't know whether you consider that wrong or right, but it is a morality song in a sense." The contents of the catalogue and McLean's comments were widely reported, but I have relied primarily on the news stories from April 8, 2015, in *The Guardian*, *The Newcastle Herald*, and *The Telegraph*.
5. From Christie's website, www.christies.com, May 2, 2015. The song's mystery and complexity are certainly part of its success and charm. The National Endowment for the Arts and the Recording Industry of America chose "American Pie" as the fifth greatest song of the twentieth century.

Works Cited

Atkinson, Michael. "Deadpan Walking: Welcome to the Droll House. American Geekhood Finds a New Icon in a Clueless Idaho Teen." *Village Voice*, June 1, 2004. Web. Accessed April 6, 2010.

Brooks, Cleanth. *The Well-Wrought Urn*. 1947. New York: Harcourt, 1975. Print.

Brooks, Cleanth, and Robert Penn Warren. *Understanding Poetry*. New York: Holt, 1938. Print.

Coleridge, Samuel Taylor. *Biographia Literaria*. 1817. Yorkshire: Scholar, 1971. Print.

Eliot, T. S. *Selected Essays*. New York: Harcourt, 1932. Print.

Keats, John. *The Letters of John Keats, 1814–1821*. 2 vols. Cambridge: Harvard UP, 1958. Print.

Moore, Marianne. *Collected Poems of Marianne Moore*. New York: Macmillan, 1935. Print.

Ransom, John Crowe. *The New Criticism*. New York: New Directions, 1941. Print.

Richards, I. A. *Practical Criticism*. New York: Harcourt, 1929. Print.

Wellek, René, and Austin Warren. *Theory of Literature*. New York: Harcourt, 1949. Print.

Wimsatt, W. K., and Monroe Beardsley. *The Verbal Icon*. Lexington: U of Kentucky P, 1954. Print.

Recommended Further Reading

Ayers, David. *Literary Theory: A Reintroduction*. Oxford: Blackwell, 2008. Print. The first two chapters, "English as a University Subject" and "The New Criticism and Beyond," offer a superbly detailed explanation of how New Criticism developed.

Berman, Art. "The New Criticism." *From the New Criticism to Deconstruction*. Urbana: U of Illinois P, 1988. 26–59. Print. A sophisticated discussion of the philosophical underpinnings of New Criticism.

Internet Public Library: Online Literary Criticism Collection. University of Michigan, School of Information and Library Studies, 2006. Web. Accessed Nov. 26, 2006. The Internet Public Library is an amazing resource, providing links to and assessment of many other biographical and literary critical websites. You can search by author, by title, by country, by period. There's a "Literary Criticism Pathfinder," suggesting strategies for finding criticism in real libraries and on the Web. Begun as a class project in 1995, on a budget of US$18 per month, the IPL exemplifies the educational and scholarly potential of the Internet.

Lynn, Steven. "René Wellek." *Modern American Critics*. Ed. Gregory Jay. Detroit: Gale Research, 1988. 290–303. Print. Discusses the career of a critic who was enormously influential in the development of New Criticism, and who (interestingly enough) did not consider himself to be a New Critic.

Searle, Leroy. "New Criticism." *The Johns Hopkins Guide to Literary Theory and Criticism*. Eds. Michael Groden and Martin Kreiswirth. Baltimore: Johns Hopkins UP, 1994. 528–534. Print. Nice overview.

Sosnoski, James. "Cleanth Brooks." *Modern American Critics*. Ed. Gregory Jay. Detroit: Gale Research, 1988. 33–42. Print. A detailed and engaging study of Brooks' stellar career, championing the principles of New Criticism and applying them brilliantly.

Tyson, Lois. "New Criticism." *Critical Theory Today: A User-Friendly Guide*. New York: Garland, 1999. 117–152. Print. A lucid and very thorough introduction.

Willingham, John. "The New Criticism: Then and Now." *Contemporary Literary Theory*. Eds. Douglas Atkins and Laura Morrow. Amherst: U of Massachusetts P, 1989. Print. Explores the continued viability of New Criticism.

Creating the Text

Reader-Response Criticism

Unless there is a response on the part of somebody, there is no significance, no meaning.

—Morse Peckham(1)

What you'll learn in this chapter:

- To identify the purpose of reader-response criticism and to recognize opportunities to use reader-response and reader-oriented strategies.
- To develop and refine ideas about texts using reader-response criticism.
- To write and revise essays, step by step, about literary texts, using reader-response techniques.
- To apply reader-oriented strategies in a variety of contexts.

THE PURPOSE OF READER-RESPONSE CRITICISM

New Criticism as the Old Criticism

Reader-response criticism can be seen as a reaction in part to some problems and limitations perceived in New Criticism. New Criticism did not suddenly fail to function: It remains to this day a popular and effective critical strategy for illuminating the complex unity of certain literary works. But some works seem to respond better than others to New Criticism's "close reading," or perhaps we should say some readers seem to respond better to some works than to others. Much of eighteenth-century literature, for instance, has generally not been shown to have the sort of paradoxical language or formal unity that New Critics have found in, say, Donne or Keats. A second problem with New Criticism, at least for some readers, is that the approach seems to find roughly the same thing in whatever work one happens to read, if it is successful: "This work has unified complexity," "So does this one," "Yep, this one too."

Further, if the work is indeed a stable object, about which careful readers can make objective statements, then why hasn't there been an emerging consensus in criticism? Instead, the history of criticism seems to be one of diversity and change, as successive critics provide innovatively different readings of the same work. Developments in literary criticism seem more like changes of fashion than the evolution of science. Even in the sciences, however, the idea of an objective point of view has been increasingly questioned. Facts, as Thomas Kuhn famously argued, emerge because of a certain system of belief, or paradigm. Scientific revolutions occur not simply when new facts are discovered, but when a new paradigm allows these "facts" to be noticed and accepted.

Such ideas about the conceptual and constructed nature of knowledge, even scientific knowledge, call a fundamental assumption of New Criticism into question. In positing the objective reality of the literary work, New Criticism was arguably emulating the sciences; but in the wake of Einstein's theory of relativity, Heisenberg's uncertainty principle, Gödel's mathematics, and much else, it seems clear that the perceiver plays an active role in the making of any meaning and that literary works in particular have a *subjective* status.

In addition, by striving to show how great works balance and harmonize opposing ideas, New Criticism has seemed to some to encourage the divorce of literature from life and politics, indirectly reinforcing the status quo. By the standards of New Criticism, any literary work that takes a strong position ought somehow to acknowledge the opposing point of view, and criticism ought to point to that complexity and balance. Further, by assuming that literary language is fundamentally different from ordinary language, New Criticism may further tend to support the idea that literary study has little or no practical value but stands apart from real life (a poem should not mean but be, MacLeish says). New Criticism sometimes seems, especially to unsympathetic eyes, like an intellectual exercise.

The perception of these shortcomings of New Criticism—its limited applicability and sameness of results, the questionable assumption of a stable object of inquiry, and the separation of literature from other discourses— no doubt helped open the door for reader-response criticism (and other approaches). But reader-response criticism has its own substantial appeals beyond not being New Criticism, as we shall see.

The Reader Emerges

In 1938, while future New Critics were formulating ideas of the text as a freestanding object, Louise Rosenblatt prophetically called for criticism that involved a "personal sense of literature" (60), "an unselfconscious, spontaneous, and honest reaction" (67). Her *Literature as Exploration* was far ahead of its day, but by the time Rosenblatt published *The Reader, the Text, the Poem* in 1978, much of the critical world had caught up with where she was 40 years before. For instance, in 1975 David Bleich championed the creative power of readers in *Readings and Feelings*, which was followed in 1978 by his *Subjective Criticism*. Because "the object of observation appears changed by the act of observation," as Bleich puts it, "knowledge is made by people and not found" (*Criticism* 17, 18).

This insight leads Bleich to embrace subjectivity. Writing about literature, he believes, should not involve suppressing readers' individual concerns, anxieties, passions, enthusiasms. "Each person's most urgent motivations are to understand himself," Bleich says (*Criticism* 297), and a response to a literary work always helps us find out something about ourselves. Bleich thus encourages introspection and spontaneity, and he is not at all worried that different readers will see different things in a text. Every act of response, he says, reflects the shifting motivations and perceptions of the reader at the moment. Even the most idiosyncratic response to a text should be shared, in Bleich's view, and moreover heard sympathetically.

It is easy to imagine that many students have found such an approach liberating and even intoxicating, and that many teachers have contemplated it with horror. In Bleich's view of criticism "There's no right or wrong," as one exasperated teacher said to me; "students can *say anything*." But Bleich actually does not imagine that the student's engagement with literature will *end* with a purely individual, purely self-oriented response; rather, he expects that students will share their responses, and then through a process of "negotiation," as he describes it in *Subjective Criticism*, they will as a community examine together their individual responses, seeking common ground while learning from each person's unique response. As training to participate in the civil discourse crucial to democracy, this process seems quite empowering.

An especially striking illustration of the benefits of Bleich's orientation appears in an essay published by Robert Crosman in 1982. Crosman recounts a student's response to William Faulkner's famous "A Rose for Emily" that is so eccentric, so obviously "wrong" (if it is possible to be wrong within this approach), that one must begin to wonder if the student really read the story with any attentiveness. The student's response seems in fact to expose the absurdity of letting students say whatever comes into their heads, for she writes that Emily, the mad recluse who apparently poisons and then sleeps with her suitor, reminds her of her kindly grandmother. Crosman's student thus ignores the horrible ending of the story, which implies that Emily has recently slept with the much-decayed remains of her murdered lover. Instead, the student writes about the qualities of her own grandmother—"endurance, faith, love"—that she also sees in Emily

(360). The student finds that her grandmother and Emily both inhabit houses that are closed up with "relics and mementos of the past"; both her grand-mother and Emily seem to think of past events and people as being "more real" than "the world of the present." She links her grandmother to Emily, one might say, by ignoring what is most distinctive, important, and grotesque about Faulkner's character.

But the value of this student's response emerges in the way Crosman uses it to modify his own reading, which is a kind of negotiation in Bleich's sense. He comes to see that his interpretation, which is of course much more typical of experienced readers, actually "suppresses a good deal of evidence" (361). Crosman has perceived Emily to be a kind of monster, but he is led by his student to see that such is not simply or entirely the case. Confronting the heroic aspects of Emily's character, Crosman notices that she triumphs, in a sense, over the men (father, lover, town fathers) who are, Crosman says, "ultimately responsible for Emily's pitiful condition" (361). By the same token, just as Crosman is able to see the positive aspects of Emily's character, making her human rather than monstrous, so is his student, by considering Crosman's response, placed in a position to see more than her grandmother's goodness in Emily.

Thus, Bleich sees the reader's response evolving by "negotiation" within a community of readers, and Rosenblatt focuses on the "transaction" between the text and the reader. While she accepts multiple interpretations, as readers actively make different works out of the text, Rosenblatt also considers some readings to be incorrect or inappropriate because they are unsupportable by the text. So the "unself-conscious, spontaneous, and honest reaction" that Rosenblatt encourages ought to be checked against the text and modified in a continuing process, or "transaction": A poem is made by the text and its readers interacting. For both Bleich and Rosenblatt, the reader ought not simply respond and move on. Rather, the reader shares a response, and considers the responses of others, and reconsiders the text, and evolves his or her responses.

The various reader-response critics all share the sense of reading as a process, an activity. Their differences stem from this question of how meaning is controlled. Who's in charge? The text? The reader? A community of readers? The case of Stanley Fish is especially interesting in this regard because over his career Fish has evolved. His early work emphasizes how the text controls the reader's experience. The task of criticism is to describe this experience, and Fish's readings seem much like watching a movie in super-slow motion as it is being analyzed by an imaginative film critic. Fish moves through a few words or phrases and then considers in clever, often brilliant detail what "the reader" makes of it. Fish repeatedly finds that admirable texts continually surprise us, evading our expectations, exposing us to "strains," "ambivalences," "complexity" (*Artifacts*, 136, 425). These values, as Jane Tompkins has suggested, are very similar to the values of New Criticism. But the way they are discovered in texts, as Fish describes it, is quite different.

In *Surprised by Sin*, for instance, Fish argues that the reader "in" Paradise Lost experiences temptations and disorientations that parallel those of Adam and Eve. Thus, the critics who have thought Satan more appealing than God have not spotted a flaw in Milton's achievement; on the contrary, they have simply succumbed to the temptation Milton meant for them to experience. Likewise, in *Self-Consuming Artifacts* Fish shows how the process of reading certain seventeenth-century texts involves creating expectations that are thwarted, complicated, reversed, and transformed as the reader goes on.

In his later work, in *Is There a Text in This Class?* and *Doing What Comes Naturally*, Fish moves away from the idea of an ideal reader who finds his or her activity marked out, implied, embedded in the text, and he moves toward the idea of a reader who creates a reading of the text using certain interpretive strategies. These strategies may be shared by other readers, and the critic's job is to persuade his or her interpretive community to accept a particular reading. Neither the text's implied activity nor the community's shared reading strategies can be said to determine interpretation, for even when readers inhabit the same interpretive community, they must struggle to persuade one another of the "facts" regarding a particular text. Such persuasion may include information about the author, or the author's audience, or the initial reception of the work, or the history of its reception, or the text itself, or the conventions of interpretation the text draws upon. But the continuing process of discussion begins with the response of the person persuading. In 1994 Fish turned his attention to the law and politics, publishing *There's No Such Thing as Free Speech: And It's a Good Thing Too*, which he followed in 1999 with *The Trouble with Principle*. These books seek to demolish the idea of universal and impersonal principles, arguing that meaning is always created in a particular context by particular people. Our values, in other words, are a kind of reader's response to our culture and history.

As our reading becomes more dependent upon screens and websites, the active role of the reader is perhaps more obvious than with a paper-and-ink text, especially when we are reading texts that have links to other texts within them. Such hypertexts, as they are usually called, offer the reader choices, allowing for different reading experiences of the same "text." With hypertext fiction, for instance, the reader may choose to pursue different story lines or add different characters or experience different endings. These alternate paths are already prepared, so the reader's active role is limited, but one can easily imagine texts that will be truly dynamic, that are in a real sense created in part by the reader, who might decide to kill off a character or add another story line or even insert his or her own contribution. It has already been predicted that computer programs will in the not-distant future be able to write news stories, perhaps replacing many journalists, and a truly dynamic hypertext story would need a program that would react and respond to the reader-become-writer.[1]

Although reader-response criticism might evolve in the future into reader-response writing, this critical approach has its roots in one of the oldest academic disciplines, the study of rhetoric, a field that for over 2,500 years has focused on how speakers and writers can shape the responses of their audiences. Rhetoric is concerned primarily with how to generate a response: how to invent material, how to arrange it, how to style it, and how to present it in such a way as to elicit the desired reaction. Audience-oriented criticism moves in the other direction, in a sense, constructing a response and analyzing how it has been produced. Rhetoric generally has been thought of in terms of political and ceremonial and judicial texts, and reader-response criticism has mostly been concerned with literary works. But the resources of rhetoric certainly can be brought to literary study, and reader-response criticism can be used on any kind of text. Literary study is in fact so valuable for such a wide range of endeavors precisely because we are asked to think about how we ought to respond, and how that response is being created. And rhetorical concepts are, not surprisingly, often quite useful. Aristotle's *Rhetoric*, for instance, says that a speaker has three major strategies to draw upon: We are influenced by how we perceive the person speaking, the appeal to "ethos"; we're influenced by logic, by agreeing with certain assumptions and their logical implications, which is the appeal to "logos"; and we are swayed by emotion, by the appeal to our fears, and self-interests, and desires, the appeal to "pathos." This simple triad is a useful tool for analyzing a presidential speech and a poem alike, helping us to think about how our responses are shaped.

HOW TO DO READER-RESPONSE CRITICISM

Preparing to Respond

Imagine that you've been asked to write about the following poem, drawing on reader-response criticism. You'll want to read the poem carefully, thinking in terms of the following possible questions:

1. How do I respond to this work?
2. How does the text shape my response?
3. How might other readers respond?

Love Poem #1
Sandra Cisneros

a red flag
woman I am
all copper
chemical
and you an ax   5
and a bruised
thumb

unlikely
pas de deux
but just let   10
us wax
it's nitro
egypt
snake
museum   15
zoo

we are
connoisseurs
and commandoes
we are rowdy   20
as a drum
not shy like Narcissus
nor pale as plum

then it is I want to hymn
and hallelujah   25
sing sweet sweet jubilee
you my religion
and I a wicked nun

(1987)

What can you say about this poem? How can audience-oriented criticism help you to understand and appreciate it?

Making Sense

My own response to this poem began when I started to annotate it. I underlined some words that I thought might be especially important or unclear, and then, on a separate sheet, I speculated on their meanings. With any approach, you may need to look up some words. If you're a little hazy on who "Narcissus" is (line 23), for instance, a dictionary definition may be all you need: "A youth who, having spurned the love of Echo, pined away in love for his own image in a pool of water and was transformed into the flower that bears his name" (*American Heritage Dictionary*). Dictionary definitions aren't always sufficient, and (it probably goes without saying) the more you know, the more experience you have as a reader, then the richer and more informed your response is likely to be. Responding to a poem always involves you in creating a context in which the sequence of words makes sense: You must ask, Who is speaking to whom? Under what circumstances would someone say these things?

Still, all responses are potentially worthwhile as starting points. You may want to underline some important or puzzling words and speculate on their meanings before you look at my annotations below. And you may want to share your responses with another reader.

a red flag woman—What does this mean? A red flag means something to watch out for, dangerous, a warning. For instance, "The temperature reading should have been a red flag." So she is dangerous?

all copper—Why copper? Because it's cold? Because it turns green?! No, I don't think so. Copper is a great conductor of electrical current and heat. She's hot; she's electrified. That is, she's passionate, emotional, responsive?

chemical—Like a chemical reaction?

an ax and a bruised thumb—Is he clumsy? He does things aggressively, in an imprecise way. He breaks or splits things like an ax, but he isn't always careful (the bruised thumb).

pas de deux—A ballet dance for two, according to Webster. The sort of grace and coordination we'd expect from a ballet is indeed unlikely for these two together, a live wire and a wild man.

nitro etc.—This is a neat list of unexpected things, each one giving a different aspect of their relationship. Nitro = explosive?; egypt = foreign, exotic, mysterious, enduring (like the pyramids)?; snake = something wicked? a phallic symbol? the garden of Eden? Are "egypt" and "snake" related? "Museum" and "zoo" point us to public institutions. "Museum" suggests their love is rare, valuable, enduring, worth showing off; "zoo" suggests perhaps they're animals?

connoisseurs and commandoes—They again appear to be radical opposites: connoisseurs are refined, tasting carefully; commandoes are reckless and go wild.

you my religion—This is about as involved in another person as you can get. There's something troubling about such devotion to another person. No human being should worship another one. But am I taking this line too seriously?

wicked nun—This image continues the religious reference. Being a wicked nun seems especially exciting, or offensive, depending on the responder, combining suggestions of the forbidden and the delayed.

Subjective Response

Thinking about the words, you're already unavoidably beginning to think about the poem as a whole and your own response to it. The next step might be to freewrite about the poem. Just focus on the poem and write quickly whatever occurs to you. Don't worry about grammar, and don't stop writing. If you can't think of anything to say, say whatever is most obvious. The important thing is to keep the pen or keyboard moving. As a last resort, write "I can't think of anything to say" until you think of something. If that fails, then read the poem again and then try once more. Set yourself a time limit for this free response; ten minutes is about right for most people. There's no way to do this exercise incorrectly: Just read carefully and respond, being as honest and involved as you can.

Here is my freewriting response:

> This poem reminds me of Carol and Bob's relationship. They are about as unlikely and mismatched a couple as this pair, an "unlikely pas de deux." But instead of "copper" and "chemical," Carol is more like plutonium and nuclear. She's incredibly energetic, especially when you compare her to Bob. He could fit "an ax / and a bruised / thumb," but I suspect the result would be an amputated thumb in his case. They are amazing, like the couple in the poem.
>
> Are Carol and Bob "nitro" together, like this couple? I don't know. There seems to me to be a good bit of energy in their marriage. I don't see Carol wanting "to hymn / and hallelujah," perhaps, but I'm really in no position to judge, am I. I don't know what happens when they "wax," whatever that means. Certainly, the two people in Cisneros's poem are not living a dull life, and I think the contrast is also stimulating to Carol and Bob. There is power in conflict or difference. Opposites not only attract; they make sparks.

Many people find this kind of freewriting exercise very useful: It generates material that you may be able to use in an essay, and it is likely to stimulate your thinking about the work. Just to give you an idea of how individualistic and personal such responses can be, here is another one:

> This poem seems to talk about an exciting relationship: She says "it's nitro." That suggests the relationship is great, but I think it's really doomed. I think this relationship, the first time it is shaken, will probably explode, just like nitro. She is emotional; he is rough and

clumsy. Where's the long-term interest and compatibility in this setup? Opposites attract, sure, but when they're so totally opposite, so far apart, the attraction may be volatile. This is, after all, only "Love Poem #1." I am wondering if there will be #2 and #3 once the relationship matures and cools off.

I think the speaker's comparison of herself to "a wicked nun" is revealing. The comparison supports my feeling that the relationship, despite its current heat, isn't going to make it. I notice that she does not see herself as a nun who has decided to give up her habit. She is just "wicked," doing something wrong and enjoying the extra excitement that doing the forbidden gives her. If her love feels that way to her, then won't that eventually put a strain on the relationship? Will she decide to give up her old life, her old religion, and become devoted to her new religion, her lover? Or will her prior life win out?

In my experience, relationships built on excitement are treacherous and fragile. I bet the nun will repent and reform.

Which of these responses is correct? Both are. Both are thoughtful and well-supported responses to the text. Taken together, these two different responses may suggest a third one that tries to determine whether the poem really does evoke some skepticism on the reader's part or if it is simply a joyous celebration. Are there some elements that would qualify the poem's enthusiasm for most readers?

After engaging the text in a personal way, you can begin to ask such questions about your own response in the context of other readers' responses. Let's see what happens when the reading process is slowed down and an effort is made to imagine how the reader is supposed to respond moving through the poem.

Receptive Response

The title, "Love Poem #1," does not seem imaginative or romantic, and the first line seems to open further the possibility that the poem is not a love poem in the usual sense: "a red flag" signals a warning, a danger, and seems more appropriate to a poem announcing the end of a love affair. So perhaps the first is the last, and the unimaginative title is ironic? The second line, "woman I am," seems to be an affirmation of the speaker's individuality and her sisterhood. In other words:

Line 1: "a red flag" = Watch out! There's something dangerous here.

Line 2: "woman I am" = The reason you should watch out: a red flag (look out!), I am woman.

But as the reader begins to wonder about these two statements—"a red flag" and "woman I am"—the possibility arises, reading backward, that these two lines go together in a different way, as a single statement: "a red flag" becomes a modifier of "woman"—I am a red-flag woman.

Without punctuation, the reader cannot decide for sure which syntax is correct, and so both readings continue on: "watch out, I'm a woman," and "I'm a dangerous kind of woman." Do the next two lines support the suggestion of an unromantic, even threatening self-portrait of the speaker? Yes, most readers will think of electrical wiring and plumbing when they read "all copper," which appears to refer back to the speaker; likewise, things that are "chemical" are perceived by most readers as dangerously reactive. Only experts should fool around with plumbing, wiring, chemistry: Pipes explode, wires spark, chemicals blow up.

The reader will find the next three lines equally disorienting, as the speaker's love is described in the decidedly unromantic terms of "an ax / and a bruised / thumb." He or she is potentially destructive and apparently dangerous. (Although some readers may assume the speaker's lover is male, the poem doesn't prescribe that response, does it?) An ax usually isn't used to build things, but rather to cut them, kill them, chop them down. Such wrecking sometimes results, especially if the worker is clumsy, in a bruised thumb, or worse. As a love poem, this one seems to be going nowhere, and the reader may well not be surprised that it is #1. How can there be any more?

Thus, I would argue that the opening of the second group of lines confirms the attentive reader's assessment: they are indeed an "unlikely / pas de deux." This admission also sets the reader up, however, for a turn. By saying they are unlikely as a pair, Cisneros implies that they may be nonetheless a couple, somehow. The rest of the poem vigorously fulfills that implication, reversing the reader's inferences, which he or she may have suspected would be reversed. Still, the explanation of their relationship is startling, as the reader encounters a list of unexpected and even puzzling comparisons:

> *nitro*—This one is easy. They are explosive together—and that seems good. But since nitroglycerine is used to blow things up (as well as to prevent heart attacks), an element of danger remains.

> *egypt*—How can the lovers be "egypt"? Perhaps the reference means they are exotic together? Hot, like the deserts? Mysterious, like the pyramids? Alluring, like Cleopatra? Fertile, like the Nile? By not saying how the lovers are like Egypt, Cisneros opens up a space in which the reader can supply all sorts of qualities.

> *snake*—This comparison is as tantalizing and amazing, at least, as "egypt." A snake is of course often considered a phallic symbol, and the reader may think of the lovers' conjunction as a kind of living version of that symbol. But it may also remind us, in the context of a couple, of Adam and Eve, suggesting that they are somehow participating

in a return to Eden together; but this time, the lovers are not ruined by the serpent but rather become one themselves? Or, is the snake, in the context of "egypt," supposed to suggest some sort of ancient fertility cult that involved the handling of snakes? We don't know, but the attentive reader will consider these and other possible responses to this rich and startling image.

museum—Another strange and disorienting comparison. How can the lovers be like a museum? Perhaps they create, in their lovemaking, something of enduring value, something so wonderful that future generations would want to preserve it, as in a museum.

zoo—This reference is perhaps the easiest for the reader to respond to: it suggests obviously that they are animals together—a collection, in fact, of all sorts of exotic and wondrous animals.

The rest of the poem continues to celebrate the lovers in unexpected ways, even though certain ideas reappear. The speaker calls them "connoisseurs and commandoes," which repeats to some degree the oppositions already set up. The reader may connect "connoisseurs" to the cultured reaction of museum-goers, but at the same time the lovers are wild "commandoes," which the reader may link to the violence of "nitro" or an "ax." The difference in this third section of the poem is that instead of each lover having distinctly different qualities, they are together "connoisseurs and commandoes," unifying opposing features in their relationship.

If the reader believes, however, that the rest of the poem will fit some sort of pattern set up thus far, the next lines seem designed to thwart that expectation. The lovers are "rowdy / as a drum," which suggests, I suppose, the rowdiness of someone beating a drum. Perhaps this simile reinforces the earlier suggestions of wildness, but it is certainly difficult to see how a drum in itself is "rowdy" or what this comparison is supposed to accomplish. The reader next learns the lovers are "not shy like Narcissus," an allusion that means obviously that they are not self-absorbed, that they don't hold back from love. But is there any deeper significance to this allusion? Why bring in Narcissus and shyness? Would any reader suspect at this point that they are shy—these commandoes, who are "nitro"? The next line seems even more elusive, as if the lovers are slowly becoming incomprehensible to the reader: "nor pale as plum." Perhaps this comparison refers to the color plum and tells us in another way that they are not shy—although the reader surely must hesitate to call "plum" a "pale" color.

But "plum" serves another function beyond befuddling the reader, as it becomes clear at this point, if not before, that a recurrent rhyme is appearing, unobtrusively: "thumb," "museum," "drum," and "plum." And with the appearance of this music, beginning to evade meaning, the poem moves to its climatic ending, comparing the speaker's feelings to a religious ecstasy:

> then it is I want to hymn
> and hallelujah
> sing sweet sweet jubilee
> you my religion
> and I a wicked nun

The reader may hear the assertion that she wants "to hymn" as a pun on "him," as if her lover has become an activity in which she can engage or as if the male role is one the speaker longs to adopt. The associations of "hymn" continue for the reader as singing hallelujah and enjoying the "jubilee" appear. Immediately these religious comparisons are carried beyond the reader's expectations (which may be, at this point, what the reader does expect), as the speaker declares her lover to be her religion. For most readers, such sacrilege is an exaggeration at the edges of propriety: Most readers are all in favor of love, but to make another person one's religion is troubling. The experienced reader probably sees this assertion as exaggeration (hyperbole), but it is nonetheless worrisome in its implications.

But the final line takes even a further step, as the speaker names herself "a wicked nun." This final move completes the effort to convey the excitement of the forbidden, the impossible, the dangerous in the relationship, leaving the reader shaken and stunned—like the speaker herself, it seems—by the power of their love. Their love is itself vigorously direct, like the poem's title; their love is also apparently unadulterated and uncompromised, pure and explosive at its very beginning.

It is quite likely that your own thinking about the reader's reception of this poem is different from mine—perhaps radically different. That's fine. Although we could argue over which one of us is insufficiently attentive to the poem's cues, in the context of reader-response criticism it makes more sense to try to learn from each other. For me, even when I'm trying to play the role of the implied reader, I'm continually aware that I'm making choices, filling in blanks and gaps, interpreting in one particular way when several other ways (some of which aren't occurring to me) are feasible. I say "the reader," and I am trying to think of an ideal or implied response, but I'm aware at several points that "the reader" may be only me. Still, it seems helpful to try to think of how other readers will respond and to read what other readers say and enrich our own responses. The real beauty of audience-oriented criticism, after all, is that the focus is on our activity: We make the text say whatever it's going to say and then try to persuade others to accept our readings.

You can apply the strategies of reader-response criticism to anything—even to objects or stimuli that we do not literally "read," such as cultural and political events, even paintings and sculptures. You simply need to be able to describe how the "reader" or viewer or listener (hypothetical or real) responds. Think, for instance, about the sequence of events at a football game, and how the spectators respond as the spectacle unfolds. Why do sporting events typically begin, for instance, with the singing of the national anthem? How are spectators expected to respond? One might argue that the national anthem tends to remind antagonistic fans of the citizenship that they have in common, encouraging them to respond to the game in a better spirit of sportsmanship. Or, perhaps the national anthem lends an air of importance to what follows, suggesting that football is somehow more than just entertainment, but somehow has some significance, and should be taken seriously and passionately. Or perhaps the national anthem marks a boundary, signaling a transition from the real world (before the anthem) to the "play" world, setting aside our concerns and worries while we think only about a game.

Whatever we're analyzing with reader-response strategies, two moves seem especially worth noting here. First, although a response might feel seamless, continuous, flowing, the description of a response must somehow be broken up into parts. Language moves through time, in sentences with subjects and verbs and the rest, and so the description of a response must move through time, forcing us to divide the response up into pieces. The immediate impression that one gets from a painting or sculpture will be difficult to describe, of course, because it feels like an all-at-once experience. You can talk about what one notices first, and second, and third, moving around the canvas or object, or through the event or the text, but you are inevitably making choices about where that first bit of response begins and ends, and the second begins and ends, and so forth. For people who want there to be one right answer, and for everyone to see and experience things the same way, reader-response criticism is bound to be pretty frustrating. For people who rejoice in the diversity of experiences and responses and opinions, reader-response criticism will be especially interesting, not only because of our different orientations and abilities, but also because of the different ways that we partition and perceive our experiences. Texts, films, objects, events generally provide us with cues about how we ought to comprehend their parts, or (depending on the perspective) we ascribe these cues to whatever we interpret. Part of your job in constructing a response, then, will be to determine the segments of whatever you're responding to.

The second move involves understanding how the perception of genre affects the response. If we recognize that a work is a detective story, or a situation comedy, or a sermon, then we have a repertoire of expectations and reactions that come into play. The *Star Trek* television shows, for instance, have all begun in ways that immediately identify the kind of thing that we are watching: The original *Star Trek*, with Captain Kirk, Mr. Spock, and the rest, feature an opening credit sequence that shows the *Enterprise* in space, coming into view in one corner of the screen, zipping across, and disappearing from the other corner in an instant. Viewers not only have a response to that scene, identified as a discrete bit of the show, but they also create certain expectations about what will follow. *Star Trek* famously depicts an optimistic vision of the future, in which science and technology will have solved many of our current problems and advanced humankind into space, "the final frontier." This opening scene, displaying a faster-than-light starship, suggests that we should view what follows as science fiction: There will be marvels, but they should be plausible within the terms of what we know and can extrapolate about science today. All the subsequent incarnations of *Star Trek—Next Generation, Deep Space Nine, Voyager,* and *Enterprise*—present some variation on this outer space vista: *Next Generation* shows incredibly beautiful planetary systems and the new *Enterprise* passing by them; *Deep Space Nine* shows us the space station and an amazing interspatial wormhole; *Voyager* depicts strange planets and phenomena, and the ship jumping into warp speed; and *Enterprise* precedes a similar jump to warp speed with various images of human exploration, from the historical past and the imagined future. Viewers familiar with the *Star Trek* series and with science fiction in general are going to respond differently from viewers unfamiliar with either or both.

Although educators may tend to think of reader-response criticism as an equal-opportunity sort of approach, allowing every reader (or respondent) to have his or her say about the work's effects, this simple reference to the beginnings of a television franchise emphasizes that our responses depend on what we know: If we understand the genre of a particular work, if we have experience with other similar works, then our responses will be more informed, quite possibly richer. Even those teachers who insist that there are no wrong responses (which is indeed a liberating principle, inviting students to boldly go where their reading and responding has never gone before) still must acknowledge that we become in some sense better at reading and responding with practice. And a key part of what we learn has to do with recognizing, at the outset, the kind of thing we are experiencing.

THE WRITING PROCESS: A SAMPLE ESSAY

Preparing to Respond

The essay that will be developed here, to illustrate reader-response criticism, focuses on "A Very Short Story" (1925) by Ernest Hemingway, a little gem of a very short story that is a part of a sequence of stories, although it can certainly be read on its own (for the whole sequence, see *Ernest Heming-way: The Short Stories*).

A Very Short Story*
Ernest Hemingway

One hot evening in Padua they carried him up onto the roof and he could look out over the top of the town. There were chimney swifts in the sky. After a while it got dark and the searchlights came out. The others went down and took the bottles with them. He and Luz could hear them below on the balcony. Luz sat on the bed. She was cool and fresh in the hot night.

Luz stayed on night duty for three months. They were glad to let her. When they operated on him she prepared him for the operating table; and they had a joke about friend or enema. He went under the anaesthetic holding tight on to himself so he would not blab about anything during the silly, talky time. After he got on crutches he used to take the temperatures so Luz would not have to get up from the bed. There were only a few patients, and they all knew about it. They all liked Luz. As he walked back along the halls he thought of Luz in his bed.

Before he went back to the front they went into the Duomo and prayed. It was dim and quiet, and there were other people praying. They wanted to get married, but there was not enough time for the banns, and neither of them had birth certificates. They felt as though they were married, but they wanted every one to know about it, and to make it so they could not lose it.

Luz wrote him many letters that he never got until after the armistice. Fifteen came in a bunch to the front and he sorted them by the dates and read them all straight through. They were all about the hospital, and how much she loved him and how it was impossible to get along without him and how terrible it was missing him at night.

After the armistice they agreed he should go home to get a job so they might be married. Luz would not come home until he had a good job and could come to New York to meet her. It was understood he would not drink, and he did not want to see his friends or any one in the States. Only to get a job and be married. On the train from Padua to Milan they quarrelled about her not being willing to come home at once. When they had to say good-bye, in the station at Milan, they kissed good-bye, but were not finished with the quarrel. He felt sick about saying good-bye like that.

He went to America on a boat from Genoa. Luz went back to Pordenone to open a hospital. It was lonely and rainy there, and there was a battalion of arditi quartered in the town. Living in the muddy, rainy town in the winter, the major of the battalion made love to Luz, and she had never known Italians before, and finally wrote to the States that theirs had been only a boy and girl affair. She was sorry, and she knew he would probably not be able to understand, but might some day forgive her, and be grateful to her, and she expected, absolutely unexpectedly, to be married in the spring. She loved him as always, but she realized now it was only a boy and girl love. She hoped he would have a great career, and believed in him absolutely. She knew it was for the best.

The major did not marry her in the spring, or any other time. Luz never got an answer to the letter to Chicago about it. A short time after he contracted gonorrhea from a sales girl in a loop department store while riding in a taxicab through Lincoln Park.

(1925)

How this story shapes the reader's response has already been suggested by Robert Scholes in *Semiotics and Interpretation*. As Scholes observes, the point of view in the story is technically third person (if it were first-person narration, it would read this way: "One hot evening in Padua they carried me up on the roof ..."). But the viewpoint, Scholes says, seems to be closer to the unnamed man than to Luz (116–117). If the narrator were equally distanced from both characters, they would both have names. But "he" apparently doesn't need a name. The reader is told in the first and second sentences what "he" could see. Also, as Scholes notes, the assertion "She was cool and fresh in the hot night" really makes sense only from his perspective: *To him*, she seemed cool and fresh. This point of view plays an important role in the reader's response, and I would like to elaborate on Scholes's view of the story by tracing out in some detail "the reader's" experience.

For starters, we might consider how the reader responds to Hemingway's opening paragraph. Our response must be problematic at that point because we know so little: Important information is being left out. But we do know something. We know "he" is in Padua, but we don't know what he is doing there or who he is. We learn that "they" carried him to the roof, but we don't know who "they" are or why he has to be carried: Is he sick or injured? Does he have a handicap? The reference to searchlights in the third sentence probably suggests to most readers that the story may be taking place during wartime: These are searchlights looking for attacking planes. If that's the case, then perhaps he is being carried because he is wounded. We also learn that he and Luz are somehow close: "they" leave them alone on the roof, and Luz sits on his bed, appearing "cool and fresh."

In this second paragraph, the implied point of view is made clearer, and additional clues are offered. The notion that he is in a hospital is confirmed here. Luz is on night duty, so she would seem to be a nurse—an inference further supported by her preparation of him for the operating table. The reader may notice, as Scholes points out, that the male character's reticence is much like the story's own restraint (119). He doesn't want to blab, and neither apparently does the story's narrator, telling us only the minimum. Letting go is the enemy and the enema; as Scholes puts it, "Logorrhea and diarrhea are equally embarrassing" (119).

Even if the reader finds the male character's fear of talking about anything problematic, the embodiment of a dumb macho stereotype, the strong silent man, we must be softened by his kindness in taking the temperatures. Here he is on crutches, and yet he gets up so Luz won't have to. What is not said by the narrator is what Luz is doing in his bed, but this is a blank that the reader easily fills in. The reader can easily discern that the "it" that the few patients "all knew about" must be an affair "he" and Luz are having. Why else would the narrator present the revelation that "they all knew about it" as if it were a kind of secret?

Recognizing what "it" is, most readers will probably acknowledge that a nurse sleeping with her patient probably does not represent the highest ethical standards. And recognizing this response perhaps makes clear why Hemingway has the narrator immediately tell us "They all liked Luz": Their affection for Luz is designed to qualify the reader's disapproval. With the paragraph's final sentence, the reader must also realize, as "he" thinks of Luz in his bed, that she apparently means a lot to a recovering man, perhaps a wounded soldier. Having immersed ourselves in "his" point of view, readers may not notice, without some consideration, that we do not know what Luz is thinking.

In the third paragraph we learn that he is, in fact, a soldier because he goes back to the front. We learn that he and Luz pray together in church, and the narrator tells us that they wish they could be married and feel as if they are married. If this feeling really is mutual, the reader may wonder about their plan. Why doesn't Luz return with him rather than waiting on his "good job"? Doesn't this condition make her seem a bit mercenary? Also, why are the restrictions on him seemingly so severe? Perhaps it makes sense that he will not drink, especially if he has a problem with drinking. But why does he not want to see his friends? In fact, he doesn't want to see anyone at all, according to their understanding. Does Luz not trust him? Does he not trust himself? The reader cannot be sure, the way this understanding is phrased, whether Luz imposes these conditions or he volunteers them; but since they restrict his behavior, the reader may assume the rules are Luz's idea.

Such subtle shaping of the reader's response prepares us for the bomb-shell in the sixth paragraph: She dumps him. In thinking about the reader's response here, we might consider (among other things) the effect of the information that "she had never known Italians before." The passage seems to offer this fact as a kind of explanation of her behavior, but it is an excuse that makes Luz seem worse, as if she wants to try Italians the way one might try a new flavor of ice cream. Hemingway does not say this excuse is disgustingly inadequate, but he sets up the story so that the reader easily comes to such a conclusion. Her letter is not quoted, but is filtered through his perspective; from that vantage point, it seems reasonable to assume that Luz has shamefully betrayed him.

There are, in fact, aspects of the letter, as it is reported, that seem so unfeeling they appear to be cruel. It is difficult for any reader to imagine what could be more devastating than saying what he thought was the love of his life was actually "only a boy and girl affair." To say "she loved him as always" similarly demeans their relationship. "I thought we were in love," she is in effect saying, "but now that I've been with this Italian, I see we were just playing like children." Her love hasn't changed, just her understanding of what that love was. Finally, to say she "believed in him absolutely" after refusing to come to America before he had a "good" job seems the height of hypocrisy and coldness.

How do we respond to the conclusion? Hemingway has led the reader, it may seem, to see Luz's own jilting by the major as just what she deserves. He adds "or any other time" to prevent the reader from assuming that Luz and the Italian had some problems but worked them out. The affair that *she said* she thought was the real thing, in comparison to their boy and girl thing, does not turn out to be real after all. But did she really believe that the Italian was different? Is Luz a "loose" woman? Is that the significance of her name?

By telling us that Luz never got an answer to her letter, Hemingway conveys indirectly the soldier's pain. The reader can imagine he is so hurt, and so thoroughly disgusted, that he can't even respond to her. The final sentence further deepens the reader's perception of his pain. As Scholes points out, first Luz wounds his heart; then the salesgirl wounds him in a different place. The reader will naturally assume that he wouldn't have been in that taxicab, fooling around recklessly and decadently, in public in Lincoln Park, if it had not been for Luz. The narrator does not say it is Luz's fault that he gets gonorrhea, but that clearly is the implication: When he loses Luz, he loses everything. "A short time after" here implies some connection. First the war wound, then Luz's, then the salesgirl's.

In moving through the story, I am carrying out and elaborating on the reading Scholes suggests. About the reader's response to this story—that is, the implied response that Hemingway marks out—Scholes says the following:

> Most male students sympathize with the protagonist and are very critical of Luz—as indeed the story asks them to be. Many female students try to read the story as sympathetic to Luz, blaming events on the "weakness" of the young man or the state of the world. This is a possible interpretation, but it is not well supported by the text. Thus, the female student must either "misread" the work (that is, she must offer the more weakly supported of two interpretations) or accept one more blow to her self-esteem as a woman. Faced with this story in a competitive classroom, women are put at a disadvantage. They are, in fact, in a double bind. (120–121)

I have thus far essentially agreed with this analysis of the implied reader's response. The text, in Scholes's opinion, makes the case against Luz. Although taking Luz's side is "a possible interpretation," Scholes says, it seems more difficult to him, a misreading. Scholes does, to be sure, place "misread" inside quotation marks, indicating his awareness of alternatives. But in truth, Scholes sees the reader—the male reader anyway—as being pulled toward one best response.

Not only does Scholes implicitly assume the text is a stable structure, marking out a particular response; he also assumes that "most" males will naturally take the soldier's side, and females will naturally try to take Luz's side. But one of the beauties of reader-response criticism is that it takes advantage of the diversity of readers in the world, reminding us of the treacherousness of generalizations about them. Reader-response criticism—by bringing the personal, the individual, even the eccentric responses to our attention—can revitalize texts that we think we have already learned how to read. Having processed the story with considerable care, attempting to play the role of a passive reader, we're ready now to take a more active part as a responding reader, entering into a debate within a community of readers.

PREPARING TO WRITE

What seems more difficult to Scholes (that is, taking Luz's side) seems to me in fact more compelling. I felt the first time I read this story that Luz was getting a raw deal, both from the soldier and from the narrator. Does that mean that I am responding from a woman's point of view? And is that point of view necessarily "at a disadvantage"? Even if we assume that women tend to side with Luz, and that the evidence for doing so is weaker than the evidence against Luz, we should still note that what is most obvious is oftentimes not very interesting in literary criticism. Making the case for Luz against the soldier is generally a more interesting endeavor than showing how Luz is cruel to the soldier.

Thus, I argue that Hemingway creates such apparent bias against Luz in order to expose it: that is, the soldier is so obviously being made into a martyr, and Luz into a villain, that the reader's response ought to resist this bias and look more carefully at the text, seeing past the narrator's obscuring point of view.

To give you an idea how I developed this response into an essay, I present below my notes and then the essay that resulted from them. Before examining these documents, you might want to sketch out your own response to Hemingway's story. What does it say to you?

> Emphasize that the narrator clearly takes his side: Hemingway is reminding us to consider the source. You can't let the player's coach call the balls in or out, and the narrator in this case is on the soldier's team.
>
> I could make Hemingway into the villain who tries to cover for the soldier, making Luz into an Eve figure. Or I could argue that Hemingway has the narrator make those moves, thus exposing him. I think the latter would be more fun.
>
> What is the absolute worst evidence against Luz? Probably the reason she gives for the breakup. Focus on that reason: "theirs had been only a boy and girl affair." The reader assumes, in the context created by the soldier's spokesman, that this excuse is cruel and cold. But maybe it isn't a rationalization, a way of getting her Italian major. Consider the possibility that Luz is right: They are immature; it is a boy/girl affair. Any evidence?
>
> > • The soldier does reveal his immaturity after Luz breaks it off: having sex in a taxicab, getting an STD—now that's really mature.
> > • We also must wonder about his decision not to respond to Luz's last letter. If he really loved Luz, wouldn't he consider forgiving her? Doesn't everyone make mistakes? Isn't it possible that Luz just got confused and mistook infatuation with the major for love? At such a distance from the soldier, in such bleak circumstances, she simply erred. But the soldier is such an immature hothead that the idea of forgiving her never occurs to him.
> > • What is after all the basis of the soldier's relationship with Luz? If she is wrong, if it is more than a boy/girl affair, what evidence is there in the story of his maturity and the depth of his love? The story, in fact, tells us nothing that suggests any great passion on his part. He seems perfectly willing to leave her behind while he goes to the United

States to get a job. What does he think of Luz? We know only two things, really: She was "cool and fresh" and "he thought of Luz in his bed." So far as we can tell, the relationship is based on sex, which isn't the strongest foundation for marriage.

- What is the evidence that Luz is a bad person? She does have sex with the soldier while he's a patient. She sleeps in his bed. She lets him get up and take the temperatures. But none of this makes her evil. He is a wounded soldier in a foreign country about to go back to the front. She is comforting him. She offers him love and affection. She is the nurse every wounded soldier no doubt dreams of. In letting the soldier get up and take the temperatures, Luz is arguably letting him act as her protector, strengthening his ego, which is likely to be fragile after his injury.

- Why is there an understanding that he won't drink and won't hang around with his friends? Is Luz being mean? Hemingway leaves this meaningful gap in the story, when he could have easily filled it in. Perhaps the soldier has a drinking problem. Early in the story other people do take away the bottles. The story doesn't say that Luz imposed this "no drinking" policy on him; perhaps he imposed it on himself to indicate his seriousness and trustworthiness to Luz.

- What does it mean when Luz breaks it off? Had there been a formal proposal, an acceptance, a ring, an engagement? All the reader knows is that the two are sleeping together and that they come to view each other as married—at least from the soldier's perspective. Hemingway says the understanding is that "he should go home so they might be married." What does "might" mean here? If they wanted to get married before he went back to the front, why didn't they arrange it when he returned? Such unexplained gaps must lead the reader to wonder about the facts. Has the soldier come to assume something that just isn't the case? He assumes, because they are sleeping together, they're going to get married? And poor Luz, feeling sorry for his wounds and his inevitable return to danger doesn't have the heart to tell him it just isn't that serious.

- If they really were in love, why might Luz fall for the Italian major? The reader isn't told anything about what things look like from her perspective. Does he write letters? Does he get a job? Does he follow through on his "no drinking" pledge? If he does get a job, then why hasn't Luz already come over? It seems likely, in fact, the more one thinks about it, that something is seriously wrong on his end. Hemingway, by withholding vital information, allows the reader to jump to conclusions—conclusions that the careful reader must eventually withdraw. The reader leaps to conclusions, much like the soldier.

Shaping

Based on these notes, which meditated on the possibility that Luz is being set up and that the reader ought to see through this unfair treatment, I sketched out a draft of the main points I might want to make in articulating my response. Here's what I wrote:

Main point: Luz is right. It was a boy and girl affair.

Evidence:

- Their relationship is apparently based on sex; plus, some questionable ethics are involved in their affair.
- The soldier appears to be unreliable: Luz is afraid he won't get a job but will just drink and run around. Since she doesn't come to the United States, it appears that she may have been right.
- Luz obviously wasn't ready to get married, or she would have married him when he returned to the front, before he returned to the States. She just couldn't break his heart so soon after the war.
- He doesn't respond to her last letter; he doesn't try to win her back. Instead he responds with reckless indulgence. Our first impulse is to feel sorry for him; our more reasoned response is to fault him.

Problems:

- If Luz has no intention of marrying him, it is only momentarily kind to string him along.
- If Luz aims to get him to the States, where he'll slowly forget about her, then why do they have this understanding about his drinking and socializing?

Drafting

At this point, I feel ready to write a draft. After several tries, and some rethinking and rewriting, here is the essay I produced.

The Longer View of Hemingway's "A Very Short Story"

The obvious response described: the setup.

Most readers of Hemingway's "A Very Short Story" will naturally pity the poor nameless soldier. He is wounded in the war, and then his fiancée breaks off their relationship when she falls for an Italian major. Her name, Luz, which might be pronounced like "lose," points to his fate: Where

Why this response occurs (point of view): more setup for an alternative response.	women are involved, he will lose. As a final indignity and injury, another woman gives him gonorrhea, emphasizing his status as a victim and a loser—because of women. Although the main villain is Luz, his experience with the salesgirl, who wounds him in a different way, suggests quite simply that women are untrustworthy, evil, dangerous—as bad as the war, it seems.

But this immediate reaction of pity is the effect of our point of view. Although the story is told in third person, Hemingway actually gives us, as Robert Scholes points out in *Semiotics and Interpretation* (Yale UP, 1982), what is essentially the soldier's point of view. Repeatedly in the brief story, we are told what he experiences and what he is thinking. In the opening, for instance, we are told that "he could look out over the top of the town." We learn that Luz "was cool and fresh in the hot night"—a perception that clearly is his. We know his motivation for trying not to talk under anesthesia (he does not want to "blab"), and we know how many letters he received and what was in them. We never know, however, what Luz is really thinking, and we learn the content of her letters from his perspective, when he reads them. The real context of their writing is hidden from the reader.

But Hemingway gives the careful reader plenty of clues that suggest we should look closer, overcoming the limitations of the narrative's point of view. Is Luz, in fact, entirely the villain, and the soldier purely the innocent victim?

Our opinion of Luz is, of course, influenced by the fact that in falling for the Italian major, she betrays the American soldier. There is little question that Luz made a mistake, but it is also clear that she pays for her mistake, for "The major did not marry her in the spring, or any other time." And when Luz writes to the soldier about the major's departure, she is perhaps attempting to resurrect her relationship with the soldier, but he fails to respond. The soldier cannot forgive her, apparently.

Nor, it seems, can many readers. The most important reason, I believe, is Luz's letter breaking off her relationship with the soldier. Specifically, her assertion that "theirs had been only a boy and girl affair" seems especially thoughtless and cruel. It is bad enough to be dumped, but it is even worse to learn that your own relationship was, in your partner's view, immature and superficial. But before we damn Luz's insensitivity, we ought to consider the possible

The marginal notes alongside the text read:

How third person seems like first.

Transition to a different response, one that looks beyond the point of view.

This focuses on the crucial factor in our response to Luz: She betrays him.

The letter is most important in shaping this negative response to Luz.

validity of her remark. In other words, is she possibly right? Was their relationship only a boy and girl affair?

What, in fact, is the basis of their relationship? It appears to be only physical. All we know of his view of Luz is that she is "cool and fresh." She sounds more like a soft drink or a vegetable than a partner for life. Luz is, after all, sleeping in the hospital with one of her patients, and another pronunciation of her name, as "loose," may also be appropriate. When she says their relationship was immature, perhaps she accurately assesses her own behavior. The conditions, to be sure, were extraordinary: It is wartime, and the wounded soldier is returning to the front. I can understand Luz's looseness, but I can also agree that she is immature.

Her assessment of the soldier's maturity also seems accurate to me. Just look at his response to her last letter. He goes from hospital-bed sex to taxicab sex. Hemingway provides the tawdry details to emphasize his poor judgment: "A short time after [her letter] he contracted gonorrhea from a sales girl in a loop department store while riding in a taxicab through Lincoln Park." The poor soldier is wounded again in "combat," but surely this problem is his own fault. It is not Luz's fault, nor even the salesgirl's fault, is it? Even if we grant that mature and thoughtful people might contract a sexually transmitted disease, and that things were much different back then, the circumstances here still do not suggest responsible behavior. In fact, it is hard for me to imagine how he could be more immature, unless perhaps he had sex on the sidewalk with a prostitute.

I also notice the soldier's promise not to drink, nor to see "his friends or anyone." Given the reference early in the story to drinking on the roof, I have to wonder if he has a drinking problem. I wonder why they did not marry when he returned from the front. There was not sufficient time before he left, but surely there is enough time when he gets back. It seems fair to suspect that the lack of time was just a convenient excuse. Likewise, why does he go ahead and leave Luz if he is unhappy with the arrangement? How long does it take him to get a job? Does he, in fact, get one? If so, then why is Luz still overseas? We are not told many things we need to know to evaluate his responsibility; but what is left out, together with what we do know, does suggest to me that Luz's view may not be thoughtless or cruel, but simply accurate. Theirs was indeed a boy and girl affair. At least Luz is perceptive enough to see it.

My response, contrasting the obvious response: Luz may be right.

I see Luz's immaturity easily.

I also see the soldier's immaturity.

Most immature: his response to Luz's breakup.

How I respond to earlier evidence of his immaturity.

I think Luz is right: I can see her side.

PRACTICING READER-RESPONSE CRITICISM

I offer here three poems and a short story, along with some questions intended to stimulate your responses and help you to develop a reader-response essay. These are just sample questions; other ones will probably occur to you. The important thing is to generate materials that allow you to evolve and articulate your response. Without you, there is no response.

Since There's No Help
Michael Drayton

Since there's no help, come, let us kiss and part,—
Nay, I have done, you get no more from me;
And I am glad, yea glad with all my heart,
That thus so cleanly I myself can free;
Shake hands for ever, cancel all our vows,   5
And when we meet at any time again,
Be it not seen in either of our brows
That we one jot of former love retain.
Now at the last gasp of Love's latest breath,
When his pulse failing, Passion speechless lies,   10
When Faith is kneeling by his bed of death,
And Innocence is closing up his eyes,—
Now if thou would'st, when all have given him over,
From death to life thou migh'st him yet recover.

                                                            (1619)

Questions

1. As you read the first line, what scene do you imagine taking place? At the end of the first line, what tone do you imagine the speaker is using?
2. How do the next three lines (2–4) affect your perception of the speaker's tone? What do the words "cleanly" and "free" suggest about the speaker's tone?
3. The speaker says about ten times (depending on how you count them) that the lovers should break it off. Why all the repetition? And why the extreme declaration that not "one jot of former love" should remain?
4. Imagine yourself as the person being addressed in this poem. How would you feel after line 8?
5. How does your view of the relationship change in the last six lines? How does presenting "Love" as a dying person affect your response?

6. The poem speaks to "you." Who is this "you"? What clues does the poem give us about the character of "you"?

7. Sometime around 1591 Michael Drayton fell totally in love with Anne Goodere (he said he lost his mind over her). This sonnet was probably written shortly after that, even though it was not published until 1619. Anne Goodere married Sir Henry Rainsford in 1596; Drayton never married. But he did spend every summer at Clifford Hall, the country home of Anne and Henry, his passion apparently turning into a deep friendship. How does this information affect your response to the poem?   ■

Killing the Bear
Judith Minty

She has strung the hammock between two birch trees at the edge of the clearing. Now she drifts in and out of the light there and drowsily studies the pattern made by the rope's weaving and the flickering leaves.

When she had the dog, he stretched out beneath the hammock. Hackles raised, growling and nipping at flies, he'd meant to save her from shadows. In truth, he startled at noises, even at shifts in the wind, and she ended up more his protector than the other way around.

There were wolves at the little zoo when she was a child. She heard them howling from her aunt's kitchen and went to see them up close. And a bear.

Three times she visited, slowly circling the bear pen, but he was always sleeping. He looked like a bundle of clothes by the dead tree. His fence was electrified and posted with signs, and she was afraid to touch the iron bars.

The wolves set off a chorus of neighborhood dogs. Their calling floated back and forth all that summer vacation.

⚮

She lies in the hammock every afternoon, her life in the rhythm of the woods. Up at dawn to the shrill pitch of bluejays. Logs tossed into the stove, match lit, breath steaming in the cabin's chill. Trip to the outhouse, coffee perking, bucket of water from the river. The rest of the morning, ping of nails driven into boards. Her porch is nearly done. One room and another room. Something inside and something out.

The afternoon silence and the sway of the hammock lull her and when she hears a low guttural, she thinks, at first, it is the dog. Then she remembers the dog is gone.

She struggles to sit up and makes the hammock sway crazily.

A bear stands beyond the pines—small jets of eyes, heavy black coat. He snuffles, then drops on all fours and weaves into the forest.

Her hands lift to cover her breasts.

⚮

Her favorite doll was a stuffed animal and she slept with it close to her heart. She was nine when her mother said, "Give me your bear for three months. Let's see if you can stop sucking your thumb."

She tried very hard to stop, and when the time was up, she asked for the bear again.

Her mother said, "Another month."

One day, as she sat in the kitchen watching a cake being stirred and poured into the pan and then put into the oven, it came to her that her bear was gone, that it had been thrown down the incinerator.

Only a few years ago, her mother told her, misspeaking even then, "I'm sorry for burning the animal in you."

❦

Her hammer has stopped its thump and echo. The roof is laid. The porch smells of fresh paint. She has hauled the old sofa out and can sit there in the evenings, if she wants.

When the bear understood that she was alone, he came closer. The first time, she was reading in the hammock and heard something like a sigh. She knew it was him, even before she caught a glimpse of black gliding through the woods. The next time, he was so close she smelled him—a terrible, rancid odor. Without looking, she swung out of the hammock and walked to the cabin. Two days later, he stood next to the birch tree, breath rattling his throat. If she'd turned, she could have touched the bristles on his shoulder.

❦

The Gilyak tribe honored him. They put his head on a stake outside their doors and made offerings to it. On Yezo Island, the Ainus thought he was a man trapped inside the body of a bear. If a hunter found a cub, he brought it to his wife who suckled it.

In Lapland he was King of Beasts. The men lived alone, purifying themselves, for three days after the hunt. At the funeral, after they had feasted, they put his bones back together in the ground.

Once she spent an evening with two Swedes. At dinner, their wineglasses held the tint of leaves. Ole, the painter, said, "You live in green light." Gunnar told magic tales. "When a woman meets a bear in the woods, she must lift her skirt. Then he will let her pass."

❦

In the travelogue about Alaska, the Kodiak caught a salmon, his claws stretched out like fingers. When the second bear approached, he reared up. He looked soft and gentle, as if he were greeting a friend, until, with a sweep of his paw, he split open the head of the other.

In college, a classmate told about the summer he'd worked at Yellowstone and got too close. He never felt the nick, only knew when blood trickled down his forehead.

There was also the news story about the woman dragged from her tent in the middle of the night, crying, "He's killing me. Oh God, he's killing me." The bear carried the woman away, his claws tangled in her hair, ripping at her arm.

⸎

When she drove to town for supplies, she bought a secondhand rifle. She keeps it loaded now, propped against the doorjamb inside the cabin.

The clerk at the hardware store showed her how to fire it, how to aim along the sights. He winked and told her she could get a man with it at twenty yards. She said she didn't need a man, just wanted to do some hunting.

She misses the dog. She carries the gun awkwardly over her shoulder when she goes to the woodpile, or to the river.

⸎

Her calendar hangs on the cabin wall, each day of summer marked with an X, the rest of the year clean and open. She turns up the wick on the lamp and starts to brush her hair, staring at her reflection in the windowpane.

She is thinking about leaving. She is thinking about driving out of the clearing.

When the scream begins, it breaks against the walls. It shudders in a moan, then rises. Everything, even the wind, holds its breath.

It is over so quickly she almost believes it didn't happen and raises the brush again, and barely recognizes herself in the glass. She runs to the lamp and blows out the flame, then to the window, hoping she will not see what must be there.

⸎

She did not shoot cleanly the first time. When he ripped the screen and tore the siding loose, she stood on the porch, gun leveled.

"Go away."

He was no more than ten feet from her when she fired. He spun around and fell to the ground, then raised himself up.

When she realized she had only wounded him, she ran into the cabin and turned the lock and leaned against the door. She could hear him thrashing and bellowing in the bushes and against the trees.

She knew she would have to step onto the porch again, go to the ripped screen, with nothing but night air between them. She would have to take aim and shoot again. And if that didn't stop him, she would have to slip the bolt and reload the rifle and stand there and shoot him again until he stopped bawling and weeping and falling down and getting up and lurching against the trees.

When they began this, she never thought she would have to kill him so slow. She never dreamed she would have to hurt him so much.

⸎

It is nearly dawn when he dies, when she gets up from her chair, when his groans stop pricking her skin. She takes the flashlight and goes out on the porch. She shines the beam around in the gray light and sees the blood dried on the new screen and on the fresh-painted sill and spattered on the leaves around the cabin. She sees the trampled bushes and broken branches and where he crawled into the weeds.

She shines the arc out, light bouncing on tree and log, until it lands on a black heap, huddled in the middle of the clearing.

As soon as the sun rises, she begins to dig, and by midafternoon she is through with it—the rope tied to him, the car backed up to the hole, the rifle and box of ammunition remembered and dropped in next to him, the musty soil put back, and branches over that.

Then she bathes with the last of the water from the river and sweeps the cabin floor, thinking that rain will wash away the blood and that, soon enough, snow will fall and cover it all.

❧

It is dark when she gets to the state line. Next summer, she will dig him up to take the claws.

(1991)

Questions

1. What associations do the first two paragraphs bring to your mind? Can you imagine yourself in a similar scene? How would you feel? How do you react to the suggestion that she ended up more the dog's protector "than the other way around"?

2. Do paragraphs 3–6 alter the mood created by the first two paragraphs? What contrasting moods are created by the third section?

3. What is your response to the following sentence? "Her hands lift to cover her breasts." For instance, what expectations does the statement create for you?

4. How do paragraphs 12–16 affect the reader's understanding of her attitude toward bears?

5. How does her construction of a porch, and the movement of her sofa onto the porch, affect your response to the bear's appearance? What does the bear's smell contribute to your response? How about the bear's sex? (The bear is a "him," not an "it.")

6. Paragraphs 19–21 observe how various cultures have honored bears, but it also has its ominous aspects. Explain how the reader's sense of danger builds in the seventh section.

7. Why are the summer days marked with an X? Does that have anything to do with bears?

8. Describe your reaction to paragraphs 32–41.

9. Is the final sentence surprising? Why, or why not?

Did I Miss Anything?
Tom Wayman

Question frequently asked by
students after missing a class

Nothing. When we realized you weren't here
we sat with our hands folded on our desks
in silence, for the full two hours

    Everything. I gave an exam worth
    40 percent of the grade for this term   5
    and assigned some reading due today
    on which I'm about to hand out a quiz
    worth 50 percent

Nothing. None of the content of this course
has value or meaning   10
Take as many days off as you like:
any activities we undertake as a class
I assure you will not matter either to you or me
and are without purpose

    Everything. A few minutes after we began last time   15
    a shaft of light suddenly descended and an angel
    or other heavenly being appeared
    and revealed to us what each woman or man must do
    to attain divine wisdom in this life and
    the hereafter   20
    This is the last time the class will meet
    before we disperse to bring the good news to all people on earth

Nothing. When you are not present
how could something significant occur?

    Everything. Contained in this classroom   25
    is a microcosm of human experience
    assembled for you to query and examine and ponder
    This is not the only place such an opportunity has been gathered

    but it was one place

And you weren't here   30

(1993)

Questions

1. How does the poem's subtitle shape your expectations for what will follow? How would you imagine most teachers would view this question?
2. How would you describe your response to the first three lines?
3. How would you describe the teacher's attitude toward the students' question?
4. The poem alternates between "Nothing" and "Everything." How is your response to the final "Everything" section different from your response to the previous sections? How is that final section different?
5. Imagine a student (perhaps one who has asked this question), a teacher, a parent of a student, a drill sergeant, and a Buddhist monk responding to this poem. Describe how their responses might differ. ■

deep as space
A. Williams

you are as constant
as post nasal drip,
i love you.
you have the body of a beach ball
with a slow leak,   5
i love you.
you have the grin of the first ant
that discovers the picnic,
i love you.
you are like a paper wasp   10
living in your desk hive of paper,
i love you.
you have a mind as deep as space
full of bright stars and flashes,
you are loved.   15

(1979)

Questions

1. Describe your expectations and responses as you move through the first three lines. After five words, what do you expect? How do the next three words undo that expectation? And then what happens with the next line?
2. After the first three-line sequence, the poem repeats this structure four times. Is your response to each of the sections the same, or similar, or does your response evolve? Where are you at the end of the poem, compared to the beginning?

3. Why is the final line different from the previous repetitions of "i love you?
4. How would you respond to this poem if it were addressed to you? As a love poem, would this appeal to you? What does this poem suggest about its author, and about the relationship between the author and the person addressed? How, in other words, does the author expect this person to respond? ■

USEFUL TERMS FOR READER-RESPONSE CRITICISM

Affect: In discussing your response, you may well talk about how something affects you. Be sure to distinguish the spelling of this word from the following one.

Effect: This word refers (usually) to what the work creates in you: The effect of the work comes from how it affects you. "Affect" is usually a verb, and "effect" a noun—although there are exceptions. Psychiatrists, for instance, talk about the "affect" of someone, referring to that person's emotions and demeanor: "He has a flat affect" means that his emotions appear to be flat. Also, "effect" can be used as a verb, meaning "to bring something into being." For instance, "We are going to effect some changes in the retirement plan" means that we are going to bring about changes.

Expectation, Anticipation: In describing your response you're likely to talk about how the text prepares you for something and then surprises or satisfies you.

Implied Reader: The reader that you think the author had in mind. In trying to respond as the implied reader, you aim to put aside your own idiosyncrasies and try to play the role of the reader the author was addressing. Obviously, the implied reader is a fiction, a composite of lots of real readers.

Subjective Response: This stance involves letting your own personality figure freely into your response. With a subjective response, you're not trying to be the implied reader (as in a receptive stance). Instead, you're trying to respond authentically, honestly, richly, personally.

✓ Checklist for Reader-Response Criticism

1. Read actively—make notes, ask questions, respond, and record.
2. Focus on details and ask how your response would change if the details were changed.
3. Decide on your purpose: a subjective, an interactive, or a receptive response.

Note

1. See Steven Levy, "Can an Algorithm Write a Better News Story Than a Human Reporter?" *Wired*, April 24, 2012, Web, accessed May 17, 2015, and Dylan Love, "If You Don't Think Robots Can Replace Journalists, Check Out This Article Written by a Computer," *Business Insider*, July 9, 2014, Web, accessed May 17, 2015. For a contrary view, see Milo Yiannopoulos, "Everyone Is Going to Hate the News Stories Written by Robots," *Business Insider*, July 11, 2014, Web, accessed May 17, 2015.

Works Cited

Bleich, David. *Readings and Feelings: An Introduction to Subjective Criticism*. Urbana: National Council of Teachers of English, 1975. Print.

___. *Subjective Criticism*. Baltimore: Johns Hopkins UP, 1978. Print.

Crosman, Robert. "How Readers Make Meaning." *College Literature*. 1982; 9: 207–215. Rpt. in *Literary Theories in Praxis*. Ed. Shirley Staton. Philadelphia: U of Pennsylvania P, 1987. 357–366. Print.

Fish, Stanley. *Doing what Comes Naturally: Change, Rhetoric, and the Practice of Theory in Literary and Legal Studies*. Durham, NC: Duke UP, 1989. Print.

___. *Is There a Text in This Class? The Authority of Interpretive Communities*. Cambridge, MA: Harvard UP, 1980. Print.

___. *Self-Consuming Artifacts: The Experience of Seventeenth-Century Literature*. Berkeley: U of California P, 1972. Print.

___. *Surprised by Sin: The Reader in Paradise Lost*. New York: St. Martins, 1967. Print.

___. *The Trouble with Principle*. Cambridge, MA: Harvard UP, 1999. Print.

___. *There's No Such Thing as Free Speech: And It's a Good Thing, Too*. Oxford: Oxford UP, 1994. Print.

Kuhn, Thomas. *The Structure of Scientific Revolutions*. 2nd ed. Chicago: U of Chicago P, 1970. Print.

Peckham, Morse. "The Problem of Interpretation." *College Literature* 6.1 (1979): 1–17. Print.

Rosenblatt, Louise. *Literature as Exploration*. 1938. Rev. ed. New York: Noble, 1968. Print.

___. *The Reader, the Text, the Poem: The Transactional Theory of the Literary Work*. Carbondale: Southern Illinois UP, 1978. Print.

Scholes, Robert. *Semiotics and Interpretation*. New Haven, CT: Yale UP, 1982. Print.

Tompkins, Jane. "The Reader in History: The Changing Shape of Literary Response." *Reader-Response Criticism*. Ed. Jane Tompkins. Baltimore: Johns Hopkins UP, 1980. Print.

Recommended Further Reading

Beach, Richard. *A Teacher's Introduction to Reader-Response Theories*. Urbana: National Council of Teachers of English, 1993. Print. A very comprehensive overview of the wide range of reader-oriented approaches.

Berg, Temma. "Psychologies of Reading." *Tracing Literary Theory*. Ed. Joseph Natoli. Urbana: U of Illinois P, 1987. 248–277. Print. A lively discussion of the way personality affects textual reception.

Brenner, Gerry. *Performative Criticism: Experiments in Reader Response*. Albany: State U of New York P, 2004. Print. In this entertaining variation on reader-response criticism, Brenner brings characters from classic literary works to life, and they respond to works that they inhabit (or rather, Brenner responds through them).

Davis, Todd, and Kenneth Womack. *Formalist Criticism and Reader-Response Theory*. New York: Palgrave-Macmillan, 2004. Print. Clearly explains these two theories, referring often to familiar texts (e.g., Conrad's *Heart of Darkness*, Fitzgerald's *Great Gatsby*).

Gaillet, Lynee Lewis. "Reading." *Keywords in Composition Studies*. Ed. Paul Heilker and Peter Vandenberg. Portsmouth, NH: Boynton/Cook, 1996. 196–200. Print. A brief yet expansive view of our current conceptions of making meaning. Includes a concise treatment of reader-response criticism in the context of the teaching of writing.

Holland, Norman. "Hamlet—My Greatest Creation." *Journal of the American Academy of Psychoanalysis*. 1975; 3: 419–427. Print. A classic essay, often reprinted and excerpted, arguing that meaning is not discovered, but is actively made as the reader responds.

Iser, Wolfgang. *The Implied Reader*. Baltimore: Johns Hopkins UP, 1974. Print. Influential and still readable, Iser's work convincingly argues that texts provide cues that indicate an implied reader—a role the real reader may assume, play, or reject.

Jauss, Hans. *Toward an Aesthetic of Reception*. Trans. by Timothy Bahti. Minneapolis: U of Minnesota P, 1982. Print. A challenging book that places reader response in historical context: How does a reader's historical position affect his or her response? Should we attempt to respond as the initial readers of a work? Is that possible?

Wimsatt, W. K. "The Affective Fallacy." In *The Verbal Icon: Studies in the Meaning of Poetry*. Ed. W. K. Wimsatt Jr. Lexington: UP of Kentucky, 1954. Print. The famous essay articulating the New Critical axiom that literary criticism is not properly concerned with the reader's response, but should focus on the work itself. Reader response critics would embrace this "fallacy."

CHAPTER 5

Opening Up the Text

Structuralism and Deconstruction

Imagine being the first to say, with confidence: uncertainty.
—Michael Blumenthal[1]

What you'll learn in this chapter:

- To identify opportunities to use structuralist and deconstructive principles.
- To develop ideas about texts using structuralism and deconstruction.
- To write and revise essays, step by step, about literary texts, using structuralism and deconstruction.
- To apply structuralism and deconstruction in a variety of contexts.

THE PURPOSES OF STRUCTURALISM AND DECONSTRUCTION

If New Criticism focuses on the work, and reader-response criticism focuses on the reader, then structuralism might be seen as a combination of these two approaches: A structure is something—a pattern, a design—that is somehow "in" a text, but a structure is also something that readers must actively perceive. Without someone reading, there is no structure; without a structure, there is no one making sense. You have an understanding of the structure of the English language, and that allows you to identify the subjects, the verbs, the modifiers, and so forth of the sentences you are reading—and thereby make sense. This drive to find organization and meaningfulness is so powerful that human beings can find shapes in clouds or the scorch marks of a tortilla. If we can find structure where no one has created it, we can also fail to detect structures, as in hidden codes or unknown languages. But when communication takes place, it occurs because these two elements, text and reader, come together: A perceiver sees how the surface experience fits into some underlying set of conventions, imagining meaning. And if structuralism aims to understand how this conveyance of meaning occurs, deconstruction aims to show how it doesn't—how the structures that we bring to language and experience inevitably fail, how meaning slips and slides and comes apart. Deconstruction is, in a literal and theoretical sense, what comes after structuralism: To see how something comes apart, one must first see how it went together, so a deconstructive analysis is possible only after some degree of structuralist analysis. Thus, this chapter deals with structuralism and deconstruction, but it focuses on deconstruction because its influence is enormous, helping to open up theory and reading to a multitude of other approaches. Deconstruction has not rendered structuralism obsolete, but it has, for many people at least, changed our thinking about what structuralism actually does, undermining the scientific exuberance of the early structuralists and becoming a pervasive part of our intellectual assumptions.

Structuralism and Semiotics

Structuralism grows from Ferdinand de Saussure's series of lectures on language, delivered between 1913 and 1915, but not translated into English or widely known until the late 1950s. Rather than thinking of a particular language in terms of its history, moving through time, a "diachronic" view, Saussure took a "synchronic" view, looking at the relationships of all the parts of a language at a given moment in time. The surface elements of language, which Saussure called *parole* (French for "speech"), may vary widely. British and American speakers of English, for instance, say the word "towel" differently: Most Americans use two syllables, while most British use one. Some people in my hometown, in fact, pronounce "towel" in the same way they say the word "tile." We may find these kinds of linguistic differences insignificant, or interesting, or amusing, or grounds for bias, but we are able to understand each other because of our understanding of the underlying structure, which Saussure called *langue* (French for "language"). This underlying structure allows us to make sense of the surface.

Saussure's structural approach to language not only provided a powerful analytical tool, but it also altered the way we think about language and meaning. In particular, the distinction between a "signifier" (a word, an image) and a "signified" (the concept that the signifier is pointing to) is crucial, exposing the arbitrary relationship between the words we use and the ideas in our heads. Anyone who can speak two languages fluently knows that some things that are easy to say in one language may be difficult or even impossible to say in another. Different languages structure the world differently: If one language has eleven different words for fog, and another language has only one, then it's reasonable to assume that speakers of these two languages look at fog differently (and probably spend different amounts of time in fog). It's not that one system of meaning is better than another—that fog either comes in eleven different kinds or one. Fog comes in however many kinds we are able to perceive (and desire to distinguish)—and this organizing of the world is based on underlying structures we perceive and create. Crucially, structure is based on difference: The word "bat" is not "cat" because of the difference in the two initial sounds. Structuralism seeks to bring a scientific approach to language, finding the underlying commonalities and distinguishing differences.

As a method, however, structuralism can be applied to anything, not just language, and "semiotics" is the term usually employed for this larger enterprise. In the late 1950s, for instance, Claude Levi-Strauss began to demonstrate how structural analysis could be applied to cultures—with fascinating results. Looking for the underlying structures of food preparation, for instance, Levi-Strauss in *The Raw and the Cooked* (1964) observed that in every culture people divide their food into three classes: raw, rotten, and cooked. This fundamental structure has resulted in some wildly different cuisines that are nonetheless organized in the same way. In one society, moldy clumps of solidified cow's milk are consumed; in another, whale blubber with maggots in it is valued. Specific rules that create systems of meaning allow both these cultures to make sense of their food. All of our meaning-making as humans—what it means to be a "person," to be "married," to be "good" or "guilty" or "in love," or not—depends upon the linguistic structures that we inhabit.

Poststructuralism and Deconstruction

The term "deconstruction" as an activity in theory and criticism derives from Jacques Derrida, a French philosopher, and his 1967 work *Of Grammatology*, and it is easily one of the most edgy and exhilarating concepts developed in the twentieth century, or one of the most scandalously outrageous ideas, depending on one's perspective. (Or both.) The term rather quickly became so pervasive and was used in so many different ways and contexts that it became hard to say what it means. As Gregory Jay put it in 1991, "deconstruction has now become an indeterminate nominative" (xi): a name without a particular reference. Derrida himself, rather than clarifying his usage, seemed much more interested in saying what deconstruction was not than what it is. But if the assumptions of deconstruction are correct, "deconstruction" always was an uncertain term, for deconstruction's supposition that all terms are unstable must apply to itself. Few efforts would appear to be more ironic, perhaps even comical, than attempting to define and explain a philosophical position that assumes the inevitability of error and misreading, the impossibility of explaining and defining in any stable way.

There are, however, at least three reasons to attempt to explain deconstruction anyway:

1. The alternative to explaining what in the final analysis cannot be explained is silence. We explain deconstruction, and we practice it, even though something is always left undone, unstated, unclear, unthought of. Another explanation can supplement this one, and then another one can supplement it. Such is the case with any term, or perhaps with any thing human. Perhaps we should have more compassion for each other, given the ultimate futility of what we endeavor every day.

2. Deconstruction makes no effort to suppress its own irony or absurdity; instead, deconstructive critics have generally indulged in a playfulness that from the perspective of traditional criticism seems at times unprofessional; in the merciless punning of some of the most prominent deconstructive critics, it has seemed occasionally almost juvenile.

3. Deconstruction as a method, or antimethod, can be learned and practiced by students, and in my experience it often stimulates a wonderfully imaginative playfulness and scrutiny. In fact, rather than being an esoteric, foreign, abstract, discouraging approach, deconstruction for most students makes tremendous sense: It articulates precisely what they have, in fact, already assumed in a vague way. Students who understand deconstruction tend to be much more adventurous, questioning, insightful readers.

So, here we go. The next little stretch is a bit theoretical and even strange, but you'll see several illustrations later on. Just fasten your seat belt and prepare for a little turbulence.

Structuralism and semiotics have produced many richly revealing and interesting analyses of texts and social phenomena—wrestling matches, detergent boxes, advertisements, anything. But some thinkers, exposing gaps and inconsistencies in the structures they examined, started to question just how far structuralist readings could be taken. This push beyond structuralism, revealing the failures of systems of meaning, came to be known as poststructuralism. Poststructuralism did not put structuralism entirely out of business: One can still do structuralist analysis today, but poststructuralism has altered our sense of what is produced by such readings. And poststructuralism is the set of assumptions and ideas that make deconstruction possible. What is deconstruction? To answer that question, let's turn to Jacques Derrida (who isn't going to tell us, but that is an intriguing part of the story...).

Derrida is without question the most important figure for deconstruction. He relentlessly and astonishingly exposed the uncertainties of using language. Derrida starts, we might say, from the recognition that words do not refer directly to things. If they did, all languages would represent the world in the same way, and the meanings of words would be stable. Instead of words referring to things, Saussure argued that the signifier (the word) and the signified (its reference, a concept) are not a unified entity, but rather an arbitrary and constantly shifting relationship. A dictionary only seems to stabilize a language, for what we actually find in a dictionary is the postponement or deferment of meaning: Words have multiple definitions, and these definitions require us to seek the meaning of other words, which are themselves defined in the same way.

Even if it were possible to construct instantaneously a dictionary that would be perfectly up-to-date, we would still find ambiguity, multiplicity, and slippage pervading the language. The reason is nicely captured in Derrida's most famous statement, *il n'y a pas de hors-texte*, which appears in *Of Grammatology* (158–159) and which has been variously translated as "There is no outside-text," "There is nothing outside the text," and "There is no outside to the text." (In itself, this uncertainty regarding translation tells us something important about language.) Derrida's point, it seems, is that in making meaning we can't get outside of language. Anything we say is contextual; words always refer to and depend upon other words.

Deconstruction reveals the arbitrariness and open-endedness of language most strikingly by exposing the contradictions in a text, thereby showing how a text undermines itself. As Barbara Johnson puts it, deconstruction proceeds by "the careful teasing out of warring forces of signification within the text itself" (5). Or, as Jonathan Culler says, "To deconstruct a discourse is to show how it undermines the philosophy it asserts, or the hierarchical oppositions on which it relies" (*Deconstruction*, 86). This exposure of a text's self-contradictions is possible, deconstruction assumes, because words cannot stabilize meaning: If we choose to say one thing, we are leaving out another thing. And there is always a gap, a space in the text, that the reader cannot ultimately fill in, as we shall see.

Deconstruction is therefore particularly valuable because of its power to open up a text that we may have seen as limited or closed. Popularly, "to deconstruct" has often been used to mean "to dismantle" or "to destroy," as if "deconstruction" were a fancier form of "destruction." But for most informed critics, deconstruction is not so much a way to obliterate the meaning of a text as it is a way to multiply meaning by taking something apart, to show the contingency of how something is put together by disassembling it. Deconstruction thus encourages us to resist a complacent acceptance of anything and to question our positions and statements in a particularly rigorous way, even reading texts against themselves.

For instance, let's take a very simple text, one appearing beside an elevator: "Seeing Eye Dogs Only." A deconstructive reading of this text might point out that although it appears to extend assistance to the visually impaired, it literally should force them to walk up the stairs, for the sign appears to say, "This elevator is reserved for seeing eye dogs. No other animals or persons can ride it." The text shifts power and privilege to a certain kind of dog, while ignoring the owners of the dogs. Here's a text ostensibly put up to help blind persons, and it actually ignores them. A blind person with a helpful friend, or a seeing eye monkey, presumably, must not ride. Plus, ironically, blind persons obviously cannot read the sign, which suggests that some other intention motivates it. Perhaps the sign is intended to make sure that someone who is fully sighted and has a retired seeing eye dog as a pet can take such a dog on the elevator? Isn't that what it says? What *is* the point of this sign?

Although such undoing of a text may seem at first glance a bit silly, it actually has the potential for enormous practical value. Imagining all the things a text *might* be saying, including even the opposite of what it may appear to say, will help us to become more creative and careful readers and writers. Some colleagues of mine wrote a policy statement that told students "You will fail your Freshman English course if you miss more than three scheduled tutoring sessions." One student read this statement as a prediction rather than a rule, and he elected to skip all his tutoring sessions in order to prove the prediction wrong. As he told me later, appealing his failing grade, "I knew I was smart enough to pass the course without any help, and I resented them telling me I couldn't do it, and I worked twice as hard as I would have otherwise." A deconstructive stance might have anticipated this reading, and precluded it by revising the sentence (although such a stance must also acknowledge that every possible misreading can't be anticipated or prevented).

But a deconstructive stance not only may help us anticipate some of the ways that even simple texts can be misread; it may also help us see what is being excluded or suppressed in a text. For instance, the J. Peterman Company advertises a reproduction of "Hemingway's Cap." The point of the advertisement is, of course, that Ernest Hemingway picked out a tough, distinctive, very masculine hat to wear, and now you can have the same. The ad conveys this message by telling us that Hemingway possibly bought the cap "on the road to Ketchum," which is where Hemingway's Idaho ranch was located, the scene of hunting, fishing, and other outdoor activities; that he found it "among the beef jerky wrapped in cellophane," which also helps create a rustic, macho atmosphere (isn't beef jerky primarily eaten by guys in a duck blind or deer stand—or wishing they were?); that the bill is longer than average, longer in fact than the advertiser has ever seen, and "impervious" to rainstorms; that the cap is the color of "scalding expresso"—a drink for tough men who need a tough cap; that there's an elastic band "to keep this treasure from blowing off your head and into the trees"; and much else. Thus, the advertisement celebrates masculine toughness, durability, endurance, and sensibility, using these values to sell the product.

But a deconstructive stance encourages an acute alertness to rhetorical strategies and even the assumptions these strategies depend upon.

Hemingway's Cap.

He possibly bought his in a gas station on the road to Ketchum, next to the cash register, among the beef jerky wrapped in cellophane. Or maybe in a tackle shop in Key West.

I had to go to some trouble to have this one made for you and me, but it had to be done. The long bill, longer than I, at least, ever saw before, makes sense.

Hemingway's Cap (No. 1537). The visor: calfskin, soft and glareless and unaffected by repeated rain squalls. The color: same as strong scalding espresso, lemon peel on the side, somewhere in the mountains in the north of Italy.

Ten-ounce cotton duck canvas. Six brass grommets for ventilation. Elastic at back to keep this treasure from blowing off your head and into the trees. Imported.

Sizes: M, L, XL.

Although the cap appears to promote and depend upon a masculine toughness, deconstruction tells us that it also unavoidably promotes and depends
upon masculine insecurity. Why would anyone want the longest bill anyone
ever saw? For the same reason one might want the fastest car anyone ever
saw. Or the biggest ranch. Such a desire for preeminence is risky because
it requires constant monitoring and measuring and exposes one to a sense
of fragility and uncertainty. Made of "calfskin," this longest bill becomes
a symbol of its owner's power and potency. The bill, one could argue, is
a phallic substitute: An earlier version of the cap was made of "deerskin,"
and it is pretty clear what part of their skin many men would consider
most "dear" (and deconstructive critics do tend to love puns). Certainly,
Hemingway was fascinated by potency and its lack: In *The Sun Also Rises*, for
instance, Jake Barnes has been emasculated by a wartime injury and loses
Brett, Lady Ashley, to a young bullfighter and then to another aristocrat.

Likewise, the idea that Hemingway may have bought his cap "on the
road to Ketchum" conjures up scenes of hunting and fishing. But Ketchum
is also where Hemingway committed suicide. Seriously ill for some time, he
put a shotgun in his mouth and pulled the trigger. Denied the sort of active,
impervious masculinity embodied in the cap, Hemingway apparently could
not face a compromised life.

How the cap relates to this weakness or insecurity is most startlingly
seen in an especially revealing (or especially disturbing) phrase, referring
to the "elastic at back to keep this treasure from blowing off your head."
In asserting that the cap is a "treasure," the ad unavoidably raises the
danger—the inevitability really—of losing it. This sentence is meant to
reassure potential owners, but it also points out how only the elastic (which
must age and wear out) stands between the owner and loss of his manly
treasure. The advertisement thus helps to foster an insecurity that the cap
covers over; but in such a value system, depending on potency and toughness, the danger of something "blowing off your head" is very real, as
Hemingway's own case reveals.

Is such a mischievous, even outrageous, allusion intended in "blowing
off your head"? Although I've had students who insist that the phrase is
a wickedly clever joke, that the ad's author must have been aware of the
implications of "blowing off your head" in the context of Hemingway, the
issue is really undecidable, and from a deconstructive point of view irrelevant because other conflicting and contradictory meanings are always
available to the attentive, creative reader. There will always be a trace of
"don't buy this hat" left in any urging to "buy this hat." And this counter-
reading can also be reversed. (I do own two of the caps.)

Let's turn now to some other examples and to the practical matter of
how structuralism and deconstruction work on more complex texts, which
often even more readily lend themselves to opening up.

HOW TO DO STRUCTURALISM AND DECONSTRUCTION

In an essay designed to question and criticize, Lawrence Lipking shows how deconstruction would deal with W. B. Yeats' famous poem "Sailing to Byzantium." Since deconstruction turns a text against itself, multiplying its meanings, it seems only appropriate that Lipking's attack on deconstruction should provide a convenient illustration of deconstruction's value.

Here is Yeats's poem.*

Sailing to Byzantium†
William Butler Yeats

I

That is no country for old men. The young
In one another's arms, birds in the trees
—Those dying generations—at their song,
The salmon-falls, the mackerel-crowded seas
Fish, flesh, or fowl, commend all summer long   5
Whatever is begotten, born and dies.
Caught in that sensual music all neglect
Monuments of unaging intellect.

II

An aged man is but a paltry thing,
A tattered coat upon a stick, unless   10
Soul clap its hands and sing, and louder sing
For every tatter in its mortal dress,
Nor is there singing school but studying
Monuments of its own magnificence;
And therefore I have sailed the seas and come   15
To the holy city of Byzantium.

---

*Reprinted with the permission of Scribner, a Division of Simon & Schuster, Inc., from THE COLLECTED WORKS OF W. B. YEATS, VOLUME 1: THE POEMS, REVISED by W. B. Yeats, edited by Richard J. Finneran. Copyright © 1928 by The Macmillan Company; renewed 1956 by Georgie Yeats. All rights reserved.

†*Byzantium:* "Byzantium" is the name of an ancient city with an unusually rich set of associations. It was the capital of the Eastern Roman Empire in the fifth and sixth centuries and was celebrated for its art, architecture, and culture. Byzantium later became Constantinople, and then Istanbul, which is of course in modern-day Turkey. The city's crucial location along the Silk Road allowed it to connect the European and Asian worlds.

III

O sages standing in God's holy fire
As in the gold mosaic of a wall,
Come from the holy fire, perne in a gyre,‡
And be the singing-masters of my soul.   20
Consume my heart away; sick with desire
And fastened to a dying animal
It knows not what it is; and gather me
Into the artifice of eternity.

IV

Once out of nature I shall never take   25
My bodily form from any natural thing,
But such a form as Grecian goldsmiths make
Of hammered gold and gold enameling
To keep a drowsy Emperor awake;
Or set upon a golden bough to sing   30
To lords and ladies of Byzantium
Of what is past, or passing, or to come.
(1927)

    Deconstruction needs a norm or a convention to work against. If we don't assume a text is logically coherent, then exposing its incoherence and self-difference is hardly remarkable. In a way, then, a deconstructive reading is like an extension of a New Critical reading: Setting aside authorial intention and the reader's response, one first identifies the unity that appears to be present in the text and then divides and dispels it. But a deconstructive reading also looks somewhat like a structuralist reading that is pushed beyond the breaking point. I want to illustrate this point by studying the classic New Critical reading of Yeats' poem that is offered by Cleanth Brooks in *The Well-Wrought Urn* (1947). Saussure asserted that

---

    ‡*perne in a gyre*: A "gyre" is a spiral or a vortex. A "perne" is a spool or cylinder or cone that one would wind thread onto. Yeats did use this unusual word "perne" in at least one other place: In *Per Amica Silentia Lunae* (New York: Macmillan, 1918, page 90), he says "I begin to study the only self that I can know, myself, and to wind the thread upon the perne again." Also, a "pern," as John Unterecker has observed in his *A Reader's Guide to W.B. Yeats* (New York: Noonday, 1959, page 173), is a kind of hawk, commonly called a "honey-buzzard." It seems possible, even though the spelling is different, that Yeats is also suggesting the image of a hawk moving in a spiral. The Latin verb "perneo," as Phyllis Katz has noted (in a conversation reported by Patrick Gillespie: see his discussion of this poem on his website "PoemShape," accessed 8 August 2015), means "spin," and its imperative form is "perne." Thus, "spin in a gyre" makes perfect sense, although we might wonder why Yeats would have used a Latin imperative verb here.

language operates by means of binary oppositions: "cold" means something because it is opposed to "hot"; "nice" makes sense because we understand "mean." Brooks' reading of Yeats' poem depends on his perception of a structure of certain tensions or oppositions, which include, for instance, "nature versus art." By this opposition, Brooks means (among other things) that the first two stanzas talk about "fish, flesh, or fowl" and about aging—aspects of nature. The second two stanzas talk about "gold mosaic," "artifice," "hammered gold"—works of art.

Brooks discusses these other oppositions:

becoming	vs.	being
sensual	vs.	intellectual
here	vs.	Byzantium
aging	vs.	timelessness

To unify these oppositions, Brooks focuses on the speaker's "prayer," which begins in the third stanza and which asks the "sages" to "come from the holy fire"; and Brooks makes the word "artifice" the crux of the poem:

> The word "artifice" fits the prayer at one level after another: the fact that he is to be taken *out of nature;* that his body is to be an artifice hammered out of gold; that it will not age but will have the finality of a work of art. (188)

In every opposition, Saussure said, one element is favored or privileged over the other. Yeats seems, Brooks says, to favor the second elements in the list above. "Artifice," however, complicates matters:

> But "artifice" unquestionably carries an ironic qualification too. The prayer, for all its passion, is a modest one. He does not ask that he be gathered into eternity—it will be enough if he is gathered into the "artifice of eternity." The qualification does not turn the prayer into mockery, but it is all-important: it limits as well as defines the power of the sages to whom the poet appeals. (189)

This move, as I pointed out in the chapter on New Criticism, is typical, as Brooks finds an ironic center that unifies the poem. Here is Brooks' thesis, as stated early in his essay, responding to the question of "which world" Yeats commits himself to:

> The question is idle—as idle as the question which the earnest schoolmarm puts to the little girl reading for the first time "L'Allegro—Il Penseroso": which does Milton *really* prefer, mirth or melancholy . . . . Yeats chooses both and neither. (187)

Yeats manages, in other words, to unify the poem's oppositions, choosing both and neither. More directly, Brooks articulates his position this way near the end of his essay:

> The irony [of the poem] is directed, it seems to me, not at our yearning to transcend the world of nature, but at the human situation itself in which supernatural and natural are intermixed—the human situation which is inevitably caught between the claims of both natural and supernatural. The golden bird whose bodily form the speaker will take in Byzantium will be withdrawn from the flux of the world of becoming. But so withdrawn, it will sing of the world of becoming— "Of what is past, or passing, or to come." (189–90)

This "intermixture" that Brooks finds is for him the force unifying the poem's complex oppositions, thereby making possible the poem's greatness.

A deconstructive reading observes the text's structure of oppositions, as Brooks has done, but it refuses to accept their unification, and instead focuses on how their apparent resolution can be teased apart. Brooks claims that Yeats chooses both art and nature. But is that really true? In the final stanza, the speaker says, "Once out of nature I shall never take / My bodily form from any natural thing." If he escapes nature and becomes a golden work of art, then he has certainly chosen one member of the opposition. Brooks tries to cover this problem by saying the bird, outside of nature and time, will sing of the world of becoming—"Of what is past, or passing, or to come." But surely singing of something is not the same thing as being in it. Yeats *does choose*—art over nature, being over becoming, the intellectual over the sensual.

Or does he? The final step of deconstruction (after finding oppositions, assessing their hierarchy, positing their resolution, and questioning that resolution) is to call the reversal into question, placing the text in uncertainty. Lawrence Lipking, who aims to illustrate a deconstructive stance in order to criticize it, repeatedly shows us how a deconstructive critic would find that the poem fails to resolve its meaning. He asks, for instance, why should soul "louder sing / For every tatter in its mortal dress"? Is it singing to distract itself or us from the tatters of its mortal dress? Then the singing is opposed to the tatters, as the soul sings in spite of physical ailments. Or is it singing in celebration of these tatters, because the body's deterioration brings the soul closer to separation from the body? Lipking ponders these alternatives and concludes that "the line does not make sense, if by sense we understand a single unequivocal meaning or even the Aristotelian logic that asserts that nothing can be itself and not itself at the same time. Language goes its own way" (431).

Likewise, Lipking raises the question of whether, in the third stanza, there is a singing school. If "Nor is there singing school" means there isn't one, which seems reasonable enough, then how come the speaker wants some singing masters in the next verse? Perhaps the speaker says there is no singing school *unless* it consists of studying monuments of the soul's magnificence. But such activity hardly sounds like a singing school, and it seems unlikely that such soul singing is learned in an academic way. In the final analysis, Lipking suggests that the poem, through a deconstructive lens anyway, is confusing.

Similarly, Lipking asks if the artifice of eternity is "something permanent (an eternal artifice) or something evanescent (an illusion without any substance)" (432). He confesses he can't decide. He also points even to the uncertain syntax of the opening "That" (which, Lipking points out, "Yeats himself said was the worst syntax he ever wrote"). In sum, Lipking finds that "the elementary polarities that seem to provide its [the poem's] frame—the dialectic of 'that country' and Byzantium, of young and old, of time and timelessness, of body and soul, above all of nature and art—do not hold up under a careful reading" (432). Thus, "Whatever is begotten, born, and dies" only appears to parallel "what is past, or passing, or to come." The word "lives" would parallel "born" better than "passing," and "begotten" does not clearly relate to "past." Even the word "dies" is not entirely satisfactory because the birds' "song" is one that lives on from generation to generation.

These points may seem rather minor but, as Lipking amusingly puts it, there is one internal contradiction "so important and obvious that it is noticed by a great many students, and even some critics":

> When the speaker claims that "Once out of nature I shall never take / My bodily form from any natural thing," he seems to ignore the blatant fact that every bodily form must be taken from nature, whether the form of a bird or simply the golden form embodied by an artist. (432–33)

In a famous letter, Sturge Moore did write to Yeats that "a goldsmith's bird is as much nature as a man's body, especially if it only sings like Homer and Shakespeare of what is past or passing or to come to Lords and Ladies" (qtd. Lipking, p. 433). In fact, art seems already to be present in the world of nature that is described so artfully in the first verse. "That" country and Byzantium, Lipking says, "are equally unreal; they acquire significance only by being contrasted with each other" (433). "That" country never appears in the poem; it is always absent. Nor does the poet arrive at Byzantium, as Lipking reminds us: He is only "sailing to" it. And the problem, deconstruction tells us, is that we "swim in a sea of language" (435), where enduring "presence" is impossible: We never arrive where we're going, linguistically. Instead, we find only oppositions and differences that defer meaning.

In making this case, Lipking is depending on, I would argue, the following assumptions:

1. Meaning is made by binary oppositions, *but* one item is unavoidably favored (or "privileged") over the other.
2. This hierarchy, favoring one item over another, is arbitrary and can be exposed and reversed.
3. Further, the text's oppositions and hierarchy can be called into question because texts contain within themselves unavoidable contradictions, gaps, spaces, and absences that defeat closure and determinate meaning. All reading is misreading.

These assumptions, I believe, lead Lipking to something like the following strategies:

1. Identify the pattern of oppositions in the text.
2. Determine which member appears to be favored and look for evidence that contradicts that favoring.
3. Expose the text's indeterminacy.

Lipking, to be sure, is demonstrating deconstruction only to attack it. He is not alone in thinking that deconstruction is disturbing and even dangerous. But many other people find it invigorating and useful. The most damning charge against deconstruction is that it allows a text to mean anything at all—or, as Lipking sees it, ultimately nothing. But deconstruction's supporters, both in Europe and America (who have somewhat different conceptions of the matter), believe that texts *always already* were unavoidably open to interpretation. Deconstruction, in this case, really changes nothing except our awareness of the complexity and "otherness" and openness of our discourse. We might think prior to deconstruction that opposing viewpoints can't both be true: If a movie critic, for instance, says that the Coen brothers' *No Country for Old Men* (based on Cormac McCarthy's novel, which alludes, of course, to Yeats' poem) is shallow and nihilistic, and another critic says that the movie is profoundly deep and inspiringly masterful, then we might reasonably assume that one is right, and the other isn't—or at least, one is more right than the other. A deconstructive stance, however, keeps leading us to "both/and" assertions, rather than "either/or" choices, as we can see how contradictions can both be true—and also not true.

The whole idea, of course, of reducing deconstruction to a formula, to a set of steps, is so wrong and inconsistent within the theory of deconstruction itself that it seems mischievously deconstructive to do so. But you need, as a deconstructive critic might put it, to (mis)understand deconstruction first in order to (mis)understand it.

Here's another example to help you get more comfortable using this approach (or abusing it), as we leave Yeats' golden bird for one of another metal.

THE WRITING PROCESS: A SAMPLE ESSAY

Here's a poem by Amy Clampitt, published on April 12, 1993, in the *The New Yorker*.

Discovery
Amy Clampitt

The week the latest rocket went	1
up, a pod (if that's the word)	
of manatees, come upriver	
to Blue Spring, where it's	
always warm, could be seen	5
lolling, jacketed, elephantine,	
on the weedy borderline	
between drowsing and waking,	
breathing and drowning.	
As they came up for air,	10
one by one, they seemed numb,	
torpid, quite incurious. No	
imagining these sirenians	
dangerously singing. Or	
gazing up yearningly: so much	15
for the Little Mermaid. True,	
the long-lashed little ones	
could have been trademarked	
"Cute" by the likes of Walt Disney.	
His world's over that way,	20
suitably for a peninsula where	
the cozy mythologies we've	
swindled ourselves with, on	
taking things easy, might even	
come true: sun-kissed nakedness	25
on the beach, year-round, guilt-free	
hibiscus and oranges, fountains	
welling up through the limestone,	
the rumor of Ponce de León, having	
found the one he was looking for,	30

living at ease in, some say
Boca Raton, others Cádiz. A last
bedtime placebo? Still, we keep
looking up. That clear morning,
just warm enough for a liftoff,   35
the fabulous itself could be seen
unwieldily, jacket by jacket,
in the act of shedding, as
a snake does its husk, or

a celebrant his vestments: 40
the fiery, the arrowy tip of it,
of the actual going invisible,
trailing its vaporous, ribboning
frond as from a kelp bed,
the umbilical roar of it   45
stumbling behind, while up in
the belly of it, out of their
element, jacketed, lolling
and treading, the discoverers
soar, clumsy in space suits.   50

What are we anyhow, we warmth-
hungry, breast-seeking animals?
At Blue Spring, a day or so later,
one of the manatees, edging
toward discovery, nudged a canoe,   55
and from across the wet, warm,
dimly imaginable tightrope,
let itself be touched.

(1993)

Preparing to Write

What does this poem describe? What does it most clearly and obviously
say? Do any oppositions or tensions seem to be involved?

It might be helpful to sketch out an initial response to the poem, to
show you as fully as possible how a deconstructive essay might be developed. Keep in mind that no reading of any literary work is likely to spring
fully formed from your brain. You should expect to tinker, ask questions,
pose answers, play around with the work and generate some ideas and
some material before a reading will emerge. So, to illustrate this process,
I'm going to divide the poem into pieces and try to say what went through
my mind as I tried to make sense of it. I'd encourage you to write your own
notes before you look through mine.

Discovery

> The week the latest rocket went
> up,   (lines 1–2)

Is the speaker referring to a fictional rocket or a real one? Perhaps the speaker is referring to NASA's space shuttles (they weren't rockets, of course, but they were launched by rockets). One of the shuttles was called "*Discovery*"; does the title refer to it?

> a pod (if that's the word)
> of manatees, come upriver
> to Blue Spring, where it's
> always warm, could be seen
> lolling, jacketed, elephantine,
> on the weedy borderline
> between drowsing and waking,
> breathing and drowning.   (lines 2–9)

Well, perhaps the poem isn't about the space shuttle or "the latest rocket." Maybe that's just the time frame. I saw manatees when I lived in Florida, and "elephantine" is right—they do seem like armless and legless elephants floating in the water. And they don't seem to swim: "lolling" is a good word for what they do. The idea that they are "between drowsing and waking" also seems just right. But how are they between "breathing and drowning"? And how are they "jacketed"? What does that mean?

> As they came up for air,
> one by one, they seemed numb,
> torpid, quite incurious.   (lines 10–12)

These lines remind me that manatees are mammals, and so they don't breathe under water. They have to come "up for air"—which explains, I guess, the idea that they're between "breathing and drowning": If they don't come up, they'll drown; so they live most of their time in a state between breathing and drowning. I still don't know why they're said to be "jacketed." Perhaps Clampitt is inviting us to see their skin, which looks sort of loose and baggy, as a kind of jacket.

> No
> imagining these sirenians
> dangerously singing. Or
> gazing up yearningly: so much
> for the Little Mermaid. True,
> the long-lashed little ones
> could have been trademarked
> "Cute" by the likes of Walt Disney.   (lines 12–19)

A number of things at this point are puzzling: for instance, why are the manatees called "sirenians"? What is a sirenian, in other words, and why might one imagine them "dangerously singing"? And what's the connection to the Little Mermaid?

Whenever something is puzzling, I usually search for help, which usually means doing some research. In this case, a quick look in *The Columbia Encyclopedia* is revealing: The entry for "manatee" refers us to "sirenian," which is the name of a biological order, "Sirenia." (The only other living sirenian, or sea cow, is called a dugong.) Right above "sirenian," we find "Siren," the name for sea nymphs in Greek mythology who sang so beautifully that sailors would crash into the rocks around their island. So, the manatees, although they're sirenians, aren't like the Sirens. So that's one puzzle solved.

The entry also reports the speculation that manatees, "which nurse on the water's surface, are the source of the mermaid legends." Clampitt's speaker finds the manatees so "numb, / torpid, quite incurious" that it's impossible to imagine them as Sirens or mermaids. Contrasting them to the Little Mermaid is of course particularly comical given the huge bulk of these floating blobs. They are, according to the entry, "sluggish, largely nocturnal bottom feeders," weighing perhaps five hundred pounds and eating as much as a hundred pounds of vegetation a day. Even so, we must note that the "long-lashed little ones" are "Cute" enough for Disney. So another puzzle is solved.

The entry also may help clear up another question: Manatees, we read, have gray skin that is "completely hairless" (except for bristles around the mouth). The skin has folds and wrinkles in it: So, maybe that is why it appears to be a jacket to the speaker.

> His world's over that way,
>
> suitably for a peninsula where
> the cozy mythologies we've
> swindled ourselves with, on
> taking things easy, might even
> come true: sun-kissed nakedness
> on the beach, year-round, guilt-free
> hibiscus and oranges, fountains
> welling up through the limestone,
> the rumor of Ponce de León, having
> found the one he was looking for,
>
> living at ease in, some say
> Boca Raton, others Cádiz. A last
> bedtime placebo?   (lines 20–33)

This section makes clear that the speaker is indeed in Florida at the Kennedy Space Center, where the shuttle launched, near Orlando and Disney World "over that way." We dream, the speaker says, of "taking things easy" in Florida, living in paradise forever like a successful Ponce de León. Such dreaming doesn't do anything, but it may make us feel better anyway, like a "placebo."

> Still, we keep
> looking up.   (lines 33–34)

What does it mean to say "Still, we keep / looking up"? Perhaps it means that our dreams of contentment ("sun-kissed nakedness / on the beach") aren't entirely satisfying: we still keep looking up, waiting for some discovery—or, in this case, for *Discovery*. We all want to see something.

> That clear morning,
> just warm enough for a liftoff,
> the fabulous itself could be seen
> unwieldily, jacket by jacket,
> in the act of shedding, as
>
> a snake does its husk, or
> a celebrant his vestments:
> the fiery, the arrowy tip of it,
> of the actual going invisible,   (lines 34–42)

These lines strike me as a wonderful way of describing a launch: The shuttle disappearing as it rises is "the actual going invisible." The shuttle's voyage becomes "the fabulous itself" in the act of "shedding"—being reborn or transformed like the snake or the celebrant. If you've seen a launch, even on television, you know that the rocket does seem to move "unwieldily," rotating slowly as it goes up, lumbering so it seems, at least at first, toward the heavens.

> trailing its vaporous, ribboning
> frond as from a kelp bed,
> the umbilical roar of it
> stumbling behind, while up in
> the belly of it, out of their
> element, jacketed, lolling
> and treading, the discoverers
> soar, clumsy in space suits.   (lines 43–50)

The comparison of the booster rocket's vapor trail to a "ribboning / frond as from a kelp bed" is very strange, isn't it? What's the point of such an odd description? It takes us, obviously, to the manatees, who eat such fronds in kelp beds. It begins to link, it seems to me, the astronauts to the manatees. The connection becomes stronger as Clampitt uses "jacketed" and "lolling" to describe the human "discoverers," the same words used to describe the manatees.

In what ways are the astronauts like the manatees? Clampitt suggests that the astronauts are also in a sense "out of their element." They are "treading," not in water, but as if they were. And they appear, like the manatees, to be "clumsy in space suits."

> What are we anyhow, we warmth-
> hungry, breast-seeking animals?
> At Blue Spring, a day or so later,
> one of the manatees, edging
> toward discovery, nudged a canoe,
> and from across the wet, warm,
> dimly imaginable tightrope,
> let itself be touched.   (lines 51–58)

If we had any doubts about what the oppositions are in this poem, and how they're brought together, this final section makes these matters very clear, doesn't it? When Clampitt asks "What are we anyhow, we warmth- / hungry, breast-seeking animals?", who is the "we" here? At the beginning of the poem, it is the manatees who "come upriver" to where "it's / always warm," and it seems clear that the "warmth-hungry" we includes both human "discoverers" as well as manatees (who breast-feed their young on the surface, we recall).

With the final scene of the manatee "edging / toward discovery," Clampitt most strikingly unites manatees and humans. The manatees are also "looking up," reaching out. They may seem clumsy, numb, quite incurious, but the astronauts, as they float around "out of their / element," also seem clumsy, lolling. Clampitt uses "jacketed" to describe both human and manatee (although I still find this word a bit confusing). In letting itself be touched, the manatee is aligned with humanity, becoming really a courageous discoverer, like the crew of *Discovery*.

But what is the "wet, warm, / dimly imaginable tightrope" that the manatee reaches "across"? It must be, I suppose, the water, or the surface of the water, and Clampitt's point would seem to be that the manatee, while appearing to be clumsy, is actually pulling off quite a feat. Inhabiting the water, living between breathing and drowning, is like walking a tightrope. Likewise, the astronauts on *Discovery* may seem clumsy "jacketed" in their suits, but they are in reality "the fabulous itself."

At this point I think I understand the poem fairly well. That is, I understand how the poem's two topics are related. The manatees lolling about in the warm water, and human beings shooting themselves into space: What could be more different? And yet Amy Clampitt brings the two together.

Or does she?

Shaping

Is it possible to turn this reading of the poem around, to tease out another, conflicting meaning? To begin to deconstruct this poem, let's think a bit about the oppositions that seem to be brought together. The worlds of manatees and humans appear to be far apart—as different as "that country" and Byzantium in Yeats' "Sailing to Byzantium." The manatees seem dramatically unlike discoverers: "numb, / torpid, quite incurious." Manatees are even unlike the partly human, the mermaids and sirens. In Yeats' poem, as we just saw, Cleanth Brooks' New Critical reading finds that the golden bird unifies the poem, combining the worlds of nature and art. Likewise, in Clampitt's poem a number of images seem to unify the opposing worlds, as the human discoverers come to seem like the manatees, "lolling," "treading," "jacketed." The closing image of one manatee "edging / toward discovery" most directly shows us how the manatee shares the human urge to "keep / looking up" and to reach out and explore. We are both, manatee and human, "warmth- / hungry, breast-seeking animals." Whereas Yeats' poem unifies art and nature, Clampitt's poem brings together the realms of animal and human. So it seems.

But if the poem appears most obviously to say that manatees and astronauts are similar or linked (out of their elements, awkward, seeking discovery), is it possible to suggest that the poem also undermines this unifying theme? What is being overlooked or suppressed in Clampitt's unifying move? Here are some notes toward a deconstructive reading.

<> Apparent unity: the manatee is said to be "edging toward discovery," like the *Discovery* astronauts, it seems.

>< Reversal: But who really is the discoverer in this situation? The manatee passively "let itself be touched" after it "nudged" the canoe. Although we may think at first that the manatee is "edging toward [its own] discovery," the more reasonable inference is that the manatee is "edging toward discovery" by the canoe-goers. Does the manatee discover anything? Not that we know. There's really no evidence that the manatee has moved beyond being "numb, / torpid, quite incurious."

<> Apparent unity: "we" are "warmth- / hungry, breast-seeking animals."

>< Reversal: This assertion connects the manatees to us only in a superficial way. More carefully considered, this description actually distances the manatees from "the discoverers" in their "space suits": The astronauts surely aren't seeking warmth or breasts in space. There is something else that drives humanity to explore, to "keep looking up," and that intellectual curiosity is not shared, so far as we can tell, by the manatees.

<> Apparent unity: "jacketed" is used to describe both manatees and astronauts.

>< Reversal: The meaning of "jacketed" as it applies to manatees is never made clear. I can think of two senses in which the astronauts are "jacketed." They're actually wearing jackets; and they're enclosed, in the sense of this definition of "jacket": "a metal casing, as the steel covering around the barrel of a gun or the core of a bullet." I don't see how the manatees are "jacketed" in either of these senses. Applied to both

manatees and astronauts, the term really emphasizes the gap between the two when we examine it closely.

<> Apparent unity: The poem says, "the fabulous itself could be seen / unwieldily, jacket by jacket, / in the act of shedding, as / a snake does its husk, or / a celebrant his vestments": The reference to a snake and a celebrant again seems to link animal and human activities, subtly implying that the "jacketed" manatees and humans are discovering "the fabulous itself."

>< Reversal: But aren't these two images actually pulling in different directions? A snake shedding its skin is not performing a voluntary, self-conscious act. The celebrant, however, makes the fabulous visible by shedding "his vestments"—a voluntary, self-conscious act. In removing his religious, ceremonial garments, the celebrant reveals somehow, Clampitt says, the mystery and the wonder he has participated in: the fabulous itself. At least, that's how I read these difficult lines.

I would have thought that the fabulous would be glimpsed in the celebrant putting on his vestments and that the act of removing them would reveal the mundane and ordinary world. But Clampitt has imagined the lift-off as an act of shedding, and so images of "shedding" become images of discovery. The gap in meaning results from the difference between a reptile engaging in an automatic, biological function and a conscious human disengaging from a spiritual event.

<> Apparent unity: The notion that the astronauts are "out of their / element" may seem to reflect the manatees' situation, living in water but breathing air.

>< Reversal: But the implicit comparison doesn't hold up because the astronauts really are out of their element, totally unsuited to live in space without the creation of an artificial environment. Manatees, on the other hand, live on the border between air and water: That is their element. Birds fly in the air and build nests in trees and other places. We wouldn't say they're "out of their element" in either situation. Again, we see how the poem's effort to unify animal and human comes apart. Manatees are different: They can't live out of their element; we can, at least for certain periods.

At this point, I'm looking at the phrase "cozy mythologies we've / swindled ourselves with," mythologies that "might even / come true" in Florida, Clampitt says, in the land of Walt Disney. And I'm thinking that the poem itself offers a "cozy mythology" about manatees and humans, suppressing the essential differences. From living in Florida for three years, I remember that a great deal of attention is paid to the manatees—they're endangered, and they're uniquely huge and strange. The state offers a manatee tag for automobiles, and the funds raised go to a "Save the Manatee" campaign. The main threat to manatees in Florida today seems to be from motorboats: As the manatees float up to the surface, boaters fail to see them and run over them, inflicting severe injuries with the propellers. A manatee hospital has even been set up to treat injured manatees, and boat speeds have been restricted in some areas. We are trying to live *with* the manatees; many tourists every year get in the water and swim with them. One could argue that we are forgetting our differences, assuming that manatees are in some crucial way like ourselves, when really perhaps we should leave them alone, banning boats and recreation in the waters they inhabit. At any rate, this reading of Clampitt's poem opens up uncertainties in our understanding of them.

Drafting

At this point I think I have enough ideas to draft an essay. Where should I start? First, I need to set up the task, letting the reader know what I'm trying to do: Namely, I'm trying to show how the poem appears to link human and manatee, but really doesn't. I want to start fast, dive right in; and since the ending most dramatically unifies manatee and human, with the two actually touching with the final word, I'm going to try starting with the ending of the poem. The word "discovery" occurs in the final lines, and since it's the title, I need to pay attention to it. The final image occurs in response to a question, it seems, and so it makes sense to move next to the question itself. Then I'll present the other evidence I've generated: "jacketed," "out of their element," and the snake/celebrant problem. That's my tentative plan as I start writing, very much aware that I may change my mind.

Here's the essay that resulted after a draft and a little polishing.

Humanity and Manatee:
Amy Clampitt's "Discovery"

This paragraph introduces the issue: why is the poem partly about manatees and partly about humans? The conclusion is crucial, asserting indirectly their unity.

The conclusion of Amy Clampitt's "Discovery" follows a profoundly challenging question: "What are we anyhow, we warmth- / hungry, breast-seeking animals?" Right before this question, the poem refers to astronauts, "discoverers" who are "clumsy in space suits," so it seems reasonable to assume that "we" refers to human beings. But rather than trying to say explicitly what "we" are anyhow, answering a question about human nature that has occupied philosophies and religions for centuries, the poem offers instead a little story about a manatee:

At Blue Spring, a day or so later,
one of the manatees, edging
toward discovery, nudged a canoe,
and from across the wet, warm,
dimly imaginable tightrope,
let itself be touched.

While this story might seem at first an evasion of the question, the poem repeatedly links manatees and humans, giving them the same qualities, using the same words to describe them both. Thus, this story implicitly answers the question about human nature by pointing once more to manatees: We are more like them, and they are more like us, than we might have thought. Like the manatee, we are "edging toward discovery," reaching out to other beings.

> This paragraph directly presents the thesis: the linking is problematic.

But a careful examination of the implied links between manatees and humans reveals that the similarities are actually questionable. Ultimately, as this paper will show, it is unclear whether the poem's comparison helps us understand the nature of either humans or manatees—or just compounds the mystery.

> The strongest evidence for unity, "edging toward discovery," is introduced here.

Let us begin with the strongest unifying agent of manatee and human, the phrase "edging toward discovery." The word "discovery" links the manatee's action to the poem's title and to the space shuttle Discovery. The poem does not say that Discovery in particular is being launched at the time the manatees "come upriver," but "the latest rocket" clearly is one of the shuttles. And the description of the astronauts, "jacketed, lolling and treading," "clumsy in space suits," seems designed to remind us of the manatees, who are described in the first section in the same terms—"lolling, jacketed" and "numb, / torpid" (which certainly suggests clumsiness).

> The manatee is not a discoverer, but an object of discovery.

But in what sense is the manatee "edging toward discovery"? Although the same words are used to describe astronaut and manatee, the similarity of their roles in the act of discovery seems uncertain. Whereas the astronauts self-consciously and actively venture out into space, the manatee passively "let itself be touched." Such a surrender may seem essentially different from the behavior of the human "discoverers," either in the shuttle or the canoe. One could argue, of course, that the manatee is discovering how it feels to be touched by human beings. But the astronauts do not rocket into space to deliver themselves to the touch or observation of other beings, and the people in the canoe are not said to be allowing the manatee to see what their hands feel like. There's no solid evidence that the manatee discovers anything or moves beyond being "numb, / torpid, quite incurious." So, "edging / toward discovery" only seems initially to unite manatee and human; upon reflection, it may exhibit their differences or at the least call their likeness into doubt.

The question itself—"What are we anyhow, we warmth- /hungry, breast-seeking animals?"—may seem

The question itself applies better to the manatee.

to refer to both manatees and humans. The poem begins by noting how the manatees have "come upriver" to Blue Spring seeking warmth; and as mammals, the manatees do breast-feed their young. But this deep question also puts a gap between manatee and human, because the astronauts surely aren't seeking warmth or breasts in space. There is something else that drives humanity to explore, to "keep / looking up," and that intellectual, self-conscious curiosity is not shared, so far as we can tell, by the manatees. Although "we" may be "warmth- / hungry" and "breast-seeking," the suggestion that these are essential qualities limits and narrows what it means to be human.

"Jacket" applies better to humans.

Likewise, "jacket" or "jacketed" appears four times in the poem and would seem to be an important term connecting manatee and human, unifying the poem's two subjects. The term is applied to both manatees, who are "lolling, jacketed, elephantine," and to the astronauts, who are "jacketed, lolling / and treading." But again the link is problematic. The astronauts are "jacketed," it would seem, because they have on jackets, and because they are encased in metal—"jacketed" in the sense of "a metal casing, as the steel covering around the barrel of a gun or the core of a bullet," as Webster's puts it. Are the manatees "jacketed" in either of these senses? The other two occurrences refer to "the fabulous itself" being revealed "jacket by jacket," which seems simply to mean "layer by layer," or "casing by casing." Thus, although the repeated use of the term may seem to bridge the poem and its subjects, it really does not in any clear or direct way. The connection is superficial, and it gives way to a gap: Manatees do not really come in jackets in any literal sense; humans do.

More evidence: other gaps.

In a number of other ways the poem's two subjects break apart upon analysis. The notion, for instance, that the astronauts are "out of their / element" may seem to reflect also the manatees' situation, living in water but breathing air. But the astronauts really are out of their element, totally unsuited to live in space without the creation of an artificial environment. Manatees, on the other hand, need to live on the border between air and water: That is their element. Humans do not need to live on the border of space and earth. Or, again, the reference to a snake and a celebrant again seems to link animal and human activities. But aren't these two images actually pulling in different directions? A snake shedding its skin is not performing a voluntary, self-conscious act. The celebrant, however,

makes the fabulous visible by shedding "his vestments"—
a voluntary, self-conscious act. In removing his religious,
ceremonial garments, the celebrant reveals somehow,
Clampitt says, the mystery and the wonder he has participated in: the fabulous itself. For the snake, the fabulous
itself would seem to be the instinctual act of shedding. The
gap in meaning results from the difference between a reptile engaging in an automatic, biological function and a conscious human disengaging from a spiritual event.

> Conclusion: the unity may be a myth, or is at least uncertain.

The poem refers to the "cozy mythologies" of paradise and eternal youth that "might even / come true" in
Florida. Another myth may be the illusion that manatees
and humans are alike in some essential way. The poem
asserts that unity, but at the same time it points out the
difference, the otherness, of the manatees. We may drive
our boats and canoes where they live; we may touch them;
but it may be misleading to think we understand them—or
even ourselves. The "discovery" may well be the question,
what are we anyhow?

PRACTICING STRUCTURALIST AND DECONSTRUCTIVE CRITICISM

I offer here four texts for you to practice on, along with some questions I
hope you find helpful.

Questions

1. What is the most obvious statement the advertisement shown on the
   following page attempts to make? What sort of attitudes, feelings, and
   assumptions does the advertisement attribute to part of its audience?
   What effect does it strive to create?

2. How might the advertisement tend also to create the attitudes, feelings, assumptions it strives to reduce or remove? That is, does the
   advertisement do contradictory things? How does this conflict influence its effectiveness?

3. Look closely at the details of the advertisement and how they reveal
   (as deconstruction insists all texts must) what is being excluded or
   suppressed. For example, what does the imperative to "Cut through
   the anxiety, the unknown, the hassle" acknowledge? If the slogan
   next to the phone number were to be spoken, what would it say?
   How does the pun in this slogan divide and complicate it?

London
William Blake

I wander thro' each charter'd street
Near where the charter'd Thames does flow,
And mark in every face I meet
Marks of weakness, marks of woe.

In every cry of every Man,   5
In every Infant's cry of fear,
In every voice, in every ban,
The mind-forg'd manacles I hear.

How the Chimney-sweeper's cry
Every blackening Church appalls,   10
And the hapless Soldier's sigh
Runs in blood down Palace walls.

But most thro' midnight streets I hear
How the youthful Harlot's curse
Blasts the new-born Infant's tear   15
And blights with plagues the Marriage hearse.
                                        (1794)

Questions

1. What is a charter? What would it mean for a street to be "charter'd"?
   How about a river (the Thames in this poem)?
2. "Charter'd" is repeated in the first two lines. What other words are
   repeated in the poem? What might be the purpose of such repetition?
3. In *The Pursuit of Signs,* Jonathan Culler reviews some of the many
   interpretations this famous poem has generated, and he notes that one
   of two different structures has been perceived to organize the entire
   poem. The first way of thinking about the poem's structure sees it, as
   Culler says, as a "synecdochic series, where a list of particulars are
   interpreted as instances of a general class to which they all belong"
   (69). What, in your opinion, might be the "general class" to which the
   particulars in the poem belong? That is, the chimney sweeper's cry,
   the hapless soldier's sigh, and the harlot's curse are instances of what?
   What do they have in common?
4. The second way of thinking about the poem's structure sees it (again
   following Culler) as an "aletheic reversal: first a false or inadequate
   vision, then its true or adequate counterpart" (69). Where, in your
   opinion, might the shift from a false vision to a true one occur?
   How would you describe these two visions? (Hint: Where does the
   poem shift from universal statements—"every," "every"—to more
   specific ones?)
5. How does the idea of "mind-forg'd manacles" contribute to the structure of the poem? (Your answer to this question may overlap with
   previous answers.) Is it a particular or a general, a member of a class,
   or a class?

6. How many examples are offered in the last two verses? What are they examples of? How are they parallel? (You might think in terms of victim—action—institution.) Is there any problem with their parallelism?

   No critic, Culler says, takes the statement that the chimney sweep's cry appalls the church at face value (*Signs* 70). How does the structure of the other two examples affect the way we think about the chimney sweep? Again, think in parallel terms. Why would critics find it necessary to explain the example of the chimney sweep?

7. What sense can you make of the last verse? What are the difficulties in understanding it?

8. The speaker of the poem marks (or hears) the sweep cry, the soldier sigh, and the harlot curse. This structural parallelism encourages us to assume a parallelism of meaning. What are the problems with determining such a unity? That is, can you argue that, in fact, the poem does not make sense—at least not any one sense, but rather that it goes in conflicting directions?

9. Are the "mind-forg'd manacles" the product of the Church, the Palace, and Marriage? (Most readers seem to assume so.) Can you turn this inference around and argue otherwise? Could the sweep, the soldier, and the harlot create their own manacles?

Ethics
Linda Pastan

In ethics class so many years ago
our teacher asked this question every fall:
if there were a fire in a museum
which would you save, a Rembrandt painting
or an old woman who hadn't many   5
years left anyhow? Restless on hard chairs
caring little for pictures or old age
we'd opt one year for life, the next for art
and always half-heartedly. Sometimes
the woman borrowed my grandmother's face   10
leaving her usual kitchen to wander
some drafty, half imagined museum.
One year, feeling clever, I replied
why not let the woman decide herself?
Linda, the teacher would report, eschews   15
the burdens of responsibility.
This fall in a real museum I stand
before a real Rembrandt, old woman,

or nearly so, myself. The colors
within this frame are darker than autumn,   20
darker even than winter—the browns of earth,
though earth's most radiant elements burn
through the canvas. I know now that woman
and painting and season are almost one
and all beyond saving by children.   25
                    (1981)

Questions

1. Consider how these oppositions work within the poem: the adult
   speaker versus the child in ethics class; the Rembrandt versus the
   old woman; accepting responsibility versus avoiding it; the students
   versus the teacher; the Rembrandt's colors versus autumn's colors;
   half-imagining versus vividly imagining; childhood versus old age.
   How are these oppositions related? (Try making a chart with one kind
   of item on one side, the other kind on the other.)
2. In what sense does the poem itself deconstruct these oppositions? How
   does the ending, in other words, affect the teacher's ethics question?
3. Does the poem itself undermine or support the assertion that woman,
   painting, and season are "beyond saving by children"? What does
   Pastan mean when she says that the woman, painting, and season "are
   almost one"? Do you agree? Does that make sense?
4. What do you think of Linda's "clever" response in line 14? How is
   it different from the response she would later make as a "nearly" old
   woman, viewing a Rembrandt herself? (Is it really different?)
5. Perhaps this poem, despite its title, isn't really about "Ethics." What
   else could it be about? What theme seems to be raised, for instance,
   by the ending? Is the speaker's age significant? What difference does it
   make that the three items are "almost one" but not exactly one? What
   difference does it make that the items are beyond saving by children?
   Was the teacher literally asking the children to save one or the other?

Death Be Not Proud
John Donne (1572–1631)

Death be not proud, though some have callèd thee
Mighty and dreadful, for thou art not so;
For those whom thou think'st thou dost overthrow
Die not, poor death, nor yet canst thou kill me.
From rest and sleep, which but thy pictures be,   5

Much pleasure, then from thee much more must flow,
And soonest our best men with thee do go,
Rest of their bones, and soul's delivery.
Thou art slave to fate, chance, kings, and desperate men,
And dost with poison, war, and sickness dwell,   10
And poppy, or charms can make us sleep as well,
And better than thy stroke; why swell'st thou then?
One short sleep past, we wake eternally,
And death shall be no more; death, thou shalt die.

                                        (about 1610)

Questions

1. What kind of poem is this? (Hint: Look at its form.) What sort of poem do we associate with this form? How does choosing this form complicate what Donne is attempting to do here?

2. What is the key reversal driving this poem? What sense does it make? That is, what assumptions would one have to hold in order to make the claim that Donne makes here? Look in particular at the last line: In what sense might the poem be turned against itself starting from this last line?

3. The poem is addressed to Death, at least ostensibly, directing Death not to assume a certain stance of pride. But is Death really the audience here? How does this question of the real audience undermine or at least complicate the poem?

4. Take one line and see if you can reverse it or tease out its warring significations: For instance, "Thou art slave to fate, chance, kings, and desperate men." This statement is applied by the speaker to death. Why is that a problematic assertion? (Who is—or who else is—a slave to these things? Is Death alive? Can one be a slave and be dead—or be Death?) Explain how this line involves a reversal and arguably even a dispersal of meaning.

USEFUL TERMS FOR DECONSTRUCTION

Arbitrariness: Language, deconstruction assumes, is ultimately arbitrary. It could be different from what it is; indeed, languages change and evolve and become different as time goes on. Different languages divide up the universe differently, and each language is itself something constructed: If all English speakers decided that black dogs weren't actually dogs, and should be called "gringats" from now on, then black dogs and other kinds of dogs, according to our language, would be distinct things. Deconstruction wants to highlight this arbitrariness in order to remind us that texts are open to interpretation, and meaning is not fixed.

Binary: Language is based, structuralists and poststructuralists say, on oppositions: "Bad" only has meaning because we can contrast it to "good"; "man" takes on its meaning in opposition to "woman," or "animal," or "boy," or some other opposing term. This opposing nature of language means that it is binary—that is, having two parts, two alternatives. Deconstruction recognizes that within this binary nature, one alternative is always suppressed, falsely simplifying reality.

Différance: This difficult term was made up by Derrida to indicate two meanings at once: difference and deferral. "Difference" is an important idea in deconstruction, which seeks to show how a text contains within itself a trace of its own contradiction. The idea that something differs from itself may seem at first insane; but we've all heard someone say, "I'm not myself today." "Difference," as deconstruction sees things, is unavoidable: We are always not entirely and strictly ourselves. The related idea of "deferral" is important too; whereas "difference" seems to be a spatial idea, dividing an apparent unity, "deferral" refers to time—specifically to the idea of putting something off. "I'm going to defer a decision on that matter today," one might say. From a deconstructive point of view, when we move through time we never quite get where we're going: The point in time we aim for is always deferred. Likewise, if we want to see what something means by traveling back to its origin, we can never pinpoint this origin: there is always some prior beginning.

Think of the story of Adam and Eve, for instance: It is a story about "in the beginning," explaining the meaning of evil and suffering, which are (in the traditional reading) the effects of the first man and woman's sin, the fall from grace and innocence. But this story does not reveal the origin of the most important agent in the story: God. Why did God create Eden in the way that he did? What is the origin of the serpent who tempts Adam and Eve? Did God create him? If so, why? If not, where did the serpent come from? Thus, the deeper meaning of the story, the origin of the origin, can always be deferred if the analysis is pressed.

Dispersal: Deconstruction does not suggest simply that meanings can be reversed, end of story. Rather, the reversal of oppositions is a gesture designed to suggest the arbitrariness of meanings. Ultimately, a text could be analyzed until its essential uncertainty resulted in its unraveling—the dispersal or scattering of its meaning.

Opposition: See "binary."

Privilege: In an opposition, one term is unavoidably favored over the other in some way, since a perfect balance in every sense seems unlikely if not impossible. Deconstruction emphasizes how one term is "privileged" over another by reversing or subverting the apparent meaning.

✔ Checklist for Deconstruction

1. Identify the pattern of oppositions in the text.

2. Determine which member appears to be favored and look for evidence that contradicts that favoring.

3. Expose the text's indeterminacy.

Note

1. From "Inventors," in *Sympathetic Magic* (San Francisco: Watermark Press, 1980).

Works Cited

Brooks, Cleanth. *The Well-Wrought Urn*. New York: Holt, 1947. Print.

Culler, Jonathan. *On Deconstruction: Theory and Criticism after Structuralism*. Ithaca, NY: Cornell UP, 1982. Print.

—. *The Pursuit of Signs: Semiotics, Literature, Deconstruction*. Ithaca, NY: Cornell UP, 1981. Print.

De Man, Paul. "Semiology and Rhetoric." *Allegories of Reading*. New Haven, CT: Yale UP, 1979. 3–20. Print.

Derrida, Jacques. *Of Grammatology*. Baltimore: Johns Hopkins UP, 1967. Print.

Jay, Gregory. *America the Scrivener*. Ithaca, NY: Cornell UP, 1991. Print.

Johnson, Barbara. *The Critical Difference*. Baltimore: Johns Hopkins UP, 1980. Print.

Lipking, Lawrence. "The Practice of Theory." *Literary Theories in Praxis*. Ed. Shirley Staton. Philadelphia: U of Pennsylvania P, 1987. 426–440. Print.

Recommended Further Reading

Barthes, Roland. *Mythologies*. Trans. Annette Lavers. New York: Hill and Wang, 1972. Engaging and influential essays from a structuralist stance on food, toys, cruises, striptease, wrestling matches, and much else.

Culler, Jonathan. *Structuralist Poetics: Structuralism, Linguistics, and the Study of Literature*. London: Routledge, 1975. A brilliantly lucid introduction to criticism that analyzes the structure of literary texts, instead of pondering the meaning of the work.

—. *On Deconstruction: Theory and Criticism After Structuralism, 25th Anniversary Edition*. Ithaca, NY: Cornell UP, 2008. A careful and nuanced introduction that manages somehow to be easy to read.

Currie, Mark. *The Invention of Deconstruction*. New York: Palgrave Macmillan, 2013. Explains deconstruction in terms of its history: Why did it arise? What needs did it meet? Whom did it threaten? How has it changed?

Derrida, Jacques. "Structure, Sign, and Play in the Discourse of the Human Sciences." *The Structuralist Controversy*. Eds. Richard Macksey and Eugenio Donato. Baltimore: Johns Hopkins UP, 1972. 247–272. Enormously influential essay. Difficult, even exasperating, but also amusing at times. If you lack the stamina to read the entire essay, you should read at least some of it carefully in order to appreciate Derrida's punning, elliptical, tightly packed style.

Eagleton, Terry. "Post-structuralism." *Literary Theory: An Introduction*. 3rd ed. Minneapolis: U of Minnesota P, 2008. An excellent (but not an objective) introduction.

Lüdemann, Susanne. *Politics of Deconstruction: A New Introduction to Jacques Derrida*. Redwood City, CA: Stanford UP, 2014. This accessible guide is especially useful for its placement of Derrida within his European context.

Lynn, Steven. *Samuel Johnson after Deconstruction*. Carbondale: Southern Illinois UP, 1992. Explains deconstruction and compares it to other kinds of skepticism, arguing that Johnson anticipates poststructuralism in some important and surprising ways.

Powell, Jim (author), and Joe Lee (illustrator). *Deconstruction for Beginners*. Danbury, CT: For Beginners Press, 2008. An entertaining and useful graphic introduction.

Tompkins, Jane. "A Short Course in Post-Structuralism." *Conversations: Contemporary Critical Theory and the Teaching of Literature*. Eds. Charles Moran and Elizabeth Penfield. Urbana, IL: NCTE, 1990. 19–37. Aimed at teachers with little or no understanding of deconstruction; helpful for a general audience.

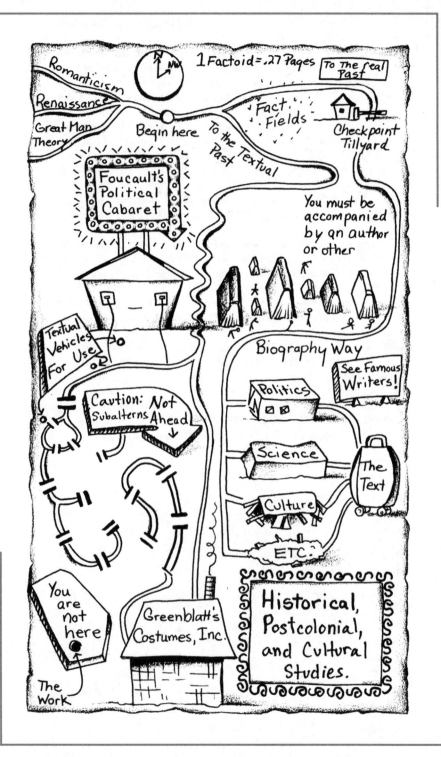

Connecting the Text

Historical and New Historical Criticism

We know somewhat, and we imagine the rest.

—Samuel Johnson[1]

What you'll learn in this chapter:

- To identify opportunities to use Historical and New Historical principles.
- To develop ideas about texts using Historical and New Historical principles.
- To write and revise essays, step by step, about literary texts, using Historical and New Historical criticism.
- To apply Historical and New Historical approaches in a variety of contexts.

THE PURPOSES OF HISTORICAL AND NEW HISTORICAL CRITICISM

In New Criticism, in reader-response criticism, and in deconstruction, our attention is primarily centered on the text itself: how it is unified, how the reader is reacting to it, how it falls apart. But there is more to life, even English professors would admit, than texts. Inquiring minds want to know about authors, their lives, how they worked, what was happening around them, who knew them and influenced them. Even the most rigorously formal New Critics or the most introspectively responding readers are likely to find biographical and historical information interesting. And if we think literature ought to have some real-world usefulness, then we ought to seek out these connections between life and text.

And yet, as we are reminded by Samuel Johnson, one of the world's great biographers, who was himself the subject of arguably the greatest biography ever written, no matter how much research we do, even if we travel and live with the person we are writing about, as was the case with James Boswell's *Life of Johnson*, we cannot fully recover the past. We must, as Johnson says in my epigraph, "imagine the rest." As we focus on the realm of biography and history in this chapter, we would do well to keep some perspective on the partiality and bias that we inevitably inhabit. This chapter focuses on the strategies we might use for imagining, on the purposes that might be served, and on the limitations of our efforts to move beyond the literary work and into politics and history. Specifically, we will consider here a variety of distinguishable but related approaches: biographical, historical, postcolonial, ethnic, Marxist, and cultural studies.

The traditional view of history and biography with regard to literature assumes that there are "facts" that we can know with some degree of certainty. As readers, we simply need to gather them and use them to enhance our understanding of literary works. In the last half-century or so, this traditional view of history has become increasingly problematic. In the wake of poststructuralism and deconstruction, which have altered our notions of language and knowledge, it has become increasingly apparent (if it wasn't already) that what we really have is not some set of stable facts, waiting on discovery, but rather a number of texts waiting on a process of interpretation. Rather than trying to determine what "really" happened, new historicists (as they are sometimes called) are interested in exploring how different versions of history are motivated and constructed. At any given moment in a culture, there may be a dominant discourse, a way of thinking and persuading that is assumed to be the norm; or there may be a swirl of competing discourses; or there may be a decaying discourse held by one segment of a culture, but under attack and falling apart, and a rising discourse, gaining adherents. There may well be, in reality, as many discourses as there are people—or even more, since some of us change our minds often, or haven't made up our minds on many things.

Whether the notion that history is somehow up for grabs—that there are competing versions of what has happened, and these stories might be put to different uses—is really a new idea is certainly arguable, but it is a crucial idea for postcolonial and cultural studies as well as new historicism. This chapter will first try to give you some sense of how to do traditional biographical and historical criticism, and then consider how other emerging and related orientations might further enhance your understanding and your critical repertoire.

Biographical and Historical Criticism

If we think of a literary work primarily as a personal achievement, the accomplishment of a great mind, then biographical criticism offers to help us understand both the work and its creator, as we relate one to the other. Take, for instance, the following poem.

When I Consider How My Light Is Spent[2]
John Milton

When I consider how my light is spent,
    Ere half my days, in this dark world and wide,
    And that one talent which is death to hide,
Lodged with me useless, though my soul more bent
To serve therewith my Maker, and present   5
    My true account, lest He returning chide;
    Doth God exact day-labor, light denied,
I fondly ask: But Patience, to prevent
That murmur, soon replies, God doth not need
    Either man's work or His own gifts. Who best   10
    Bear his mild yoke, they serve Him best: His state
Is kingly; thousands at his bidding speed,
And post o'er land and ocean without rest;
They also serve who only stand and wait.

(1655?)

Biographical criticism would insist on the importance of knowing something about the author—perhaps most importantly, in this case, that Milton had lost his eyesight to glaucoma sometime around 1648, before composing this poem sometime between 1652 and 1655. Without this fact, it could be argued, the reader might wonder what sense to make of the phrase "how my light is spent," since "going blind" would be only one of many possible meanings (how my day is spent, how my insight is used up, how my lover is tired out, and more). But knowing about Milton's life also alters our appreciation of the poem: The speaker of the poem is not merely a fiction, an assumed character, contemplating some hypothesis. Rather, the speaker in the poem has some connection to the author. Milton seems to be writing in his own voice, contemplating his own blindness.

Of course, as one guide to writing about literature puts it, you should "avoid equating the work's contents with the author's life" (Griffith 115). Still, although the writing and the life "are never the same," surely sometimes writers do try to express themselves truthfully. If we think that "When I Consider" is "fictional" in the same sense that *Star Wars* is fictional, then we arguably lose some of the poem's power. And just as Milton's life may illuminate the poem, the poem may also help us to understand his life. Milton, as *The Concise Oxford Companion to English Literature* puts it, has sometimes been portrayed as a "sociable" and "good-natured" person, but he also has also persistently been depicted as "a domestic tyrant who bullied his daughters," a "misogynist" who sternly dictated to his three successive wives (468). This poem may suggest, perhaps, that Milton tended to think of the entire universe in terms of servants and masters, and that he viewed himself as a servant to God. Although God employs thousands speeding "o'er land and ocean without rest," Milton considers His "yoke" to be "mild." Since "God doth not need / Either man's work or His own gifts," it is our honor to serve in whatever capacity we can, even if that means simply standing, waiting. The submissiveness in the poem thus arguably reflects the sort of subservience Milton apparently expected (and thought he had earned) from those who served him. Milton likely would have been dictating this poem to someone who was standing and waiting upon him. He may have treated those family members around him as if they were his servants, but he also saw himself in the same role, in service to another higher master.

Biographical criticism is the natural ally of historical criticism. We can hardly understand one person's life without some sense of the time and place in which he or she lived, and we can hardly understand human history without trying to think about the individual humans who made it. Historical criticism considers how military, social, cultural, economic, scientific, intellectual, literary, and (potentially) every other kind of history might help us to understand the author and work. In the case of Milton's poem, the most obvious historical context might well be the political situation of England: In 1655, about the time the poem is supposed to have been written, England was struggling to recover from a civil war that had ended with the beheading of King Charles I in 1649. After this regicide, of which he approved, Milton was deeply involved in politics, serving as Latin secretary to the newly formed Council of State and writing on numerous political and religious controversies. Against the backdrop of this political turmoil, the references in the poem to the "one talent" and the urgency of using it might suggest additional meanings. (He is alluding, of course, to Jesus' parable, in Matthew 25:14–30, of the disappointing servant who simply buried his talent, literally a very valuable coin, rather than putting it to work. The good servants used their "talents" for profit.)

So, given this context, Milton may well have felt called to straighten out his country by employing his gift for language; the government and the church must have seemed at times to be falling apart before his (failing) eyes.

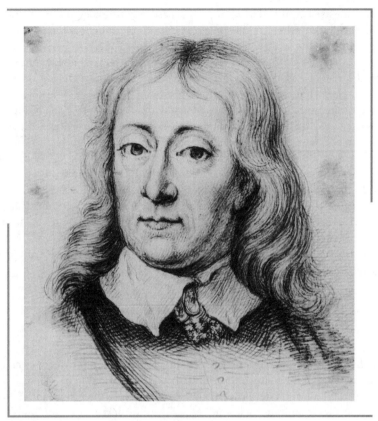

© Hulton–Deutsch Collection/CORBIS

With his talent, his gift for writing, perhaps Milton felt he should be saving the nation. But he puts this self-imposed burden in a new light in the poem when he reminds himself that God does not need his help—that others do God's bidding, and that his own job description may have changed dramatically with his impairment. He is telling himself that all he must do now is "stand and wait," ready to serve when he can. (As it turns out, Milton's accomplishments were prodigious while he "waited" to write his masterwork, *Paradise Lost*.)

The history of literature itself is also useful for understanding particular works. If Milton's readers recognize that "When I Consider" is a sonnet, in the Italian or Petrarchan form, for instance, they might usefully consider what sonnets Milton would have read, and how his sonnet relates to the history of sonnets and other kinds of works. Such literary background is almost always helpful, alerting us in this case, for instance, to the likelihood of a "turn" somewhere in the development of the sonnet—which is here in the eighth line.

In the study of Renaissance literature, in fact, students have for decades read E. M. W. Tillyard's *The Elizabethan World Picture* in order to understand what Shakespeare, Ben Jonson, Christopher Marlowe, and other Elizabethan writers would have known and assumed. Tillyard aimed, he said, to explain the Elizabethans' "most ordinary beliefs about the constitution of the world" (viii). For example, Tillyard says English citizens who lived during the reign of Elizabeth (1558–1603) believed in "a doctrine of plenitude." They imagined an order in the universe whereby every entity filled a particular position in a "chain of being," stretching from the lowest to the highest inert elements, plants, and creatures (25–33). In *Paradise Lost*, Milton's Raphael, an angel, explains this "chain of being" to Adam, showing him how everything is ranked, and every level of possible being is filled. And Adam explains to Eve one consequence of this hierarchical "plenitude," as Tillyard notes (32):

> Millions of spiritual Creatures walk the Earth
> Unseen, both when we wake, and when we sleep:
> All these with ceaseless praise his works behold
> Both day and night.

Imagining that Milton inherited the Elizabethan idea of the chain of being may help us to understand the ending of "When I Consider." Specifically, we get a better sense of the reference to the "thousands" who speed at God's bidding, without rest. They are part of the "millions" of possible creatures existing in the scale between Milton and God; and, if God has a place (but not a need) for this plentitude who actively serve him, he also must allow in the scheme of things for some who serve in every other possible way—including standing and waiting. Thus, Milton's passive role is required of him; it is right; it is his current place in the universal chain of being.

Cultural Studies

"History" includes, of course, not only those great and obviously influential persons and events that we usually think of, but also the ordinary, the everyday, the apparently trivial. The development of plumbing is clearly very important to civilization, but few people, I would venture, know much about its evolution. And who would think that the history of sewers and toilets would be pertinent to the study of literature? And yet, to take only one example, Jonathan Swift's famous poem "A Description of a City Shower" (1710) makes considerably more sense if we know that the residents of London in 1710, lacking flushing toilets and sewer systems, collected their waste in chamber pots, which were often emptied into open trenches (called "kennels"). Swift's contemporaries, no doubt expecting "A Description of a City Shower" to be an idyllic celebration of the beauty of the urban rain, were no doubt stunned by the poem's grandiose depiction of their grossly smelly reality. The modern reader who is unaware of the sanitary problems in Swift's day may find the poem's imagery incredible. Consider, for instance, the poem's resounding conclusion:

> Now from all parts the swelling kennels flow,
> And bear their trophies with them as they go:
> Filth of all hues and odours seem to tell
> What streets they sailed from, by the sight and smell.
> They, as each torrent drives, with rapid force   5
> From Smithfield or St. Pulchre's shape their course,
> And in huge confluent join at Snow Hill ridge,
> Fall from the Conduit prone to Holborn Bridge.
> Sweepings from butcher's stalls, dung, guts, and blood,
> Drowned puppies, stinking sprats, all drenched in mud,   10
> Dead cats and turnip-tops come tumbling down the flood.

For Swift's reader, or for the modern reader who knows a little something about everyday eighteenth-century life, the poem is a reflection of the city's repulsiveness, describing in serious and inflated language what everyone saw and tried to overlook every time it rained—and thus Swift's vision becomes both strangely amusing and disturbing.

If the history of everything is potentially enlightening for the study of literature, then we should also note that the historical significance of literature itself extends beyond those works that have been most valued. If, in other words, "history" ought to encompass everything, from international treaties to eating utensils, by the same token "literature" should be seen as more than just the great works that we usually consider. It should include also the second-rate, third-rate, and even too-bad-to-rate writings that actually compose the bulk of literary history. It is, in fact, probably presumptuous for us to assume the accuracy of our own perspective on what is historically important, in literature or society. The stock of many writers, including Milton, has gone up and down dramatically over the centuries.

Indeed, in the last few decades, many scholars have even expanded their view of literature to include those "texts" that aren't in the usual sense "literary" at all—advertisements, cartoons, films, romances, television shows, popular music, and much more. "Cultural studies," as this ambitious field of research has often come to be called, considers any cultural phenomenon to be worthy of serious analysis. Take body piercing, for instance. Have you ever wondered why it has recently become so popular in Western countries? Why are so many people getting their belly buttons, nipples, noses, and/ or other parts pierced? What are they trying to communicate through this action? How is this activity related to other cultural events, such as tattooing? While such questions might be investigated by sociologists or anthropologists or psychologists, a "cultural studies" stance would encourage an interdisciplinary and interconnected approach to such phenomena, relating them to the whole spectrum of popular and literary culture. Cultural studies in its inclusiveness has thus brought attention to neglected and suppressed writers, providing a richer understanding of the contributions of minorities, the excluded, the oppressed. Cultural studies is, in fact, often associated with a kind of scholarly activism, as literary and historical study is brought to bear on contemporary concerns.

We have ventured, no doubt, light-years from Milton (who had no pierced parts whatsoever, so far as I know), but let us adopt a cultural studies stance and imagine the possibility of linking contemporary body piercing to Milton's poem. (You may smile skeptically here if you like.) Body piercing, like tattooing, is surely an effort to draw attention to the self, to stand out from other people, to say, "I am extraordinary, even doing nothing; I am significant." In tribal cultures, body markings, scarrings, deformations, and ornamental punctures allow for quick identification of one's membership and status. My former student who had purple-striped hair and a large ring in his nose was simultaneously declaring his distance from the conventional culture, and his membership in another alternative community.

Although the precise coding for body piercing in early twenty-first-century Western culture may not be uniformly established, jewelry through one's nose or eyebrow or cheek or tongue undeniably makes a statement. It says *something*. In his cultural studies classic *Subculture: The Meaning of Style* (1979), Dick Hebdige noted how the outrageous styles of British lower-class youth—rockers, mods, punks, skinheads, and others—created an alternative value system. By their "style" (in the largest sense), the members of these various groups indicated that they did not belong to the mainstream culture, but that they were clearly part of some other culture. Their personal value might be negligible by the standards of conventional society, but they were rejecting that society, making themselves by their very appearance virtually unable to find ordinary employment.

Milton's poem certainly focuses on the problems of assessing one's own value, and of finding one's place in society. Milton has not intentionally deformed himself, but he did think his eyesight had been weakened by excessive study. He thus finds himself unable to contribute to his community in any ordinary sense. What he is able to do, his "talent," seems "useless" (line 4) in his present physical state. Milton's problem is how he sees, and not how he is seen, but the poem indicates that he considers himself as unemployable as a facially-tatooed skinhead applying to be a bank teller. He has become what cultural critics would call a "subaltern" writer—someone who is excluded from power, an "other." But Milton also invokes an alternative value system, for his talent is "useless" only from the point of view of ordinary utilitarian society. For Milton's life to have value in the alternative community, he does not need to make any meaningful contribution. He doesn't need to work or *do* anything to be valuable. His burden of blindness, which is also his warrant for inactivity, he calls a "mild yoke," as if it were no more than a minor inconvenience. He has value simply in being his own unique self, waiting, serving by doing nothing but waiting as one of the community of faithful.

Thus, both Milton and someone with facial piercings and a bone through the nose might find themselves rendered physically unsuited for work in the conventional sense. Their lives, which might therefore seem to be of questionable value, are made meaningful in terms of an alternative community. No productive action is required.

New Historicism

The kind of historical background provided by Tillyard depends, as Jean Howard says, on three assumptions:

1. "that history is knowable";
2. "that literature mirrors or at least by indirection reflects historical reality"; and
3. "that historians and critics can see the facts of history objectively" (18).

These assumptions, which seem reasonable enough at first glance, have been persuasively called into question. The starting point for this reformative work is a simple observation: "History" is textual. We read about it; we experience it in words, which are used to explain the physical evidence. We don't have access directly to the past; we instead have a "story" about it. The Battle of Antietam, for instance, is now a textual phenomenon. It does not exist. Our tendency to separate history and literature—seeing one as fact, the other as fiction, one as the background to the other—is arguably collapsed by this insight. So we cannot directly observe history, nor be entirely scientific or objective about its facts or remains, because history must be interpreted. Our reading of it is as subjective as our reading of any other texts.

If you've experienced accounts of the same event in newspapers or on networks with significantly different political stances, you're already aware that there is no objective historical "reality" out there. The past is always absent, gone by, removed from us. As Hayden White puts it, history becomes "a story of a particular kind" (60). History is shaped by its necessary textuality; its content and meaning are unavoidably open to interpretation. For some people, the tentative nature of historical explanations has been underscored by what is called "chaos theory." In the 1960s and 1970s, Edward Lorenz concluded that long-range weather forecasting was inevitably unreliable because weather patterns were in the final analysis chaotic. Any patterns that we might see in the short term tend to evaporate in the long run—in part because a huge cause may have a tiny effect, and a tiny cause may have a huge effect. The air currents moved by a butterfly's wings, as Lorenz's most famous illustration goes, might set off a chain of meteorological events that would result in a hurricane on another continent. Chaos theory, starting from Lorenz's notion of the strange and potentially unfathomable connections between causes and effects, has been extended to many diverse fields, including literary criticism. For history, chaos theory obviously compounds the problem of history's textual nature by proposing that the reality historians try to describe is itself random, non-linear, ever-changing, chaotic. But a problem is always also an opportunity, and while one might despair of the uncertainty of historical insight, of drawing cause-and-effect connections, another might celebrate the wider spaces opened up for innovation and creativity.

History as Text

If history and literature are both texts, then literature is potentially as much a context for history as history is for literature. Elizabethan plays may be seen to "reflect" political events, but Elizabethan politics may also be seen as the consequence of theatrical conventions. We may think of certain political events—the coronation of Elizabeth or state trials for treason, for instance—as being "staged" like plays. In this light, let's consider "When I Consider."

Even the reality of Milton's blindness as a "background" for the poem is produced textually for us, and it must be interpreted. It cannot be taken simply as a freestanding fact. What did blindness mean for Milton personally and for anyone in his day? Would it have been seen as a punishment? As a special gift or calling? Would Milton see himself as a Homeric figure, in the tradition of ancient Greece's great blind poet? Was Milton's blindness a kind of protection, affording him some exemption from prosecution when the new government failed and Charles II restored the monarchy? Why does Milton see himself as essentially helpless, unable to work, to do "day-labor," even though he can still compose—as the poem itself testifies? Was writing not considered work?

Although such speculative questions might also be pursued by traditional biographical and historical criticism, new historicism encourages a new way of addressing them. A new historicist critic might elect to examine the whole issue of vision in Milton's day, of "light" versus "darkness," of insight versus sight, of writing versus working, and much more, as a textual matter. The new historicist would feel free to read Milton's poem in the light of medical texts, economic texts, optics texts, rhetoric, and any other texts that might help explain how "blindness" functions in seventeenth-century discourse, regardless of whether Milton himself knew any of these sources. A new historicist critic might be more likely than the traditional historical critic to consider the possibility that Milton's blindness was psychosomatic, or feigned, or any other hypothesis that might be productive, because the new historicist assumes that history is a story, a construct, necessarily written and rewritten.

One of the most catalytic figures in this rethinking of history has been Michel Foucault, who persistently attempted, in the words of Eve Tavor Bannet, "to break down the familiar units, categories, continuities and totalities through which history, society and the symbolic order are traditionally interpreted" (96). We should note that Tillyard did not himself claim that every Elizabethan endorsed every aspect of "the Elizabethan world picture"; in fact, he repeatedly qualified his position by citing contrary opinions. Still, Tillyard does definitively call his work *The Elizabethan World Picture*, and the exceptions are designed to support his generalizations. New historicists, following Foucault, endeavor to expose the complexities, exceptions, divergences, gaps, and anachronisms in our characterizations of any period. While Tillyard sees the chain of being as a reassuring and pervasive principle of order for Elizabethan thinkers, Stephen Greenblatt considers how such myths serve the ideological interests of Elizabethan culture, discouraging dissent and subversion, and he shows how *King Lear*, for example, both affirms and undermines such cultural directives. Greenblatt's argument thus becomes an intervention into the traditional way of looking at Elizabethan England.

In addition to opposing or questioning traditional schemes of history, new historicism also tends to focus on the production of "knowledge" at a particular time and place. Foucault, for example, shows how the modern conception of "the mentally ill" came into being, as the insane are assigned to the same cultural position that those with leprosy had previously held. Most startling, Foucault argues that "madness" has not been a stable historical event, but is rather an invention, a construct, creating an excluded "other" category. Reversing the idea of asylums as benevolent and rehabilitative, Foucault describes their character as judicial and punitive—judging without appeal and incarcerating without trial. Similarly, Foucault reverses the widespread view that sexuality has been repressed in modern Western culture, arguing instead that sexual behavior has been increasingly discussed, classified, prohibited, authorized, and exposed. Drawing on texts from widely diverse fields, Foucault describes how the categories of the perverse and abnormal have been invented and constructed and perpetuated.

Since new historicists are interested in how historical "knowledge" is produced, they are naturally interested in the effects of power and ideology, whether these appear in "literature" in the usual sense or in any other texts. How we see the "facts"—indeed, whether we see a set of facts—depends to some degree upon the controlling system of assumptions and operations or ideology. This unavoidable interest in power has made new historicism especially appealing to those critics interested in economy and class—who are often designated as engaging in Marxist criticism. Marxist critics see the individual person as a product of society's system of value; therefore, exposing how the individual is constructed by class and economy is vitally important.

Marxist Criticism

Marxism is a theory of history, a way of thinking about labor, society, and economy that predicts the inevitable demise of capitalism. Marxist theory begins, of course, with Karl Marx, whose response to the Industrial Revolution in the nineteenth century focused on the way that profits are generated in capitalism. The laborer, Marx noted, adds value to raw materials, but only part of that value is returned to the laborer because the business owner takes out a profit. The laborer becomes nothing more than a commodity himself and is "alienated" from his work, losing his humanity. The worker is just a tool for the owner. How can this economic base of society, given its fundamental unfairness, possibly survive? Why do the workers continue to allow themselves to be exploited? Marx's answers focus on what he called the "superstructure," which consists of all the cultural directions, blatant and subtle, that support the status quo. Art, literature, philosophy, religion, political institutions—everything that shapes the ideas of the workers, the culture's "ideology"—all serve to reinforce the injustice of the capitalist system, making it seem right and normal. This superstructure, Marx argued, is an illusion, and the workers (or the proletariat) will eventually recognize their exploitation and revolt.

Marxist thinkers who followed after Marx have noted that culture, in fact, doesn't always support the economic base. A novel, a film, a political speech, a sermon, any human creation, may also challenge or undermine the capitalist system. In fact, cultural works may have complex and even contradictory relationships to the superstructure. The work of Marxist analysis involves understanding how a culture's ideology creates the individual's self-perception. The Western tradition, especially from the Renaissance and the Enlightenment, thinks in terms of a stable self, a person who has an identity. Although it may feel as if you are discovering yourself, or perhaps as if you have invented yourself, Marxists assert that the self is actually socially constructed, the product of the various ideologies that one inhabits. Rather than referring to a "self," Marxists talk about a "subject," emphasizing the way in which one's identity is subservient to myriad cultural forces.

For Louis Althusser, for instance, a culture's system of ideas, its ideology, tells us who we are. "Interpellation" is Althusser's term for the process whereby a culture creates a space that a "subject" then fills. Consider how any advertisement offers a role for the viewer: I am looking at an ad in the *New York Times* for Tourneau watches which has a picture of a watch, a listed price of $3,950, and the caption "Time for Elegance." This ad, as Althusser would say, is "hailing" or calling me, saying that I'm supposed to be the sort of person who appreciates elegance, expensive watches, and puns, a savvy guy who knows what time it is. I may not answer this call (I may deny this subject position), but I am nonetheless responding to it, registering my awareness of the lack of this watch. For Mikhail Bakhtin, what is most important about the relationship between the viewer/reader and the work is the kind of language that is used. Bakhtin famously opposes monologic (one-voiced) language to dialogic (two or more voices), preferring subject relationships in which multiple meanings and voices appear. Similarly, Michel Foucault exposes the various ways that culture restricts meaning and disciplines its citizens.

We do not have to decide whether Marxism is hopelessly flawed as a political philosophy in order to see that it is often strikingly useful as an analytical strategy. Certain features of "When I Consider," for instance, can be highlighted by Marxism's drive to see the world in terms of economic classes, to identify who is being oppressed and exploited and by whom. Let's look in particular at the reference to "day-labor" in line 7, which may seem merely a synonym for "work," a longer word for "labor." The line "Doth God exact day-labor, light denied," appears clearly to be a question, although Milton's text lacks a question mark. Some later editors have added a question mark, and sometimes quotation marks too, and the question seems clear enough, once the reader straightens out who is talking—that the "I" is speaking, and not "He." But "day-labor" is an unusual word, and one might well wonder if Milton intends it to mean something more than just "work."

To find out about the meaning of "day-labor," one could research the history of labor or of economy in the seventeenth century. Or one could see how the term is used by other writers at that time and place.

Those investigations could well be fascinating but time-consuming. More directly, we could look in the *Oxford English Dictionary*, which gives the meanings for words at various points in their histories. Or, even more directly, we could see how the term is defined in a dictionary of that time period. The first great dictionary of the English language is Samuel Johnson's famous *Dictionary* of 1755, which defines "daylabour" as "Labour by the day; labour divided into tasks." Johnson then offers illustrations, the first of which, interestingly enough, is the line we are talking about: "Doth God exact *daylabour*, light deny'd, / I fondly ask." Here's the second:

> Did either his legs or his arms fail him? No; but daylabour was but an hard and a dry kind of livelihood to a man, that could get an estate with two or three strokes of his pen.
>
> *Southey*

Johnson's definition and the Southey illustration begin to suggest how "daylabour" differs from "work." Someone who is employed by the day, or part of a day, is more likely to be a worker at the bottom of the social hierarchy than someone who has a position. Today we distinguish between those workers who are paid an hourly wage (they "punch the clock") and those who are salaried. Johnson's illustrations for "Daylabourer," which also include an example by Milton, make these hierarchical implications clearer:

> In one night, ere glimpse of morn,
> His shadowy flail hath thresh'd the corn
> That ten *daylabourers* could not end.
>
> *Milton*

> The *daylabourer*, in a country village, has commonly but a small pittance of courage.
>
> *Locke*

A "daylabourer," the Milton quotation implies, is the kind of worker who does such messy, mind-numbing jobs as threshing corn. The pay would be poor for such nonspecialized labor, and the social status would be somewhere below the seventeenth century's equivalent of a hamburger flipper. Locke's quotation further indicates the lowly standing of a "daylabourer" by disparaging the character of that whole group.

From a Marxist perspective, Locke's attitude would also suggest precisely why the working class (the proletariat) should unite and overthrow the middle and upper classes. According to Marx's labor theory of value, the true value of something reflects the amount of labor used to make it. Within a capitalist system, someone who does "day-labor" would be unjustly undervalued: rather than being compensated fairly for "the amount of labor" contributed, the underclass worker would instead be exploited by the private owner. Naturally (as Marxist thinking would go), someone like Locke, a physician and philosopher, certainly not part of the working class, would seek to justify the economic system's suppression of day-laborers by assuming their inferiority: No wonder they're poorly compensated; they have very little courage, for starters.

Such a Marxist stance, focusing on the economic and social implications of "day-labor" alone, certainly deepens and complicates our sense of Milton's poem. Let's consider what happens for a moment, beginning by looking only at the poem's first seven lines:

> When I consider how my light is spent,
> Ere half my days in this dark world and wide,
> And that one talent which is death to hide
> Lodged with me useless, though my soul more bent
> To serve therewith my Maker, and present   5
> My true account, lest He returning chide,
> Doth God exact day-labor, light denied, . . .

Notice that, observing the poem's original punctuation, we must initially assume on a first reading that it is "my Maker," returning to chide, who says "Doth God exact day-labor, light denied." Spoken by God, the statement would seem to be a rhetorical question: "Does God expect anyone to do the sort of work that day-laborers do, picking crops, threshing corn, digging ditches, etc., when there's no daylight?" The answer in this case might well appear to be "no": no day, no day-labor. Of course God wouldn't require such a silly thing.

The beginning of line 8, "I fondly ask," completely reorients our reading, however, assigning the statement to the speaker. Rather than a rhetorical question, line 7 instantly becomes a complaint, and the level of Milton's frustration is indicated by "day-labor." The absurdity of God expecting anything of him, now that his "light is spent" and his talent is "useless," is reflected in the absurdity of the image of one of the most learned men in Europe, who has devoted his life to cultivating his literary talent, engaging in "day-labor." It's as if a rocket scientist has been asked to deliver pizza. Surely God cannot require anything like day-labor of Milton.

The word "fondly," however, necessitates another level of reversal, for in Milton's day "fondly" meant, as Johnson's *Dictionary* defines it, "Foolishly; weakly, imprudently; injudiciously." To be "fond" of something was to be "foolishly tender" or "injudiciously indulgent." The question that Milton asks is, therefore, a really foolish one, as the rest of the poem reveals. Its answer shouldn't be "no"; it should be "yes indeed." In fact, however,

as the rest of line 8 begins to disclose, Milton's voice does not ask this question that we have just encountered, because "Patience" is able to "prevent /
That murmur" by pointing out that (1) God doesn't need anyone's day-
labor or any other kind of labor and (2) some people, even though they may
seem incapable of having a job, have the job of simply waiting to see if they
have a job of any sort to do. The poem is thus creating a subject position
for the reader, as we are interpellated here, to use Althusser's term: We
should all be happy, the poem seems to assert, to serve in whatever fashion
we are called upon.

Marxist criticism strives to see literature in terms of its relationship to
society, and a work is assumed to reinforce the current social structure, or
undermine it, or some combination of the two. The reading of "When I
Consider" that I have just rehearsed—a reading that considers the experience of moving through the poem (and is indebted to Stanley Fish's famous
reader-response version of this poem in "Interpreting the *Variorum*")—takes
on yet another dimension in this Marxist context: the poem becomes propaganda for the status quo. It is part of a discourse that disciplines and controls the laboring classes, as Foucault might put it; and the key to this insight
is, again, "day-labor." How so? Specifically, the experience of the poem
reinforces the emerging capitalist system in Milton's England by undermining any potential resistance by the lower classes to their exploitation. The
poem first poses the idea of resisting unreasonable demands for labor, then
immediately dispels such opposition. All workers, the poem indicates, need
to do their jobs, whatever they might be. This poetic message, in Bahktin's
terms, is monologic, silencing in a sense other voices about labor and resistance. Marx says that all should give according to their means and take
according to their needs. Milton stresses the value of work even for those
who don't work: "They also serve who only stand and wait."

Postcolonial and Ethnic Studies

New historicist critics not only highlight the way power has produced
"knowledge" in the past, but they are also often self-consciously aware of
the possibility that literary criticism might be used as a political instrument
in the here and now. When Greenblatt shows how Elizabethan culture discouraged dissent, he is unavoidably suggesting questions about how other
cultures, including our own, have suppressed, shaped, or encouraged dissent. When Foucault strives to expose the invented status of madness or
perversity in the past, he is inevitably challenging the authority of current
sexual or psychological norms. Such boundaries, Foucault is teaching us,
are based on fictions, not facts; nurture, not nature.

This creative relationship between power and knowledge is especially
evident when strikingly different cultures interact. "Knowledge" for a

nuclear physicist in California may not be "knowledge" for a pygmy tribes-
man in central Africa. Is one form of knowledge better than the other?
Wouldn't anyone reading this text agree that the physicist is likely to have
a more accurate understanding of the universe than the pygmy? When I
am sick, I think that a virus or a bacterium, not an evil spirit, has probably
invaded my body. But isn't it unfair and inaccurate to value one culture
over another? Aren't I being ethnocentric, placing my own ethnic group at
the center of things, assuming that my own Western worldview is superior,
when it is in fact just different? To be sure, characterizing whole groups is
always dangerous: Some very wacky people live in California (even perhaps
some nuclear physicists), and some very sensible pygmies no doubt live in
Africa. On some issues, the pygmy and the Californian might agree that
my ideas are absurd. Such considerations have obviously helped to ener-
gize multiculturalism, which seeks to appreciate, understand, and respect
the uniquely different viewpoints of different cultures—even if we disagree.
Some practices and beliefs, however, seem so obviously unethical and
erroneous that a simple multicultural celebration of difference becomes
problematic. At the least, a multicultural stance invites us to attempt to
understand the subjectivity of our own views—to see where we are standing within our own culture as we look in on other cultures.

The powerful effects of cultural bias were compellingly exposed in
1978 when Edward Said published *Orientalism*, showing how European
culture in the nineteenth century created and perpetuated the idea that
Middle Eastern and Asian cultures were inferior to European culture. The
idea that "Oriental" cultures were less advanced was used, as Said demon-
strates, to justify European colonization and exploitation. Following Said,
in-depth examinations of the various relationships between dominant and
subjugated cultures, races, and ethnic groups have been carried out by a
growing number of scholars. "Postcolonial studies," the name now usually
given to such investigations, explores in particular the effects of this history
upon formerly colonized peoples. Postcolonial criticism thus considers the
role that literature has played as an agent of oppression and resistance, dis-
tortion and understanding. What did European imperialists say about the
people they colonized? How did the colonized people talk about themselves
and their masters?

The playing field for postcolonial, racial, and ethnic studies is huge,
as indicated by its diversity and geographical expansiveness (from Canada
to Sri Lanka, from Australia to Jamaica, from India to Senegal) or by its
theoretical sophistication and diversity (as suggested, for example, by *The
Empire Writes Back: Theory and Practice in Post-Colonial Literatures*, the landmark
1989 study by Bill Ashcroft, Gareth Griffiths, and Helen Tiffin). Still, as a
special kind of historical interpretation, postcolonial studies would appear
to be limited in scope, focusing upon certain authors and works (those who

write in or about European colonies). By the same token, racial and ethnic studies that are oriented toward a historical stance might also seem somewhat restricted.

Milton's "When I Consider," for instance, might seem to be an unpromising work from a postcolonial perspective, as it was written well before England's massive global expansion in the eighteenth and nineteenth centuries, and it says nothing at all about colonies or colonizing. Still, one might note that European nations were already striving toward empires well before the mid-seventeenth century. And shouldn't it be possible, in theory, to decipher England's imperialistic aspirations from almost any text, just as any one cell thoroughly analyzed may tell us a great deal about the body it was taken from? Indeed, if we return once more to "When I Consider" with a postcolonial vision, we may notice that Milton does, in fact, depict God as an autocrat ("His state / Is kingly") who lives elsewhere (we are in a colonial state), but who might "returning chide" the speaker for a lack of production, for a falsified account. Milton thus sees himself (or the speaker) as a kind of subjugated person, one who is, in fact, in colonial servitude, although the absent master's "yoke" is "mild," and he is willingly in service.

Milton thus cannot avoid implicating the ideology he inhabits, and therefore in his effort to glorify God, he thinks of "Him" as a king who appropriately controls the most extensive empire. With "thousands at his bidding" posting "o'er land and ocean without rest," we can imagine that the sun never sets on His subjects, just as the sun in later centuries would never set on the British Empire. Milton's poem thus reinforces concepts essential to justifying British expansion and exploitation, as we see implicitly that the master rightly expects complete loyalty and service from an inferior being. The speaker in this poem, the "subaltern" (as Gayatri Spivak would put it), has no business questioning his particular situation. The speaker indeed relinquishes his rights, since his place is simply to do whatever is asked of him—including even to stand and wait. Those who are blind, as a group, have some common ground, and some distinct differences, from the status and perception of ethnic and racial groups.

To notice the logic assumed by Milton's poem is to begin to question it, and it is easy to see how the potential for political activism in postcolonial criticism in particular and in new historicism in general would be especially appealing to many scholars who may understandably have wondered through the years if their research is having any real influence on the world beyond academe. From one point of view, new historicism simply acknowledges that some political agenda has always inevitably been involved in historical and critical work. The implications of new historicist work are just more visible, radical, and compelling.

In other words, against the assumptions of the traditional history of the sort practiced by Tillyard, we may place the assumptions of the new historicism:

1. History is knowable only in the sense that all texts are knowable—that is, by interpretation, argument, speculation.
2. Literature is not simply a mirror of historical reality; history, in fact, isn't a mirror of historical reality. Literature is shaped by history and even shapes history; it is also distorted by history and is even discontinuous with history.
3. Historians and critics must view "the facts" of history subjectively; in fact, the "facts" must be viewed as their creation.

HOW TO DO BIOGRAPHICAL AND HISTORICAL CRITICISM

To do biographical criticism, you need to know as much as you can about the life of the author and then apply that knowledge, being careful not to equate the author with a narrator or character. You will want to draw your conclusions cautiously, and support them solidly with evidence from the literary text itself, and not only from the author's life.

To do historical criticism, you need to know the relevant history and use it in some way. The difficulty here, besides the work of mastering history, is determining just what is relevant. One way to look at this: If the history helps you to understand the work, then it's relevant. New historicism complicates things a bit, because you ought to know the author's biography—even though the author's personality is a cultural construct, a textual effect; and you ought to know the history (or histories)—even though the "facts" are always subject to questioning, supplementation, and opposition. Thinking from a new historical point of view, you are encouraged to be particularly imaginative in making connections, and to think about how particular documents participate in, or help to create, systems of assumptions and meanings.

To do postcolonial criticism, you need to know the history (social, economic, political, cultural) of the imperial and the colonized peoples, and you want to apply that history somehow to literary texts (or art, music, fashion, whatever). The most influential work in postcolonial theory has dealt with India, Africa, Australia, Canada, the Caribbean, and New Zealand, and typical moves (following after Said) involve revealing how the colonial power depicts the native population as in need of domination. The men of India, according to pervasive cultural propaganda, are effeminate and unambitious; Africans are savage and lazy; Oriental people are mysterious and threatening. Postcolonial criticism can show how these images are perpetuated or undermined or transformed in various literary works.

Similarly, cultural studies might be most accurately presented as more of a set of goals than a clear-cut method. The fundamental idea of cultural studies, one could argue, is that the products of a culture are shaped by underlying assumptions and values; and a variety of strategies, ranging from psychoanalysis to deconstruction to feminist criticism and so forth, can be used to explain the artifacts and activities of a culture. In *The Life and Times of Cultural Studies* (Duke UP, 2003), Richard Lee notes a shift in cultural studies from issues of working-class culture toward questions involving race and gender. Whatever the object of cultural studies—high culture, low culture, popular culture, elite culture; class, race, gender—"doing" cultural studies means not only attempting to illuminate culture but also intervening in it. Part of the academic popularity of cultural studies no doubt stems from this commitment, allowing scholars and teachers to act on their political allegiances, working for change by producing knowledge. Given the origins of cultural studies in the 1960s in Great Britain's New Left, and particularly in Birmingham University's Centre for Contemporary Cultural Studies, the social change that cultural studies typically advocates is progressive and liberal. In bringing an academic rigor to the analysis of all sorts of things previously ignored or dismissed, such as motorcycle gangs, soap operas, tattoos, advertising, or rock music, cultural studies has indeed made some startling contributions to our understanding.

The whole idea of cultural studies as an "approach" might indeed be questionable for some people. Michael Bérubé has observed, lamenting its porous boundaries, that "cultural studies now means everything and nothing. It has been associated with a cheery 'Pop culture is fun!' approach" (B10). One could, in fact, argue that cultural studies is really distinguished by the objects of its attention (the products of popular culture and subcultures) or its goals (progressive social change), and not by any distinctive method. Like all the approaches covered in this chapter, a cultural studies stance encourages you to make connections (which can include breaking down fences) between and among the products of history, biography, and culture. Literature, from this perspective, is not something that we study for its own sake. Literature is part of life. And what we call "literature," or at least give a literary sort of attention to, may well be a text or object or activity that is not "literature" in a traditional sense.

However we demarcate historical, postcolonial, and cultural studies, some general guidance about how to use these approaches to write about a text can now be offered:

1. Determine the historical setting of the work—when and where it was written and under what conditions. Investigate the author's biography, including—of course—race, class, gender, and so forth.

2. Consider how the historical background helps us to understand the work, or consider how the work contradicts or stands apart from the consensus historical or biographical background. Are there individuals or groups that are characterized in politically significant ways?

3. Identify other texts of the same time period that might be related to the text under analysis. Identify the ideology (or ideologies) driving these texts, constructing a system of meaning. Expose the cultural significance of the literary text.

Although these approaches require some research and patience, they are interesting and often very rewarding. With the ongoing expansion of electronic resources, historical materials are becoming increasingly accessible. There is no substitute for the thrill of examining (carefully) a first edition of Samuel Johnson's great 1755 *Dictionary of the English Language*; but the digital version allows one to search the entire massive work for a particular word or phrase. Doing historical research has never been so easy. Museums and libraries allow scholars to access treasure troves of original sources. Historical organizations provide links to scholarly journals and primary sources. You need information about railroads in the nineteenth century? Check out the Railroad History Database. Or maybe it's the history of the Air Force: There's the Air Force Historical Research Agency, of course. Although chat rooms and email and online shopping are nice, the Internet's most stunning potential lies in its power to teach us. The vastness of resources available may seem overwhelming at times, so don't hesitate to seek advice. Librarians and teachers are ordinarily delighted to help. As I'm sure you know, not everything you can find online is reliable, so when you're doing historical and biographical research, be careful and cautious, relying on scholarly journals and university presses whenever possible.

THE WRITING PROCESS: SAMPLE ESSAYS

The work I want to focus on in this section is a compelling short story, first published in the October 27, 1962, issue of *The New Yorker*.

Reunion
John Cheever

The last time I saw my father was in Grand Central Station. I was going from my grandmother's in the Adirondacks to a cottage on the Cape that my mother had rented, and I wrote my father that I would be in New York between trains for an hour and a half, and asked if we could have lunch together. His secretary wrote to say that he would meet me at the information booth at noon, and twelve o'clock sharp I saw him coming through the crowd. He was a stranger to me—my mother divorced him three years ago and I hadn't been with him since—but as soon as I saw him I felt that he was my father, my flesh and blood, my future and my doom. I knew that when I was grown I would be something like him; I would have to plan my campaigns within his limitations. He was a big, good-looking man, and I was terribly happy to see him again. He struck me on the back and shook my hand. "Hi, Charlie," he said. "Hi, boy. I'd like to take you up to my club, but it's in the Sixties, and if you have to catch an early train I guess we'd better get something to eat around here." He put his arm around me, and I smelled my father the way my mother sniffs a rose. It was a rich compound of whiskey, after-shave lotion, shoe polish, woollens, and the rankness of a mature male. I hoped that someone would see us together. I wished that we could be photographed. I wanted some record of our having been together.

We went out of the station and up a side street to a restaurant. It was still early and the place was empty. The bartender was quarreling with a delivery boy, and there was one very old waiter in a red coat down by the kitchen door. We sat down, and my father hailed the waiter in a loud voice. *"Kellner!"* he shouted. *"Garçon! Cameriere! You!"* His boisterousness in the empty restaurant seemed out of place. "Could we have a little service here!" he shouted. "Chop-chop." Then he clapped his hands. This caught the waiter's attention, and he shuffled over to our table.

"Were you clapping your hands at me?" he asked.

"Calm down, calm down, *sommelier*," my father said. "If it isn't too much to ask of you—if it wouldn't be too much above and beyond the call of duty, we would like a couple of Beefeater Gibsons."

"I don't like to be clapped at," the waiter said.

"I should have brought my whistle," my father said. "I have a whistle that is audible only to the ears of old waiters. Now, take out your little pad and your little pencil and see if you can get this straight: two Beefeater Gibsons. Repeat after me: two Beefeater Gibsons."

"I think you'd better go someplace else," the waiter said quietly.

"That," said my father, "is one of the most brilliant suggestions I have ever heard. Come on, Charlie, let's get the hell out of here."

I followed my father out of that restaurant into another. He was not so boisterous this time. Our drinks came, and he cross-questioned me about the baseball season. He then struck the edge of his empty glass with his knife and began shouting again. *"Garçon! Kellner! Cameriere! You!* Could we trouble you to bring us two more of the same."

"How old is the boy?" the waiter asked.

"That," my father said, "is none of your God-damned business."

"I'm sorry, sir," the waiter said, "but I won't serve the boy another drink."

"Well, I have some news for you," my father said. "I have some very interesting news for you. This doesn't happen to be the only restaurant in New York. They've opened another on the corner. Come on, Charlie."

He paid the bill, and I followed him out of that restaurant into another. Here the waiters wore pink jackets like hunting coats, and there was a lot of horse tack on the walls. We sat down, and my father began to shout again. "Master of the hounds! Tallyho and all that sort of thing. We'd like a little something in the way of a stirrup cup. Namely, two Bibson Geefeaters."

"Two Bibson Geefeaters?" the waiter asked, smiling.

"You know damned well what I want," my father said angrily. "I want two Beefeater Gibsons, and make it snappy. Things have changed in jolly old England. So my friend the duke tells me. Let's see what England can produce in the way of a cocktail."

"This isn't England," the waiter said.

"Don't argue with me," my father said. "Just do as you're told."

"I just thought you might like to know where you are," the waiter said.

"If there is one thing I cannot tolerate," my father said, "it is an impudent domestic. Come on, Charlie."

The fourth place we went to was Italian. "Buon giorno," my father said. "Per favore, possiamo avere due cocktail americani, forti, forti. Molto gin, poco vermut."

"I don't understand Italian," the waiter said.

"Oh, come off it," my father said. "You understand Italian, and you know damned well you do. *Vogliamo due cocktail americani. Subito.*"

The waiter left us and spoke with the captain, who came over to our table and said, "I'm sorry, sir, but this table is reserved."

"All right," my father said, "Get us another table."

"All the tables are reserved," the captain said.

"I get it," my father said. "You don't desire our patronage. Is that it? Well, the hell with you. *Vada all'inferno.* Let's go, Charlie."

"I have to get my train," I said.

"I'm sorry, sonny," my father said. "I'm terribly sorry." He put his arm around me and pressed me against him. "I'll walk you back to the station. If there had only been time to go up to my club."

"That's all right, Daddy," I said.

"I'll get you a paper," he said. "I'll get you a paper to read on the train."

Then he went up to a newsstand and said, "Kind sir, will you be good enough to favor me with one of your God-damned, no-good, ten-cent afternoon papers?" The clerk turned away from him and stared at a magazine cover. "Is it asking too much, kind sir," my father said, "is it asking too much for you to sell me one of your disgusting specimens of yellow journalism?"

"I have to go, Daddy," I said. "It's late."

"Now, just wait a second, sonny," he said. "Just wait a second. I want to get a rise out of this chap."

"Goodbye, Daddy," I said, and I went down the stairs and got my train, and that was the last time I saw my father.

In what follows we turn from the primary text to other texts, seeking connections—how the story might reflect Cheever's personal history and feelings, and how the story is shaped by a system of ideas regarding prestige, identity, suicide, and alcohol.

A BIOGRAPHICAL ESSAY

Preparing to Write

A search of the electronic card catalogue at my school's library revealed thirteen books with John Cheever as their subject. I retrieved the seven that weren't checked out and requested the others to be held for me. Then I started skimming and reading, looking especially for materials relating to "Reunion," but also learning as much about Cheever as I could. What follows is a sampling of the notes I took. You want to keep track of where you're getting information so that you'll be able to cite it later. So the first thing I wrote down was this:

• From *John Cheever* by Lynne Waldeland (Boston: Twayne, 1979):

Then I began to take notes and make observations. At first, I just wrote down anything that seemed interesting:

• "Reunion" is from *The Brigadier and the Golf Widow*, Cheever's "best volume of short stories," according to William Peden (quoted on p. 91).

At this point I didn't really know what I was looking for, and after poking around for a while, I moved on to another volume and made these notes:

• From *The Letters of John Cheever*, edited by Cheever's son, Benjamin (New York: Simon and Schuster, 1988):
• Regarding the original publication of "The Brigadier and the Golf Widow," the title story of the volume in which "Reunion" would later appear: Cheever writes in a letter to a friend that he (Cheever) went into *The New Yorker* offices to correct the galleys (the trial printing) of the story and found that Bill Maxwell, the magazine's editor, had cut the story "in half." Cheever says that he went along with the cuts while in Maxwell's office. But then he later called from a bar and cursed Maxwell, who was at home entertaining "Elizabeth Bowen and Eudora Welty" (two famous writers), telling Maxwell that if he cut the story, "I'll never write another story for your [sic] or anybody else" (232).
• Cheever's letter about this incident concludes this way: "Anyhow the magazine had gone to press and they had to remake the whole back of the book and stay up all night but they ran it without the cut" (232–233).

- Maxwell's recollection, reported by Benjamin, is very different: Maxwell says he thought the story had two endings, and so he was going to see how Cheever liked it with only one. He had no plan to cut the story at all without Cheever's approval; the story wasn't about to go to press (Cheever had found it on Maxwell's desk), and there was no all-night reworking; Bowen and Welty had visited his house, but never at the same time (233). This is an interesting discrepancy.

Looking at these sources, I had to wonder how John Cheever could have gotten the story so wrong. Did he have no allegiance to the truth, preferring to spin a good tale? Or did his letter describe the truth, at least as he remembered it? The letter seems to have been written immediately afterward: How could his memory have been so immediately faulty? Intrigued by this problem, I turned to the introduction to the volume of letters, written by Cheever's son, Benjamin. And I find Benjamin Cheever saying that "my father's interest in telling a good story was greater than his interest in what we might consider the facts" (20). Cheever's letters thus become a kind of rehearsal for his fiction, it appears, as he practices shaping reality into better narrative material. Benjamin notes that he "included excerpts from his [father's] journals and his fiction, so that one can see the life— sometimes the same incident—reflected differently through the prism of his prose" (20).

For anyone undertaking biographical criticism, the implications here are clear: We should be particularly cautious regarding the "facts," especially as reported by Cheever (or any author really); at the same time, we should also be aware that Cheever does work his life into his stories, apparently sometimes in rather direct ways.

The following passages also caught my attention:

- Benjamin writes:

> The most difficult revelation for me, as a son, was the extent of my father's homosexuality. It's impossible for me to be objective about this, or to separate his fears from my own, but he was certainly troubled by the issue. (16)

- Benjamin also writes:

> He used to say that I must wish I had a father who didn't drink so much, and I'd always say no. I suppose this makes me what Alcoholics Anonymous would call an enabler, somebody who makes it all right for the alcoholic to destroy himself. Maybe so, but I thought then and think now that you have to take the people you love pretty much the way you find them. Their worst qualities are often linked with their very best ones. (18)

- Benjamin also says (reminding me of the father's smells in "Reunion"):

> And I have sometimes thought of him with bitterness, but it remains that while I am not a heavy drinker myself, or a smoker, I still find the smell of gin and tobacco a delicious combination. (18)

And, finally, the following passage is especially interesting in the context of biographical criticism.

- Benjamin Cheever says:

> The connection between his life and his work was intimate, but it was also mysterious. My father was fond of saying that fiction was 'crypto-autobiography.' One obvious reason for this statement is that it protected him from the attacks of friends and family who felt that they'd been libeled in his prose. (21)

Next I looked through a variety of other sources, taking these notes:

- From the first chapter of *John Cheever* by Samuel Coale, "Cheever's Life" (New York: Frederick Ungar, 1977):

> Cheever's father was a shoe salesman who was out of work late in life, and his mother opened a shop for the family to survive, selling first their own belongings. Cheever's father resented, apparently, her independence and competence and his own helplessness. (23)

- From *Home before Dark*, a biography of Cheever by his daughter, Susan (Boston: Houghton, 1984):

Susan Cheever says that e. e. cummings was her father's "first model" (59)—which is a really interesting idea considering the sort of writer Cheever became. Susan Cheever remembers attending with her father a poetry reading by cummings. When cummings saw Cheever, she says, "The force and openness of their affection for one another seemed to shake that airless, heavily draped room" (60). Susan remembers particularly, she says, sitting with her father as cummings read "my father moved through dooms of love" (60), which is of course cummings's famous elegy to his father. I noted also that cummings died in 1962, the same year "Reunion" was published, which is probably irrelevant, but intriguing to me.

- And here is a passage from Susan Cheever's book that's interesting in the context of the father's use of foreign languages to attract waiters in "Reunion":

Although he spoke minimal French, he always called the French classics by their original names: *Les Faux-Monnayeurs, La Chartreuse de Parme, Le Rouge et le Noir.* In his last years—a time when he was so well respected that a lot of people assumed he spoke two or three languages—he began dropping French words into his conversation. When he was sent his own books in French translations, he kept them on the desk or his bedside table. With Italian, he was even worse. He spoke a stilted, conversational Italian, but he used it at every opportunity, and he even insisted on re-Italianizing all Americanized Italian words or names. (He always insisted on calling my editor Nan Talese 'Nan Talayzee,' for instance.) 'Che cosa di buona oggi?' he would ask any dark-haired waiter, whether he was at the Four Seasons or the Highland Diner on Route 9 in Ossining. They were always very polite. (113–114)

- Susan Cheever also offers this passage, which reminds me of Charlie's awareness of the smell of his father and suggests that Cheever longed for the sort of father that his character, Charlie, did not have:

There is the presence of a father—stern, unintelligent and with a gamey odor—but a force of counsel and support that would have carried one into manhood,' my father wrote in his journal. 'One does not invest the image with brilliance or wealth; it is simply a man in a salt and pepper tweed, sometimes loving, sometimes irascible and sometimes drunk but always responsible to his son.' My father didn't have this ideal, tweedy parent he dreamed of in his journal who would have 'equipped him for manhood.' He spent much of his life looking for counsel and support from surrogate fathers and ultimately, painfully, rejecting them. (128)

- Late in Cheever's life, according to Susan, when he had achieved some fame:

He dropped names shamelessly. It was no longer safe to tease him about favorable reviews. In restaurants, he let headwaiters know that he was someone important. Since this kind of behavior was new to him, he wasn't particularly graceful about it. Walking down Park Avenue with him once, after a lunch at the Four Seasons ('Che cosa di buona oggi?'), I noticed that he was smiling his public smile at everyone who passed—just in case they recognized him, I suppose. (210–211)

- From Scott Donaldson's biography, *John Cheever* (New York: Random, 1988), I find other information that relates to how Cheever thought about fathers and fatherhood:

Cheever's mother told him he was a mistake: "If I hadn't drunk two Manhattans one afternoon, you never would have been conceived." Cheever's father, Donaldson reports, supposedly wanted him aborted, even inviting the abortionist to dinner, an event that appears in both *The Wapshot Chronicle* and *Falconer*. (13)

In the story "National Pastime," Donaldson notes, the father won't teach the son to play baseball, which causes the son real embarrassment and trauma (20).

- From *The Journals of John Cheever*, edited by Robert Gottlieb (New York: Knopf, 1991):

Cheever writes:

Having drunk less than usual, having, as my father would say, gone light on the hooch, I find myself, for the first time in a long time, free of the cafarde. Quarter to nine. Eastern day-light-saving time. It would be pleasant to consider this a simple matter of self-discipline. Thunder and rain in the middle of the afternoon; the first of the month. Our primordial anxiety about drought and its effect on the crops, the crops in this case being three acres of lawn and forty-two rosebushes. (135–136)

I dislike writing here about boozefighting, but I must do something about it. A friend comes to call. In my anxiety to communicate, to feel the most in warmth and intimacy, I drink too much, which can be two drinks these days. In the morning I am deeply depressed, my insides barely function, my kidney is painful, my hands shake, and walking down Madison Avenue I am in fear of death. But evening comes or even noon and some combination of nervous tensions obscures my memories of what whiskey costs me in the way of physical and intellectual well-being. I could very easily destroy myself. It is ten o'clock now and I am thinking of the noontime snort. (103)

Year after year I read in here that I am drinking too much, and there can be no doubt of the fact that this is progressive. I waste more days, I suffer deeper pangs of guilt, I wake up at three in the morning with the feelings of a temperance worker. Drink, its implements, environments, and effects all seem disgusting. And yet each noon I reach for the whiskey bottle. I don't seem able to drink temperately and yet I don't seem able to stop. (103)

Never having known the love of a father has forced me into love so engulfing and passionate that there is no margin of choice. (177)

At this point I had invested about twelve hours in doing research—skimming, reading, taking notes. I decided to move on to the next phase: organizing this material and relating it to "Reunion."

Shaping

Simply by selecting some observations rather than others, I was already in a sense organizing my materials. But I wasn't quite sure why I was attracted to these materials, and so I spent some time reading over my notes and looking for links and patterns. For each note, I tried to think of some words or phrases that would characterize the material. The following topics seemed the most obvious:

1. Fiction as "crypto-autobiography"
2. The need for the father's love
3. Alcoholism
4. The father's smells
5. The father's coldness
6. The father's love
7. The father's failure
8. Foreign languages (and name-dropping)

Next, I went through the materials again and numbered them according to the list above, thus allowing me to group together all of the materials that dealt, for instance, with the relationship of Cheever's fiction to his life.

At this point, before I could tell how to arrange my organized materials, I needed a main idea: I couldn't tell how to order my materials if I didn't know what I was trying to accomplish. In general, knowing that I wanted to do a biographical project, I knew that I was trying to determine how our understanding of Cheever's life enlarges or affects our understanding of his story. In Cheever's case, such an approach seems especially promising, given his own acknowledgment of the intimate relationship between his life and art. But how would I characterize that relationship? Before I launch into that speculation, I encourage you to take a few moments to see where you would go with this biographical information. What would your main idea be?

One striking finding is that Cheever and the father in "Reunion" resemble each other: Each is an alcoholic father afraid that he is neglecting or hurting his children. Cheever struggles not to drink before noon and then, losing that battle, struggles not to get out of control. The father in the story also seems to be fixated on his drinking, forgetting—apparently—about feeding Charlie lunch. After only one drink with Charlie, he orders "Bibson Geefeater," suggesting perhaps that he has already been drinking beforehand. The father in the story also seems to be like Cheever in his desire to show off his knowledge of foreign languages, and the father also does a bit of name-dropping. Although Cheever and his wife never divorced, they seem to have lived most of their lives on the edge of that gulf. Seeing Cheever in the father, seeing Cheever's awareness of his own shortcomings reflected in the father, I tend to have more sympathy for the father.

But there are also significant ways in which the young boy, Charlie, is like Cheever. Cheever felt distanced from his father, even as he longed for his love. He felt his father to be mysteriously cold—"the greatest and most bitter mystery in my life." Even Cheever's sensitivity to the way his father smelled, recorded in his journal, is a trait we see in Charlie. Cheever did not have a secretary, but his father did, at least until he lost his job. We know that Cheever felt his father neglected him, just as Charlie's father, who has not seen him in three years, is "a stranger." In fact, Cheever believed his father wanted him aborted.

But so what if Charlie's father is like Cheever's father, and like Cheever? And Charlie is also like Cheever and perhaps like Cheever's son? What do these parallels explain? Well, what *needs* to be explained? What do you find most remarkable or puzzling about the story? For me, two things seem obviously strange:

1. Charlie says his father will be "my future and my doom." Why will his father be his doom? What leads him to say "that when I was grown I would be something like him"?

2. Charlie provides a portrait of his father that is at first perhaps a bit amusing but is ultimately grotesque. In the end Charlie's father seems to be a kind of monster, obsessed with getting "a rise" out of the newsstand clerk while the son he hasn't seen in three years is leaving. Why does Charlie, after telling us how "terribly happy" he was to see his father, reveal nothing of his feelings? We can guess how Charlie felt, but we do not know. Why the absence of feeling—at least in the telling (which may not be truthful)?

Does Cheever's relationship to the two characters offer any sort of explanation to both questions? I think so, and that idea becomes my tentative thesis:

> Cheever resented his father's alcoholism and inattention and at the same time longed for his love; he desired to turn away from his father, putting the pain of his neglect behind him, and at the same time he wanted to turn toward his father, to bridge their distance.

This love/hate conflict is intensified by Cheever's awareness that he is in certain crucial ways like his father. In "Reunion" Charlie does not directly express his disgust and rage at his father because his position is essentially the same as Cheever's: In hating his father, Charlie (like Cheever) is closing off the possibility of resolution; in hating his father, Charlie (like Cheever) is hating himself.

This thesis, as is usually the case, suggests an organization for the essay:

1. Cheever's fiction meaningfully echoes his life: thesis
2. Charlie's father and Cheever's father
3. Charlie and Cheever
4. Charlie's father and Cheever himself
5. Conclusion

Drafting

You might want to sketch out your own draft of an essay based on the plan above before you read the one that follows.

John Cheever's "Reunion" as "Crypto-Autobiography"

The intro sets up the problem: Why is Charlie's father unsympathetically portrayed?	In John Cheever's "Reunion," the portrait of Charlie's father seems in the final analysis harsh and unforgiving. Not having seen his son in three years, the father proceeds at their meeting to drink himself into an abusive, obsessive state. He is never overtly mean to Charlie to be sure, but he is also far from attentive. Before the meeting, he did not respond personally to his son's letter asking about the lunch, letting his secretary arrange it instead; and throughout the visit, he seems intent only on getting drinks and exerting his authority over waiters, showing little or no interest in the well-being of his son. As Charlie leaves, his father is unable even to say goodbye appropriately because he is so intent on getting "a rise" out of the newspaper clerk.
Yet Charlie's opinion is not explicitly presented.	And yet, despite his father's distressing behavior, Charlie does not directly express his feelings about the day's events. In the first paragraph he tells us that he was "terribly happy" to see his father, that he even wished they could be photographed together, but at the same time he says he immediately knew, the moment he saw his father, that he was "my future and my doom." Even

with this emotional load, Charlie appears simply to report what happened without betraying his own reaction. But much is left out, leaving the reader to guess what Charlie is feeling, how this event has affected him, why this was the "last time I saw my father." Was he so outraged, hurt, saddened, confused, embarrassed, or something else that he determined never to see him again? Or did his father die soon afterward? The story is so brief that it is difficult to speculate with any confidence on Charlie's motivations, or even on his accuracy, yet it is so vividly told that it is difficult not to speculate.

> Thesis is
> introduced here.

Perhaps this distancing is precisely what Cheever wanted: to tell a story about a father and a son, presenting deeply moving events without really exposing what they mean. To understand Cheever's purpose, and thereby understand his story better, we need to look at Cheever's own experience of father/son relationships. The justification for relating life to fiction is particularly strong in Cheever's case since the same incident oftentimes is recounted in his letters and journals and then

> Cheever's life
> connects to the
> story.

employed in his fiction. Even when Cheever was supposedly reporting a real event, his "interest in telling a good story was greater than his interest in what we might consider the facts," as his son Benjamin put it (20). As Benjamin wrote, "The connection between his life and his work was intimate," and Cheever was even "fond of saying that fiction was 'crypto-autobiography'" (21). In fact, there are obvious autobiographical elements in "Reunion," and decoding them does shed some light on the story.

> Cheever's father
> and Charlie's
> father.

First, we should note that Cheever was profoundly troubled by his relationship to his father: Late in life he called his father "the greatest and the most bitter mystery in my life," and he revealed that the problem of learning to love a father "appears in all the books and stories" (qtd. Susan Cheever 209–210). We do not need to know much about Cheever's childhood to imagine why he kept trying to sort it out. Not only did Cheever's mother tell him he was a mistake ("If I hadn't drunk two Manhattans one afternoon, you never would have been conceived"), but also, as Scott Donaldson's biography says, "his father wanted him aborted, even inviting the abortionist to dinner, an event that appears in both *The Wapshot Chronicle* and *Falconer*" (19). Charlie's father is in some crucial aspects like Cheever's father: alcoholic, insecure, sarcastic, self-centered. Unlike Charlie's father, Cheever's father was not divorced, but there were tremendous hostilities between his parents, leading to drunken infidelities, threatened suicides, and violent arguments—which formed much of the substance of Cheever's fiction.

Charlie and Cheever.

If Charlie's father is like Cheever's father, Charlie is also a reflection of Cheever. Charlie, like Cheever, wants to love his father, but he finds a man who is apparently uninterested in him and careening out of control. In his hunger for love, Charlie tries to connect with his father on some more primitive level, smelling his father "the way my mother sniffs a rose" and finding "a rich compound of whiskey, after-shave lotion, shoe polish, woollens, and the rankness of a mature male." Cheever was also extraordinarily moved by smells, telling his publisher he was "a very olfactory fellow" and that he should not remove any of the smells in his book (Donaldson 150).

Cheever and his father.

But Cheever does not seem to express his rage and disappointment very directly through Charlie. Surely part of the obstruction is Cheever's realization that he is in many ways like his father, Frederick Cheever, a shoe salesman who became unemployed and bitter in the mid-1920s. John Cheever was not technically out of work, but he did not have a regular job, and he struggled for much of his life to make ends meet. Most obviously, like his father—like Charlie's father—Cheever could not control his drinking. In an entry from the early journals (late forties and fifties), Cheever writes, "Year after year I read in here [in his journal] that I am drinking too much, and there can be no doubt of the fact that this is progressive" (103). Although Cheever finds everything about his drinking "disgusting," still "each noon I reach for the whiskey bottle." Cheever was evidently aware of the effect of such behavior on a son, as Cheever's own son, Benjamin, writes (in *The Letters of John Cheever*), "He used to say that I must wish I had a father who didn't drink so much, and I'd always say no" (18).

Cheever and Charlie's father.

In fact, Charlie's father's habit of baiting waiters in foreign tongues may have been modeled on Cheever's own behavior, as a passage from Susan Cheever's biography of her father reveals. After commenting on how Cheever, even though "he spoke minimal French," began "dropping French words into his conversation," she goes on to say, "With Italian, he was even worse," using it "at every opportunity," especially in restaurants (113).

Summary Thus, Charlie's statement that his father was "my future and my doom" resonates on several levels. Cheever, the model for Charlie, had become "something like" his father. And Cheever's father was "something like" Charlie's father, just as Charlie would become "something like" Cheever himself. For Charlie to hate his father would involve hating himself, his own future self; yet he could hardly approve affectionately of his father. But more than that: For Charlie to express his hatred toward his father, Cheever would have to acknowledge his own hatred for his father, which would likewise involve a self-destructive disgust. Cheever could not find a way to love his father, but he could not find a way to hate him either. And so he was driven to write about him endlessly, searching for a way to describe the relationship and resolve it.

Works Cited

Cheever, John. *The Brigadier and the Golf Widow.* New York: Harper, 1964. Print.

——. *The Journals of John Cheever.* Ed. Robert Gottlieb. New York: Knopf, 1991. Print.

——. *The Letters of John Cheever.* Ed. Benjamin Cheever. New York: Simon, 1988. Print.

Cheever, Susan. *Home before Dark.* Boston: Houghton, 1984. Print.

Donaldson, Scott. *John Cheever.* New York: Random, 1988. Print.

A NEW HISTORICAL ESSAY

Preparing to Write

Where could I look for some clues to the ideology shaping Cheever's story? I decided that one place to look, thinking of "Reunion" as part of a cultural system, would be *The New Yorker* magazine in which the story was first published. Knowing the story came out in 1962, I found it in the October 27 issue; the whole story appears on page 45.

I studied the magazine, trying to absorb the culture of 1962, the book and movie reviews, the current events, the articles, the advertisements. I did not imagine one issue of one magazine could contain an entire culture, but I did think one issue might tell me about the world *The New Yorker* presented to its readers. I tried to imagine myself as an anthropologist studying a foreign and unknown culture—in this case, the culture of *The New Yorker's* writers, advertisers, and readers. I was struck very quickly by two messages in the magazine, which seemed to appear relentlessly in various ways. Both messages arguably still permeate our culture, but they seemed especially prominent in this "foreign" setting. Perhaps I was simply paying close attention to what I ordinarily try to ignore.

Put bluntly, I found the magazine telling its readers again and again to consume—to purchase, to view, to possess, to ingest—and to display the quality of their discerning consumption. Most insistently, it seemed that readers were being told to consume superior alcoholic beverages: directly in some 36 ads and indirectly in ads for other products. An ad for Japan Airlines pictured a happy couple in the act of taking drinks from an attentive hostess, for instance; another for Caron perfumes depicted a beautiful woman clinking a brandy glass with her lover. Products that had nothing to do with drinking alcohol featured that activity.

I was also struck by the invitations to wear superior clothing, urging readers to display their wealth and excellent taste. Such exhibition was motivated, sometimes blatantly, sometimes subtly, by the promise of acceptance and affection. These messages—consume and display—appeared most obviously in the advertisements, but they could also be discerned in the articles and even the cartoons. They often appeared together.

Shaping

If we recognize that Cheever's story appears in a context saturated with recurrent encouragements to drink (for status and success) and to display one's status and success, what difference does it make? How does this context affect our reading of the story? How does the story affect our reading of the context, for that matter? One effect might be to reconsider our assessment of Charlie's father's drinking. In new historicist fashion, stressing ideology over individuals, I would argue that Charlie's father is not an autonomous agent, fully responsible for his failures. Rather, Charlie's father is to some degree a product of a value system he has learned too well. He has simply learned to seek affection and status in alcohol. His efforts to display his sophistication in languages and to demonstrate his dominance over the various waiters are also the effect of a powerful (but pitiful) desire for status.

This view of the father's fundamental insecurity and loneliness, which he attempts to erase by drinking and asserting himself, reminds me of passages in Cheever's journal. For instance, writing about his inability to control his drinking, Cheever says: "I could very easily destroy myself" (103). And Charlie's father, like Cheever, is destroying himself slowly. Cheever and his character are being driven by emotional pain and insecurity to seek relief in the way that their culture has prescribed—asserting their status, consuming alcohol.

We do not know in "Reunion" why Charlie's father and mother were divorced, and we might want to assume that Charlie has not seen his father for three years because his father is uncaring. Cheever's journal, however, may help us to consider other possibilities consistent with the facts of the story—namely that Charlie's mother may have prevented his father from seeing him. Perhaps she considered his father so worthless or repulsive that she did not want Charlie to see him again. Perhaps Charlie's father feels so guilty that he considers himself unworthy of his son's attention.

Finally, I should mention one more journal entry in which Cheever records the visit of a friend: "in my anxiety to communicate, to feel the most in warmth and intimacy, I drink too much, which can be two drinks these days" (103). The advertisements and cartoons link intimacy and affection to alcohol, and Cheever does the same thing here. Again, Charlie's father's behavior can be reconsidered in this light.

At this point, it seems clear that I have way too much material for a brief essay—which means that I'm in good shape. But don't I need to dig further, examining all *The New Yorker* issues of 1962, and *Good Housekeeping* and *Reader's Digest* also, and everything else that can be recovered? Although it's always nice to know as much as you can, my claim is simply that a certain community (the readers of *The New Yorker*) at a certain slice of time (1962) were being exposed to a certain set of messages that illuminate Cheever's story. Rather than having to dig up a whole city, the new historicist can construct a tentative system of meaning from the close analysis of selected artifacts. The point is not that one document influenced another, but rather that at this moment within this community all documents participated in certain common assumptions.

So, looking over my notes, freewriting and brainstorming, I come back to my focus on Charlie's father as a reflection of a system of meaning. I try organizing my material in the following way:

The emotional view: Charlie's father as a deviant jerk

Thesis: The analytical view—Charlie's father as a product of his time

Advertisements and cartoons suggest alcohol confers status and affection: manliness

Cheever and Charlie's father: drowning self and pain in drink

Drafting

You might wish to draft an essay yourself at this point, then compare your application of the materials to mine.

> The opening orients the reader to the story and the issue: the father's lack of affection.

How to Make an Alcoholic Drink: Cheever's "Reunion" in Its Context

In John Cheever's "Reunion," Charlie's father appears to be the worst sort of parent. After three years of separation (following a divorce), the father doesn't respond

to his son's letter but rather has his secretary arrange
their meeting. He greets his son in a strange way, with no
apparent affection:

> "Hi Charlie," he said. "Hi, boy. I'd like to take
> you up to my club, but it's in the Sixties, and if
> you have to catch an early train I guess we'd bet-
> ter get something to eat around here."

Although he puts his arm around Charlie, his
subsequent behavior seems to confirm his callous self-
absorption, as he apparently forgets about lunch and thinks
only of drinking and insulting waiters. The visit ends with
Charlie saying good-bye, for the last time, to a father who
seems interested only in harassing a newsstand clerk.

This paragraph
introduces a pos-
sible explanation:
the father's values
are shaped by his
culture.

But before we entirely dismiss Charlie's father, we
might consider his motivation. What does he think he is
doing? Where has he learned such behavior? Certainly
Charlie is a victim of his father's indulgent inattention; but
is Charlie's father also a victim in any way? In *The New
Yorker* magazine in which "Reunion" first appeared, we find
a set of directives that helps to explain the behavior of
Charlie's father, which may well be motivated not by any
sort of disregard or animosity toward Charlie, but rather
by the desire for status and affection. This desire is fueled
by a system of values reflected in and even shaped by
The New Yorker.

Evidence: Ads
for alcoholic
beverages focus
on status.

Again and again advertisements in the October 26
issue of 1962 convey to the readers the paramount importance of status, rank, superiority. One of the most blatant
of these ads asks the question "Are you a status seeker?"
If you like "Italian restaurants," the ad continues, "foreign
cars," "antique furniture," and finally "Lord Calvert" whiskey, then you apparently are a status seeker (as you should
be, the ad implies). The association of alcoholic beverages with nobility, and therefore "status," is a recurrent
theme. Grand Marnier is "The Emperor of Liqueurs," and
another scotch is named "House of Lords." Old Hickory
is drunk by "all the nicest people," and several couples
in formal evening attire are depicted. The drink identifies
you as a superior being, among "the nicest people," which
does not in this context seem to mean the most polite or
philanthropic.

Other ads and
status.

Other ads for nonalcoholic products also reinforce
this desire for status. One ad pictures an aristocratic man,
sneering slightly, in an overcoat, standing behind a large,

exotic-looking dog, with the caption "Which has the pedigree?" Of course, it isn't the dog, or the man; it's the coat. Buying this coat, the ad implies, gives you a pedigree you can wear. This anxiety about the status of one's clothing, or how one's clothing expresses one's status, is also employed by advertisements for alcoholic drinks. One ad depicts a man from the neck down, dressed in a tuxedo, carrying a fur coat with a large label clearly exposed. The caption says, "When a label counts, it's Imported O.F.C.," and we can easily see that the label in the fur coat is the same as the label on the bottle of whiskey to the right of the text.

> Clothing and status.

When does a label count? When one is concerned about the display of status and superiority, a concern that this and many other ads serve to amplify and exploit. A tuxedo and a fur coat represent the pinnacle of fashion, and we can imagine that the physically fit man, draping the fur coat over his arm, is waiting for his companion to come claim the coat. The man's head is not pictured because with the right label, his appearance doesn't really matter—and the reader can imagine his own head on that body. Tellingly, the ad says almost nothing about how the whiskey tastes ("Rich. Light.") but stresses rather that it is "In immaculate good taste." This designer whiskey confers status, prestige, and even companionship; who cares what it tastes like?

> Here the focus on labels is applied to clothing and whiskey.

This anxiety about one's status and the implication that drinking alcoholic beverages will elevate it, which pervade the advertisements and even the cartoons in *The New Yorker*, arguably shape the character of Charlie's father, and Cheever as well. Charlie's father has his secretary make the arrangements for meeting his son in order to establish that he has a secretary. He wants his son to realize that he has status—because he has absorbed the cultural lesson that his self-worth depends on it. He mentions "my club" for the same reason, I would argue: to convey that he has a club, even though it is conveniently too distant to be used. Likewise, his display of foreign languages and his manic rudeness toward the various waiters are pitiful efforts to impress his son with his sophistication and power. At the end, as he struggles to "get a rise" out of the newsstand clerk, he is trying desperately to show his son how clever and superior he is. That is why he says "just wait a second, sonny": He is putting on this performance for his son, not for his own amusement. His interest in his son and his excitement are subtly suggested by

> The claim: Charlie's father is motivated by anxiety, created in part by these cultural values.

his arrival "at twelve o'clock sharp." He's eager to see his son; he simply does not know how to impress his son, and his response is an effort to establish his status.

> Even his alcoholism is related.

Even Charlie's father's desperate pursuit of alcohol reflects his anxiety about his status. Not only can we speculate that his nervousness drives him to medicate himself with liquid depressants; we can also see how his pursuit of drinks reflects his awareness of the association, created in advertisements and other cultural messages, between alcoholic consumption and affection. Charlie's father is seeking to create a bond with Charlie in a way that advertisements even today continue to promote. Charlie's father wants to create an "it-doesn't-get-any-better-than-this" moment; when the second waiter refuses to serve Charlie, his father immediately leaves because he wants more than a drink for himself; he hopes the drinks will lead to affection and bonding.

> Conclusion: these values are destructive

But he is really self-destructive, as Cheever makes clear. Charlie's father does not establish his status, and his quest for drinks does not create a bond. Instead, the day's events extinguish the contact between father and son, just as the father's drinking represents a slow self-extinction. Cheever has exposed the lie in the advertisements surrounding his story.

PRACTICING HISTORICAL CRITICISM

Here are four suggestions to get you started.

1. If you were going to begin today to write a screenplay, a short story, a novel, a poem, or a play, what would it be about? Sketch out a rough draft or outline, or write the work if possible. Then consider how biographical, historical, or new historical criticism might relate to your work.

2. Choose another magazine from 1962 (*Good Housekeeping, Life, Reader's Digest*, the *Atlantic*, for instance) and compare its system of values to *The New Yorker*'s, as I've described it. How does this expanded vision of 1962 affect your view of "Reunion"? What if "Reunion" had appeared in *Good Housekeeping*, for instance?

3. On the next two pages are two cartoons from the same *The New Yorker* issue containing "Reunion." Discuss the system of values they imply. How might they be related to "Reunion"?

"You're going to get a great summation! He's smashed!"

4. Select two or three movies from the same year, and an issue of *Time* or *Newsweek* or a similar magazine from the same year. What connections can you make? How do the movies illuminate their time and/or each other?

USEFUL TERMS FOR HISTORICAL, CULTURAL, AND POSTCOLONIAL CRITICISM

Author: Perhaps the most important thing to gain from this chapter is an awareness of the radically different ways an author is viewed by different critical approaches. Biographical criticism assumes that it matters who wrote something, and under what conditions it was written. Studying the life of a writer is intrinsically interesting and useful—probably anyone's life holds instructive insights; but the purpose of literary biography, ultimately, is to shed some light on an author's work. The risks of biographical criticism are thus fairly transparent, but it is nonetheless important to keep them in mind. First, there's the problem of recovering

"He's got this gimmick, see. He's completely honest."

the author's life and times. For some writers, biographical information is
sparse or suspect: for J. D. Salinger (fiercely reclusive) or Homer (perhaps
not even a single person), we'd like to know a whole lot more. For other
writers, there is a wealth of information, sometimes contradictory and
confusing: To understand Samuel Johnson, for instance, you'd need to
study Boswell's magnificent and massive *Life of Johnson* (five volumes in
the standard edition), as well as at least a dozen other biographies and
memoirs, not to mention the life and works of those around Johnson
(not to mention Boswell's drafts and notebooks, which have some surprising differences with what he published), and so on.

Second, once we think we have biographical information, there's
the problem of how to use it to illuminate creative work. We know
Hemingway was wounded in World War I, and "A Very Short Story"
features a soldier who was wounded, so can we conclude that the
soldier is Hemingway? No, we can't. What if the soldier in the story is
recovering in the same town in which Hemingway recovered, and is
involved with a nurse who sounds a bit like a nurse Hemingway was

involved with? We would still diminish the literary work, rather than enhance it, if we assume that Hemingway's story is simply covert autobiography. By insisting on a distinction between the author and his or her creations, we're in a better position to appreciate the literary work and the artistic choices the author made in crafting it. At the same time, even as we acknowledge the difficulties and risk of recovering an author's life, we can certainly learn much that adds interest and insight to the literary work. We shouldn't naïvely draw a one-to-one parallel between Hemingway and the wounded soldier, but we also shouldn't pretend that literary biography doesn't enrich our understanding of and interest in a work, and vice versa.

A larger historical perspective sees the work of an author within the context of his or her time and place. Hemingway and his work can be illuminated by a better understanding of World War I, its battles, its hospitals and medical practices, and the values and ideas at work in Hemingway's culture. From a new historical perspective, the author is indeed so much a function of the time and place he or she inhabits that the author as individual tends to dissolve. From this viewpoint, the language and the patterns of thinking available to an author, at a particular time and place, determine what he or she will say—so thoroughly that it is possible to speak (as Roland Barthes has) of "the death of the author." It's more reasonable, within new historical assumptions at least, to think about an "author" as a part of a system of discourse (language, logic, values, assumptions, etc.), rather than as an individual entity or freestanding agent.

Autobiography: A writer's story of his or her own life—an autobiography—offers (potentially) an especially interesting version of what happened. But it's important to remember that the use of autobiographical material in literary study is subject to the same scrutiny as the use of biographical material. Sometimes we forget what happened, or we only thought we understood what happened, or we decide to place what happened in a certain light, or we may just flat-out lie. Interestingly, autobiographies are rather rare prior to the seventeenth century, when there was a rapid expansion of interest in self-analysis and introspection.

Bourgeoisie: The upper class, the powerful, the privileged. Karl Marx (with Friedrich Engels) uses this term in *The Communist Manifesto* (1848).

Confessional: In some literary works, the writer seems to express his or her strong emotional feelings directly, in his or her own voice and person. We call such works "confessional" because they appear to be about the writer's life, and they often explore uncomfortable, ordinarily private issues (as in a "confession"). The speaker in a poem and the creator of that poem may seem to be united. For some critics, such apparent self-exposure is daring and exhilarating; for others, the work and the life disturbingly collapse into one another, blurring the critic's function. Is the critic judging the writer's life or work? Are we engaging in artistic or aesthetic assessment or psychological analysis? On the other hand, one might argue that confessional works simply expose the personal character that is inevitable in all expressions, insisting that we unite the person and the work, violating the usual critical assumption that the speaker and the author are distinct.

Cultural Materialism: This term is often used for the British counterpart to New Historicism, which is generally more political and activist.

Culture: Biographical and historical approaches to literary works assume that it is possible to make some meaningful generalizations, not only about an individual but about the society around him or her. "Culture" refers to the whole of a particular society—the beliefs, habits, facts, laws, values, and more that we may use to distinguish one group of people from another. It certainly makes sense to distinguish one culture from another: Early seventeenth-century English culture is different from early twenty-first-century English culture; Islamic culture is different from Jewish culture. To understand better a literary work written in an Islamic culture, one should seek a better understanding of that culture. And yet, every individual within a culture does not, of course, embrace every aspect of that culture. Any attempt to describe anything so complicated as a "culture" is bound to be partial—a construct of imagination, to some degree.

Despite such difficulties, the study of literature and culture together is powerfully appealing, as we strive to see how literature and culture shape and influence each other.

Discourse: Literary critics who employ biographical and historical materials have found "discourse" to be a particularly useful term because it allows them to make useful connections between the writer and the work. If one individual is speaking to another one who can be reasonably expected to understand the speaker, then they share, to some degree, a discourse. They are participants in a conversation, which means that they share (for starters) a language. "Discourse" refers to more than just language, including the assumptions and protocols shared by a community. So, it's possible for critics to talk about "the discourse of nineteenth-century biology," or "the discourse of the eighteenth-century penal system," or "the discourse of late twentieth-century capitalism." Particular writers and their works can then be made sense of within these discourses.

Episteme: Michel Foucault's term for the ideas that control a particular historical period. Rather than focus on history as a series of causes and effects, Foucault tries to see particular moments as complex systems of meaning.

Implied author: This term distinguishes usefully between the real-life person who writes (who may be sitting in his pajamas, worried about his mortgage, with children yelling in the background, with a slight hangover and a sore throat) and the written construction of that person (which might project calm, confidence, energy). This term can be compared to "the implied reader"—an idea distinguishing the reader that the author seems to have imagined from the real-life person who is experiencing the text. The implied reader for some eighteenth-century works, for instance, might well be someone who has some familiarity with the history of armed conflict between France and England, and who has a working knowledge of Latin. A real reader, sitting in his or her twenty-first-century living room, might be very different from this implied reader. By the same token, the real author might be very different from the implied author, as he or she is reflected in the text.

Influence: Historical critics are often interested in seeing how some prior work (or body of works) has affected another work (or body of works). Themes, strategies, forms, words, plot devices—anything might be picked up from a prior work and reused by an author. The idea of influence has gotten particular emphasis because of the work of Walter Jackson Bate and Harold Bloom, who drew attention to the way some writers confront "the burden of the past" (Bate) or "the anxiety of influence" (Bloom). Rather than following after a prior writer, accepting an influence, a writer (Bate and Bloom argued) may struggle to hide or overcome an influence, attempting to assert his or her originality.

Intention: Biographical criticism brings the problematic relationship between intention and meaning to the forefront. If the meaning of a text depends on what the author meant to say (a reasonable enough assumption, it would seem), then biographical criticism may hold powerful keys to meaning. As we become removed in time from an author, we face greater difficulties in discerning what he or she might have meant, and biographical information may offer help. Intention is, however, a controversial basis for meaning: How can we know for sure what another person meant? After Freud, how can another person know what he or she meant—there may be unconscious motivations at work. It seems problematic to assume that we can say with any confidence what an author intended. Thus, intention is an especially fruitful ground for literary argument and engagement.

Literary history: Literary history not only describes the nature of individual texts but inevitably makes some generalizations about groups of texts. If we have simply a succession of random, unrelated events, then we can't realistically be said to have "history," which connects and relates discrete events. Likewise, literary history aims to connect and relate certain works. In this endeavor, the construction of distinct literary periods is helpful.

Paradigm: This term and any number of related ones ("worldview," "episteme," "ideology") draw our attention to a complex set of assumptions at work within a particular culture at a particular time. A solar eclipse means something very different from within the paradigm of the ancient Egyptians, on the one hand, and the paradigm of a modern astronomer, on the other hand. We may read individual literary works, if we employ historical approaches, in order to make sense of the different paradigms that people have inhabited. At any one moment, in any one place, however, it is quite likely that different people will hold conflicting and overlapping paradigms in their heads—the same person may even have access to conflicting paradigms. A paradigm, in other words, might be thought of as a set of instructions for making meaning. As more people accept this way of making sense, the paradigm grows in importance.

Period: For convenience, we divide history of all sorts, including literary history, into segments or periods. Although these divisions are based on evidence, they are ultimately arbitrary. There are useful generalizations about medieval literature, and about how Renaissance literature differs from medieval literature; but like all generalizations, they're subject to exceptions and challenges. The study of eighteenth-century literature has traditionally been distinct from the study of nineteenth-century literature, but it would be unreasonable to think that writers uniformly adjusted their ideas and styles and goals as the calendar shifted. The idea of a period, in other words, is a useful convenience (most useful, perhaps, as you begin to see the limitations of any particular set of generalizations).

Proletariat: The working classes, in Marx and Engel's terminology.

Subaltern: The one below, the other, the dispossessed, the oppressed. These are some of the meanings of this word, which was invented by the Marxist critic Antonio Gramsci.

Tradition: Just as we divide literary history into distinct periods, we also connect literary works across time with the idea of a "tradition." The most visible sort of tradition is probably that of genre: Milton's *Paradise Lost* can hardly be understood without some sense of the epic tradition, for example. Shakespeare's sonnets are part of a tradition of sonnets. The idea of tradition highlights the limits of formal analysis in New Criticism (and the power of biographical and historical approaches): The text itself is rarely meant to stand by itself. Writers inevitably position their works in one or more traditions of literary effort.

✔ Checklist for Historical Criticism

1. Research the author's life and relate that information to the work. (But do not assume that any character in the work simply stands for the author.)

2. Research the author's time (political history, intellectual history, economic history, etc.) and relate that information to the work.

3. Research the systems of meaning available to the author and relate those systems to the work.

Notes

1. From "The Life of Roscommon," in Johnson's *Lives of the Poets*, ed. Roger Lonsdale (Oxford: OUP, 2006), p. 20.

2. I am following the version of Milton's poem presented in Thomas Warton, *Poems upon Several Occasions, English, Italian, and Latin, with Translations, by John Milton*. London: Dodsley, 1791. In a note (p. 359), Warton says that he has introduced quotation marks (which he calls "turned commas") enclosing the question and the answer in the poem, but he acknowledges that there is no "authority" for doing so, and I have therefore removed Warton's quotation marks.

Works Cited

Althusser, Louis. "Ideology and Ideological State Apparatuses Notes Toward an Investigation." In *Lenin and Philosophy and Other Essays*. Trans. By Ben Brewster. New York: Monthly Review Press, 1971. 85–126. Print.

Bakhtin, M. M. *The Dialogic Imagination: Four Essays*. Ed. Michael Holquist. Trans. Caryl Emerson and Michael Holquist. Austin: U of Texas P, 1981. Print.

Bannet, Eve Tavor. *Structuralism and the Logic of Dissent: Barthes, Derrida, Foucault, Lacan*. Urbana: U of Illinois P, 1989. Print.

Barthes, Roland. "The Death of the Author." In *Image / Music / Text*. Trans. Stephen Heath. New York: Hill and Wang, 1977. 142–7. Print.

Bate, Walter Jackson. *The Burden of the Past*. Cambridge, MA: Harvard UP, 1970. Print.

Bérubé, Michael. "What's the Matter with Cultural Studies?" *Chronicle Review* (*Chronicle of Higher Education*), 14 September, 2009: B6–7. http://chronicle. com/article/Whats-the-Matter-With/ 48334/. Web.

Birch, Dinah, and Katy Hooper, eds. "Milton." In *The Concise Oxford Companion to English Literature*. Oxford: OUP, 2012. Page 468. Print.
Bloom, Harold. *The Anxiety of Influence*. Oxford: Oxford UP, 1973. Print.
Cheever, John. *The Brigadier and the Golf Widow*. New York: Harper, 1964. Print.
———. *The Journals of John Cheever*. Ed. Robert Gottlieb. New York: Knopf, 1991. Print.
———. *The Letters of John Cheever*. Ed. Benjamin Cheever. New York: Simon, 1988. Print.
Cheever, Susan. *Home before Dark*. Boston: Houghton, 1984. Print.
Donaldson, Scott. *John Cheever*. New York: Random, 1988. Print.
Fish, Stanley. "Interpreting the *Variorum*." *Critical Inquiry*. 1980; 2: 465–486. Print.
Foucault, Michel. *Discipline and Punish: The Birth of the Prison*. Trans. Alan Sheridan. New York: Pantheon, 1977. Print.
——. *The History of Sexuality*. Trans. R. Hurley. Vol. 1. New York: Pantheon, 1978. Print.
Griffith, Kelley, Jr. *Writing Essays about Literature*. San Diego: Harcourt, 1986. Print.
Hebdige, Dick. *Subculture: The Meaning of Style*. London: Routledge, 1979. Print.
Howard, Jean. "The New Historicism in Renaissance Studies." *ELR*. Winter 1986; 16: 13–43. Print.
Spivak, Gayatri Chakravorty. "Can the Subaltern Speak?" In *Marxism and the Interpretation of Culture*. Eds. Cary Nelson and Lawrence Grossberg. Urbana, IL: U of Illinois P, 1988. 271–313. Print.
Tillyard, E. M. W. *The Elizabethan World Picture*. New York: MacMillan, 1944. Print.
Waldeland, Lynne. *John Cheever*. Boston: Twayne, 1979. Print.
White, Hayden. *Tropics of Discourse: Essays in Cultural Criticism*. Baltimore: Johns Hopkins UP, 1978. Print.
Woodhouse, A. S. P. "The Historical Criticism of Milton." *PMLA*. 1951; 66 (1951): 1033-10–44.

Recommended Further Reading

Auerbach, Erich. *Mimesis: The Representation of Reality in Western Literature*. Princeton, NJ: Princeton UP, 1953. Print. A classic study of the rhetorical devices texts use in order to construct "reality."
Cadzow, Hunter. "New Historicism." *The Johns Hopkins Guide to Literary Theory and Criticism*. Ed. Michael Groden and Martin Kreiswirth. Baltimore: Johns Hopkins UP, 1994. 534–540. Print. A clear, brief, and reliable overview.
Gallagher, Catherine, and Stephen Greenblatt. *Practicing New Historicism*. Chicago: U of Chicago P, 2001. Print. A spellbinding discussion of the great variety of literary criticism informed by historical research.
Greenblatt, Stephen. "The Politics of Culture." *Falling Into Theory: Conflicting Views on Reading Literature*. Ed. David Richter. Boston: St. Martin's, 1994. 288–290. An introductory essay by the scholar usually credited with popularizing the term "new historicism."
Hamilton, Paul. *Historicism: The New Critical Idiom*. 2nd ed. New York: Routledge, 2003. Print. A sophisticated, valuable introduction, relating "historicism" (including new historicism) to modernist, postmodernist, feminist, and postcolonial approaches.

Harrison, Nicholas. *Postcolonial Criticism: History, Theory and the Work of Fiction.* Cambridge: Polity, 2003. Print. Major works (Conrad's *Heart of Darkness*, Camus' *The Outsider*, for example) are used to provide an illustrated introduction to post-colonial studies, while at the same time undermining some established ideas. Challenging, but accessible to students with some critical grounding.

Montrose, Louis. "Of Gentlemen and Shepherds: The Politics of Elizabethan Pastoral Form." *ELH* 50 (1983): 415–459. An influential and insightful essay, widely considered to be a classic and theoretically transparent study in New Historicism.

Patterson, Annabel. "Historical Scholarship." *An Introduction to Scholarship in Modern Languages and Literatures.* Ed. Joseph Gibaldi. 2nd ed. New York: MLA, 1992. 183–200. Print. An excellent survey in a standard reference work.

Thomas, Brook. "The Historical Necessity for—and Difficulties with—New Historical Analysis in Introductory Literature Courses." *College English.* 1987; 49: 509–522. Print. A useful introduction to the ideas of New Historicism and a thoughtful consideration of their implications for teaching.

Veeser, H. Aram, ed. *The New Historicism.* New York: Routledge, 1989. Print. A collection of influential essays theorizing, applying, exploring new historicism.

Young, Robert J. C. *Postcolonialism: A Very Short Introduction.* Oxford: Oxford UP, 2003. Print. A spirited introduction that uses a series of specific situations (a montage) to explain postcolonialism. Young vividly describes, for instance, what it would be like to be a refugee and to be African and Caribbean activists who migrated to Harlem in 1924—that is, he reveals from the bottom up what it would be like to have a postcolonialist stance.

Historical Research

- For detailed surveys of literary history—the *Oxford English Literary History*, edited by Jonathan Bate (13 volumes), or (more portably) F. E. Halliday, *A Concise History of England, from Stonehenge to the Atomic Age* and *Robert Adams, The Land and Literature of England.* A delightful miniview of American literature appears in the first chapter of Judy Jones's *An Incomplete Education.* For a detailed American history, see *The Cambridge History of American Literature*, edited by Sacvan Bercovitch. *A Short History of American Literature* is also available from Cambridge UP, edited by W. P. Trent et al.

New Historical Research

Some suggestions for places to look for materials:

- Popular or noncanonical literature—children's stories, adolescent fiction, romances, adventure stories, and so forth.
- Primary materials for other disciplines—music theory, psychology, criminology, architecture, and so forth.
- Newspapers and magazines—these can offer you descriptions of events and leads to other texts.
- Artifacts from the period—think like an archeologist trying to make sense of the physical remains of a particular time. For instance, a delicate and ornate snuffbox from the eighteenth century may illuminate the sort of cultural environment in which, say, Mozart's delicate and ornate music could be written.

Biographical Research

- For convenient access to essential facts about the life of a major figure—*Encyclopedia Britannica* or another major encyclopedia. As a rule, however, you don't want to cite general encyclopedias in your essay; just use them to get started.
- For more details—the *Dictionary of National Biography* (British), the *Dictionary of American Biography*, or the *Dictionary of Literary Biography*.
- For information on contemporary authors—*Contemporary Authors*.
- Also useful—*Biography Index, Oxford Companion to English Literature, Oxford Companion to American Literature*, and the other Oxford Companions. An especially appealing resource is *The Atlantic Brief Lives*, which offers authoritative scholars' brief and often brilliant biographies of writers and other artists.
- For book-length biographies—check the catalog in your library. Check the publication date of the biography; new facts and resources are coming to light all the time, although a newer biography is not necessarily a better one. Also, book reviews can help you evaluate a particular biography. *Book Review Index* covers the most sources; *Book Review Digest* includes excerpts from the reviews.

CHAPTER 7

Minding the Work

Psychological Criticism

When a member of my family complains that he or she has bitten his tongue, bruised her finger, and so on, instead of the expected sympathy I put the question, "Why did you do that?"
—Sigmund Freud, *The Psychopathology of Everyday Life* (201)

What you'll learn in this chapter:

- To identify opportunities to use psychological principles.
- To develop ideas about texts using psychological criticism.
- To write and revise essays, step by step, about literary texts, using psychological criticism.
- To apply psychological principles in a variety of contexts.

THE PURPOSE OF PSYCHOLOGICAL CRITICISM

Psychology began in a sense when the first person, rather than just reacting to another person's behavior, wondered instead, Why did you do that? Most people would agree that modern psychology begins with Freud, not simply because he wonders so intensely, but because he offers a compelling answer: We do things, Freud asserted, really weird and silly things sometimes, for reasons that are to some degree hidden, inaccessible, beyond our direct control or awareness. These hidden motivations come from what Freud called *das Unbewusste*, which means literally "the unknown" but is usually translated into English as "the unconscious," that part or activity of one's mind that is unknown even to its possessor. Although both the term "unconscious" and the general concept predated Freud, his theories revolutionized the study of the mind.

There is, in fact, only one major form of psychotherapy that is not based in some important respect on Freudian concepts: behavior therapy. For a psychological theory, behaviorism seems strangely unconcerned with the mind. Basing their approaches on B. F. Skinner's work, who in turn drew largely on Ivan Pavlov, behaviorists view psychological problems as bad habits: The patient has learned unproductive or destructive behaviors and must unlearn them and take up others. Every other therapy, despite some vast differences, depends in crucial ways on Freud. To understand modern psychology and to practice psychological criticism, you might well start with Freud and particularly with his conception of the unconscious mind.

Obviously, you needn't stop there. Maslow's hierarchy of needs, or Erikson's theory of adult development, or any other psychological theories (including your own) may prove very illuminating. I focus here on Freud because his work is historically the starting point, because his ideas are so familiar to educated people, because his works continue to generate challenge and controversy, and because Freud's work nicely illustrates the application of psychology to literature. His theories, in fact, were based in significant ways on literary works. There's just no way to survey here the whole field of psychology. So, I encourage you to study psychology, expanding your understanding of Freud and exploring also the theories of others.

The therapeutic procedure Freud developed was designed to help those patients whose conscious lives were being troubled or even overtaken by unconscious fears or desires. It involved having the patient lie on a couch and talk freely about whatever came to mind, roaming back through childhood, dreams, fantasies, whatever, thereby allowing the patient and the analyst to gather enough data to speculate about what was going on in the hidden country of the unconscious. By slowly exposing the effects of the unconscious, peeling back layer after layer of disguised and suppressed fears and desires, Freud's "talking cure" was designed to enlarge the mental "territory" of the conscious mind. When the patient, with the analyst's help, could expose these unconscious materials, Freud believed that their power over the patient would be lessened and even dissipated.

When Freud failed to comfort his injured family members, he was not simply creating work for future therapists (unconsciously?), but he was rather assuming that an apparently irrational action like biting one's own tongue might actually have some important underlying explanation. Freud surely did not expect his family to express their unconscious motivations ("I bit my tongue because I want to tell you to drop dead, but I know I shouldn't," for instance). Rather, he hoped to unearth some evidence of how an unconscious desire was being first covered up or denied and then expressed in a disguised way.

Freud's theory of the unconscious, presented in 1901 in *The Interpretation of Dreams*, also revolutionized the study of the mind and launched modern psychology by assuming that the unconscious is inherently sexual. Even children are sexual beings, Freud pointed out, thus scandalizing many of his Victorian contemporaries. More than a few people continue to be scandalized. How this unsettling insight affected Freud's work can be seen in the story of "Little Hans," one of his most famous and remarkable cases. When Hans was brought to Freud at age five, he refused to go outside because he was hysterically terrified that a horse would bite him. Through Hans' father, Freud was able to learn that at age three-and-a-half the child's mother had tried to discourage him from touching his own genitals by saying that if he didn't stop, the doctor would come to "cut off your widdler and then what will you widdle with?" Freud deduced that Little Hans had noticed that horses had large genitalia and that his mother did not appear to have any, apparently proving that she knew what she was talking about. In the uncanny logic of Little Hans' unconscious mind, castration and horses became all jumbled up with his love for his mother, and the competition with his father for that love. Freud helped the father reassure Little Hans that his own penis was in no danger, apparently curing his irrational fear.

It is, however, incorrect to think of Freud simply as that guy who thought of everything in terms of sex. For one thing, Freud's idea of sexuality includes much more than simply the act of sex. Rather, Freud focused on the entire drive toward physical pleasure, the "pleasure principle" as he called it, which he saw as being constantly in conflict with opposing forces, or the "reality principle." This conflict is necessary for rather obvious reasons: Without it, we would be unable to function in a civilized society. We cannot simply do whatever we feel like. But our desires, when they cannot be expressed and released, must go somewhere. Hence, the need for an unconscious, a kind of storage vault for psychic energy. And in this mental hydraulic system, as Freud sees it, some of the repressed energy does leak out in various disguised ways—in dreams, slips of the tongue, jokes, creative writing. This mechanism for submerging unacceptable desires is well known today as "repression," and it is for Freud an essential activity. Mental illness, then, in which the unconscious is unable to contain satisfactorily the repressed material, becomes different only in degree, not kind, from "normal" mental health.

There's already plenty in the little bit I've discussed to make anyone uneasy: We don't know what's going on in our minds even though that activity is influencing our thinking and behavior. The mechanism whereby our fears and desires are being repressed is the same mechanism that leads to mental illness—meaning that "normal" is a relative term, since we're all unavoidably a little out of touch. The drive toward pleasure is relentlessly struggling to overpower our grip on the realities of our culture. I haven't even gotten to the Oedipus complex, which, despite its "utter centrality to Freud's work," as Terry Eagleton says (156), is nonetheless outrageous— so bizarre and disturbing that, from a Freudian perspective, there must be something to it.

Freud concisely describes this fundamental sexual phenomenon of early childhood in "The Ego and the Id" (1923). In this accessible paper he explains how the young boy invests his desire and affection in his mother, developing an "object-cathexis" for her. The baby's desire for physical contact with his mother obviously begins with the mother's breasts, but the boy will ultimately want to possess his mother entirely. As his "sexual wishes in regard to his mother become more intense," Freud says, his father is increasingly "perceived as an obstacle to them." At this point, desiring his mother, blocked by his father, the young boy has acquired what Freud calls "the simple positive Oedipus complex" (640). Freud is alluding to the ancient myth in which Oedipus, in the course of saving a city, happens unknowingly to kill his father and marry his mother.

Obviously, the desire to do away with the father and join with the mother cannot be acted out without disastrous consequences, and it must therefore be repressed, put out of sight. This "primal repression," as Freud calls it, is, in fact, what creates the unconscious, making a place for repressed desires. But if nothing more than this repression happens, then the Oedipus complex will persist in the unconscious, exerting its relentless pressure and eventually creating psychological trouble—a "pathogenic effect." This ill effect is avoided, Freud says, when the Oedipus complex is destroyed, a process that is brought about by the boy's perception that his father is superior.

And here is where most readers of Freud tend to drop their jaws or even toss the book across the room, because the threat of the father is focused, Freud believes, in the threat of castration. Fearing that the father may negate his affection for the mother by castrating him, the boy (understandably enough!) begins a process of transferring his desires elsewhere. (What Little Hans was experiencing was thus a more intense variation of a "normal" process.) The part of the mind that "retains the character of the father," who comes to stand for the restraints of "authority, religious teaching, schooling, and reading," Freud calls the "superego." In struggling to control the ego, the superego is opposed by the id, the repository of basic instincts and desires. The relationship between the id and ego, as Freud puts it in his *New Introductory Lectures on Psychoanalysis*, is like that "between a rider and his horse" (108). The rider is supposed to direct the horse's energy, but sometimes the rider has "to guide his horse in the direction in which it itself wants to go."

Thus, Freud offers two maps of the mind. First, conscious versus unconscious, then later, this division is refined into the id, ego, superego

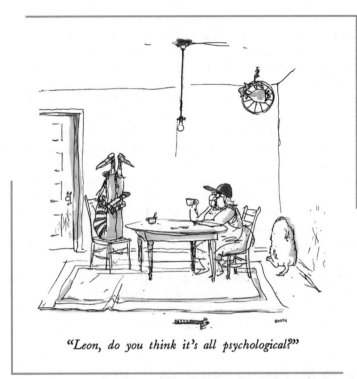

"*Leon, do you think it's all psychological?*"

model. The id is largely the territory of the unconscious, and the ego and superego are mostly conscious.

Freud's earliest followers rather quickly offered major additions, divergences, and rejections of various Freudian features. Melanie Klein, for instance, emphasized the turbulence of the pre-Oedipal period when the child wants to possess and destroy the mother. Harry Stack Sullivan turned from Freud's emphasis on internal conflicts to concentrate on the individual's relationships with important people in his life. The "good" mother, Sullivan says, conveys security and contentment to the child, whereas the "bad" mother communicates her anxiety and distress to the child, who must adjust his or her own behavior to modify the mother's stress. Carl Jung downplayed Freud's emphasis on sex and supplemented the individual unconscious with the idea of a "collective unconscious" that contains themes and images inherited by all humans. Jungian approaches to psychological criticism look for such recurrent themes and images across time and across cultures, seeing them as clues to the structuring of the collective unconscious mind.

Today little of Freud's work is accepted without substantial modification or challenge. Fortunately, in order to do psychological criticism, you don't need to wait until you have sorted out exactly what you believe. You don't need to understand all the various refinements and refutations and wholesale reconsiderations of Freud that continue to appear. The more you know about psychology, to be sure, the more options you're likely to have as a critic. But all you really need to understand in order to do psychological criticism is Freud's fundamental concept of the unconscious—a concept that has remained the unchallenged starting point for most subsequent psychological theories. The purpose of psychology depends on bringing to consciousness the hidden fears and desires that disturb and control our lives. And the purpose of psychological criticism likewise is to direct Freud's question—"Why did you do that?"—to authors or characters or readers.

Looking at the author, psychological criticism tries to go beyond the biographical facts to expose the underlying motivations—motivations and meanings that the author herself or himself may not have glimpsed. Looking at a character, psychological criticism treats the author's creation as a person whose behavior can be explained psychologically. Looking at the reader, psychological criticism considers how the reader's motivations shape the meaning of the work. Let's consider now how to carry out such tasks.

How to Do Psychological Criticism

In "Creative Writers and Day-Dreaming" (1908) Freud lays the foundation for applying psychology to literature. The author's creative production is, for Freud, like the material of a dream: It is a "day-dream," shaped and therefore disguised substantially by the unconscious mind. A work of literature then is like the material the analyst receives from his or her patients. Acts of literary criticism and psychological analysis begin to look very much alike, if they are not, in fact, the same. In both cases, the interpreter examines a text and reconstructs an underlying meaning and significance. (A text cannot, of course, respond to interrogation—at least not in the way that a patient can.) Freud's practice of using literary works to illustrate his theories, or test them, or even suggest them, has been continued by psychological thinkers of every variety. Alfred Adler, for instance, one of the earliest theorists to break away from Freud, believed his own psychological insights were drawn largely from literary works; he even asserted that "the artist is the leader of mankind on the road to absolute truth" (329).

Since these underlying meanings of the patient's or the author's stories belong by definition to the realm of the hidden and directly unknowable, a certain amount of creativity and imagination on the part of the interpreter are not only authorized but also called for. In addition to creativity, some basic concepts and terms will be useful. These originate with Freud, but they've become part of the psychological vocabulary, and to varying degrees they've even filtered into the common language.

I've already mentioned *repression*, the mind's essential strategy for hiding desires and fears. But out of sight does not mean out of mind in this case. Consider for a moment the following poem, which despite its simplicity has received much critical attention:

A Slumber Did My Spirit Seal
William Wordsworth

A slumber did my spirit seal;
I had no human fears:
She seemed a thing that could not feel
The touch of earthly years.
No motion has she now, no force;   5
She neither hears nor sees;
Rolled round in earth's diurnal course,
With rocks, and stones, and trees.

(1800)

This poem appears in a series of poems about "Lucy," a girl who died young. No historical "Lucy" has been found by researchers, and she appears to have been a fiction. If we ask Freud's question of Wordsworth, Why did you do that?, we will have to make up our own answer: Even if he were alive, Wordsworth's answer could not be trusted because the real reason for the poem might well be hidden in his unconscious. So let us ask ourselves: What wish or fear or desire might Wordsworth be expressing here in a disguised form? When Wordsworth wrote this poem, he was living with his sister in deep poverty in Germany, enduring an extremely cold winter. His sister, Dorothy, was his lifelong companion, even living with him throughout his marriage. Several of Wordsworth's poems are dedicated to her; several of his poems in fact borrow from her quite brilliant journals. Wordsworth and his sister were very close.

When Wordsworth sent this poem to Samuel Coleridge, Coleridge wrote to another friend that "in some gloomier moment" Wordsworth had "fancied the moment in which his sister might die" (1.479). If the poem is in some way about the imaginary death of Wordsworth's sister, then it certainly does represent a profound fear for Wordsworth. And yet, the poem is oddly unemotional. The speaker "had" no fears; "she" feels nothing; the speaker's "spirit" is sleeping and sealed off.

To a psychologist (or a psychological critic), the experience of an event without any of the expected response is called "isolation." In Cheever's "Reunion," I would argue, Charlie employs isolation to deal with the last time he saw his father. He doesn't overtly deny his emotions, or try to explain them away, or express them; he appears simply to ignore them, disconnecting from them, selectively telling us what happened. One could also argue, I think, that Hemingway's soldier exhibits isolation in "A Very Short Story."

But why would Wordsworth refuse to acknowledge the profound grief one would expect to arise at the idea of his sister's death? A psychological view, looking at the intimacy of Wordsworth's relationship with his sister, would have to wonder if perhaps he isn't protecting himself against desires he cannot acknowledge. If Wordsworth did have, for example, an incestuous desire for his sister, whom he certainly loved deeply, acknowledging that desire would almost certainly cause him great psychological pain. In fantasy, in his poetry, he could deal with that desire indirectly by imagining his sister, or her surrogate Lucy, as being dead. Channeling an unacceptable urge into some artistic creation or fantasy is called "sublimation." Sublimation is no doubt at work in Mary Astell's *Proposal* (see Chapter 8), in which her inevitable rage against an oppressive patriarchy becomes the driving force behind her proposal for women to secede. If Wordsworth is substituting Lucy for Dorothy, he is also engaging in *displacement,* which inserts a safe object of emotion for a dangerous one. We might argue, for example, that Milton's focus on his blindness, in "When I Consider How My Light Is Spent," is a substitute for a more frightening loss of light and capability, his death.

But perhaps we're on entirely the wrong track here, or perhaps there are simply other tracks available. My own initial reading of Wordsworth's poem was that "she" is his own spirit. Otherwise, what sense does the initial line make, "A slumber did my spirit seal"? He imagines his own death and depicts his soul as being feminine. "I had no human fears" becomes an instance then of *denial,* in which one simply falsifies reality, flatly and directly refusing to accept it. While repression buries the emotion and other strategies hide or disguise it, denial looks right at it and says it isn't there. Denial can be a more ominous symptom as it signals a break with reality. When Hemingway's soldier in "A Very Short Story" says he doesn't want to see any of his friends, it seems likely he's engaging in denial.

One could also argue, pursuing a different angle, that the critic who claims Wordsworth's poem deals with his incestuous desires is practicing *projection:* "Oh yeah, I see Wordsworth's repressed incestuous desires," the critic says, when it is actually his or her own incestuous desires, projected onto Wordsworth, that are being seen and avoided. Or one could argue the whole enterprise of criticism is motivated by *intellectualization,* a strategy for avoiding uncomfortable emotions by rationalizing them, analyzing them, talking and talking and talking about them. Intellectualization is isolation for intellectuals.

If we imagine that Wordsworth was terrified of ghosts and spirits, that he feared they were wandering all over the place, and that he was especially convinced that he would become a restless ghoul himself, then we could see the poem as a *reaction formation*, in which one is convinced that the opposite of a terrible situation is actually the case. Although Wordsworth, in this scenario, is convinced that spirits roam the earth, he keeps telling himself insistently that "slumber" actually seals one's spirit, leaving it as dead as a rock. In "My Father's Martial Art," Stephen Shu-ning Liu says his father and his Master are sitting on O Mei mountain (Chapter 3). To the extent that the speaker believes this statement, he is arguably employing a reaction formation, for the poem makes rather clear that his father is dead. He cannot come down and hush the traffic. He isn't really sitting anywhere, at least not in any physical sense.

As you're thinking about how to apply psychological theories to literature in specific ways, you might also consider the more general effects of a psychological perspective. I'd like to bring two consequences to your attention. First, students often ask English teachers, "Do you really think the author intended to mean all that?" Which often means, of course, "Aren't you being too clever, reading too much into this, making a big deal out of something that isn't there?" After Freud, such a question becomes irrelevant. The author himself or herself can't really know what was intended because of the inevitable involvement of the unconscious mind. We may think we intend one thing, but our unconscious intentions may be very different and much more complex. Our intention may even be contradictory because the unconscious mind isn't worried about logical consistency. By analyzing the work closely, we may gain some insight into what the author really intended—but we're always just guessing. At the least, we can be confident that the meaning of any statement is richer than it seems.

This point brings me to the second consequence of an awareness of psychological criticism, which is closely related to the first one. After Freud, what idea could possibly be too far out to consider? Psychological theories ought to encourage you to be creative in speculating about the motivations of characters, authors, or readers. When students write uninteresting papers, it's often because they're too vague on the one hand or too cautious on the other. I would like to think that an acquaintance with psychological criticism will tend to loosen your imagination.

THE WRITING PROCESS: A SAMPLE ESSAY

Shakespeare's *Hamlet*, as you might imagine, has been the subject of considerable psychological analysis, beginning most notably with Ernst Jones' *Hamlet and Oedipus*, which made much of Hamlet's bedroom scene with his mother. In some film versions of the play, Sir Laurence Olivier's for instance (1948), Hamlet's physical attraction to his mother is shockingly obvious, as Hamlet pushes his mother onto her bed, holding her down, ranting and raving about her affection for Claudius, his uncle, the murderer of his father, now his stepfather. In Franco Zeffirelli's 1990 film, Mel Gibson's Hamlet and Glenn Close's Gertrude make the incest theme especially explicit in what is known as "the bedroom scene." I'm going to look at a passage that seems to me much less promising. If there are psychological analyses of this passage, I'm not aware of them. In fact, I thought at first, after picking the passage at random, that a psychological reading wouldn't work. So, you're going to see the evolution of a psychological reading from the ground up.

But first you'll see the passage. In this scene, from Act IV, scene vi, Hamlet has just observed the army of Fortinbras moving to attack a part of Poland. The land the two armies are fighting over is insignificant; Fortinbras' captain says he wouldn't pay "five ducats" to farm it. And yet thousands of men and thousands of ducats will be wasted to fight over it. Hearing this, Hamlet speaks the soliloquy below. Read it carefully and consider what you might say about it from a psychological perspective.

Hamlet 4.4.32–66
William Shakespeare

°*inform against*: accuse	How all occasions do inform against° me,
	And spur my dull revenge! What is a man,
°*market*: product	If his chief good and market° of his time
°*discourse*: reasoning power, language	Be but to sleep and feed? a beast, no more. 35
	Sure He that made us with such large
	discourse,°
	Looking before and after, gave us not
	That capability and godlike reason
°*fust*: develop mold	To fust° in us unus'd. Now whether it be
°*craven*: cowardly	Bestial oblivion, or some craven° scruple 40
°*event*: the result	Of thinking too precisely on th' event°—
	A thought which quarter'd hath but
	one part wisdom
	And ever three parts coward—I do not know
	Why yet I live to say, "This thing's to do,"
°*Sith*: since	Sith° I have cause, and will, and strength, 45
	and means
°*gross*: huge, obvious	To do't. Examples gross° as earth exhort me:
	Witness this army of such mass and charge,
	Led by a delicate and tender prince,
°*Makes mouths*: taunts, scorns	Whose spirit with divine ambition puff'd
	Makes mouths° at the invisible event, 50

Exposing what is mortal and unsure
To all that fortune, death, and danger dare,
Even for an egg-shell. Rightly to be great
Is not to stir without great argument,
But greatly to find quarrel in a straw   55
When honor's at the stake. How stand I then,
That have a father kill'd, a mother stain'd,
Excitements of my reason and my blood,
And let all sleep, while to my shame I see
The imminent death of twenty thousand   60
   men,
That for a fantasy and trick of fame
Go to their graves like beds, fight for a plot
Whereon the numbers cannot try the cause,
Which is not tomb enough and continent
To hide the slain? O, from this time forth,   65
My thoughts be bloody, or be nothing worth!
                                                           (1600)

Preparing to Write

One strategy to generate ideas would be simply to run through various psychological concepts and see how each one relates to the play. To see how this heuristic (or invention strategy) would work, let's first review the concepts that have been mentioned in this chapter (which are by no means all the psychological ideas you might draw upon):

- *Isolation:* Understanding something that should be upsetting, but failing to react to it. The person thus *isolates* an event or stimulus, separating it from his or her feelings. "Yes, my uncle murdered my father and married my mother, but so what? I've got a theology exam next Tuesday at the University of Wittenberg, and I just can't worry about it now."

- *Intellectualization:* Analyzing and rationalizing rather than feeling and reacting. The topic isn't forgotten or ignored; it's just turned into an intellectual issue. "I am conducting a study on the incidence of ghost appearances here in Denmark, and I am especially interested in how often the ghost is the father appearing to his son, as in my own case."

- *Repression:* Selectively forgetting about whatever is troubling. "Ghost? What ghost? We'd better go get some lunch right now."

- *Projection:* Denying thoughts and feelings by attributing them to someone else. "You know, Horatio is just about paralyzed with uncertainties and doubts. And I think he may be sexually attracted to my mother, too."

- *Displacement:* Shifting an emotion from its real target to another one. Usually, a threatening, powerful target is exchanged for a safer one. "Don't talk to me about Claudius right now. I'm busy plotting to kill those sorry traitors Rosencrantz and Guildenstern."
- *Denial:* Falsifying reality. "I didn't see any ghost. My father is still alive."
- *Reversal:* Asserting the opposite of the truth, turning an emotion around. "I'm not attracted to my mother. I've noticed that she's attracted to me, however."
- *Reaction formation:* A pattern of behavior that repeatedly reverses the truth; an obsessive kind of denial. "First, I'll shine Claudius's boots. Then I'll sharpen and polish his sword. Then I'll dust his desk off and see what else I can do. He's my uncle, and in spite of everything I like him so much."

Now, let's see how these concepts apply to that particular passage from Act IV, scene vi, lines 32–66. The idea here is to think about each term and then brainstorm about the passage in relation to that concept. You may want to brainstorm some on your own before you check out my own meditations below:

Isolation: What is Hamlet not feeling that he should be feeling? This question seems easy to answer. Hamlet himself tells us that he should be feeling bloodthirsty rage, yet his revenge is "dull." So he tries to exhort himself to feel what he should, rather than existing in a "Bestial oblivion," feeling nothing.

Intellectualization: Hamlet offers two possible explanations for his delay in lines 39–41. "Bestial oblivion" (or isolation) is one; "thinking too precisely on th' event" (or intellectualization) is the other. Both these strategies are used to avoid feeling emotions—which is precisely what Hamlet sees himself doing.

Repression: What is Hamlet ignoring? What obvious feeling does he totally pass over? Certainly he recognizes that he should be vengeful but isn't; but Hamlet seems to look right past what would seem most important: he doesn't want to die. If Hamlet kills Claudius, he may lose his own life. He may have, as he says, "cause, and will, and strength, and means / To do't," but he has no guarantee that he can do it safely. This avoidance is, I think, a major repression, and it is bound to express itself somewhere. In fact, this whole passage can be seen as an effort to ignore what he is most pressed to say: that he fears throwing away his life.

Projection: Does Hamlet use projection to disguise his feeling that taking his revenge will mean throwing away his life? There is his reference to the "delicate and tender prince" who is willing to expose "what is mortal and unsure" for the sake of "an egg-shell." Of course, Hamlet does not know how the other prince feels, or really whether he is "delicate and tender." The other prince may well believe that the upcoming battle is a small but glorious part of an epic campaign—not that he is fighting for an eggshell, but that the battle is strategically, symbolically, historically, personally of major proportions. It is, in fact, Hamlet who, deep inside, feels that he, a delicate and tender prince, a student and theater-goer, is being asked to act like a warrior and throw away his life for an eggshell. He says, "That guy is throwing his life away for an eggshell." His unconscious meaning: "I'm throwing my life away for an eggshell."

A problem here: Can we really say that Hamlet views his cause as an eggshell? He has "a father kill'd, a mother stain'd." These would seem to be more than an eggshell. But his revenge will not alter his father's death. He'll be just as dead after Hamlet acts. Nor will Hamlet's revenge undo the stain on his mother. Although men will "find quarrel in a straw / When honor's at the stake," her honor has already been tarnished by Claudius, hasn't it? Early in the play Hamlet has referred to his world as "an unweeded garden / That grows to seed, things rank and gross in nature / Possess it merely" (1.2.135–137). So perhaps the world and his cause are no more than an eggshell for Hamlet.

Displacement: Instead of venting his anger at Claudius, who is dangerous, Hamlet is attacking himself.

Denial: Hamlet says he does not know why he hasn't acted, but the reason is right in front of him: he doesn't want to be like the 20,000 men already marching to their meaningless deaths. He is denying that he knows.

Reversal: Hamlet says that the 20,000 men are marching to their "imminent" deaths "to my shame." Isn't he turning that around, however? Isn't it really to their own shame? Hamlet acknowledges that their deaths will not mean anything significant; shouldn't they be ashamed of such senseless slaughter? The ground won't even be able to hold them, Hamlet says; but that has already been true of the bodies Hamlet has encountered: his father won't stay put; Polonius' body eludes the court; Ophelia's body floats away and surfaces again in her grave. One must wonder if the ground can ever contain the bodies put into it.

Reaction formation: Does Hamlet convince himself that the exact opposite of something bad, something that he doesn't want to confront, is going on, and that it is good? Hamlet knows that he must eventually carry out his revenge, giving in to a need for revenge that does not make conscious sense to him. His ego is being pressed by the superego, who is literally his father figure, calling for justice. His ego is also being pressed by his id, which hungers for violence, indulgence. He wants to give in to something bad: the violent energy of his id. But he tells himself he doesn't want to.

Let's try that again. Hamlet knows unconsciously that he must behave violently, like an animal, a savage, in order to carry out his revenge. He must become a beast. Yet, he tells himself the opposite. He is a beast, he says, if he doesn't carry out his revenge. The conflict in Hamlet's mind over whether he should be a beast or not, whether he should exercise "godlike reason" or not, seems designed for relating to the id, ego, and superego. So, those terms could also be used as prompts in the invention phase.

Id—Hamlet says all occasions "spur" his revenge—as if it were a horse. Freud, in fact, compares the id to a horse. It is Hamlet's id that will have to motivate his revenge: Logically, he can't do it. But Hamlet doesn't want to be "a beast," in "bestial oblivion." If he lets the id's horse run, however, that's exactly what he'll be.

Ego—So, his ego is caught in the middle, driven to commit suicide without any consciously satisfying reason.

Superego—Justice, the moral code, the stand-in for the father: In this case, the ghost of the father isn't just in his head; he's walking about. Like the id, Hamlet's superego calls for revenge, which the ego recognizes as requiring its own extinction. No wonder Hamlet is caught in the middle, unable to act. He says at the end his thoughts will be bloody—but he doesn't say anything about his actions.

Is this enough material for an essay? How would you organize it?

Shaping

Is there a thesis floating around in the brainstorming above? It seems clear that I'm returning again and again to the question of why Hamlet is not taking his revenge. Why is he standing there talking rather than doing something? He thinks he should be killing people, or at least one particular person, yet he hasn't done it. And the conclusion of his speech, which seems to announce his action, on closer analysis just says his thoughts will be bloody. The next scene in the play isn't Hamlet bursting in on Claudius and cutting his throat.

So, my thesis might be that this passage helps us understand Hamlet's hesitation—his mental conflict. First, I list what I think I know:

1. Hamlet's father and his superego (one stands in for the other) call for justice. Morality has been violated and it must be set right. "Honor's at the stake," as Hamlet says.

2. For some reason, this call to violence is insufficient. Hamlet avoids coming to terms with it for much of the play.

3. I said when I was developing ideas that Hamlet's unconscious wants to be bloody. But does that really make sense?

Let us imagine that Freud's comparison of the id to a horse is very appropriate. Let us further imagine that when Hamlet says the occasions should "spur" his revenge, he is speaking about the kinds of urges and passions that Freud assigns to the unconscious. So, why is Hamlet's unconscious unwilling to kill Claudius? For the reader who assumes Hamlet's behavior is motivated—that "Hamlet" can be discussed as if he were a personality and not a set of lines in a play, a fiction—this unwillingness is the nub of the problem.

Acting as a psychological critic, I want to persuade my audience to accept my explanation of Hamlet's behavior. To do that, I need to look some more at the text and ask a few more questions. Why would anyone be unwilling to kill someone who deserved it? I've already noted above that Hamlet doesn't want to throw away his life. He's not convinced, even though his superego or his father tell him he should be, that killing Claudius is worth it. But this stuff is logical: This is the "thinking too precisely" that Hamlet mentions. The other reason, the "bestial oblivion," is more primitive.

I haven't yet drawn on Freud's crucial Oedipal complex, and it finally occurs to me that here's where it could come into play: Perhaps Hamlet doesn't want to kill Claudius because at some level he can't blame Claudius. When Hamlet says he stands with "a father kill'd, a mother stain'd," he is in exactly the Oedipal position that Freud says the unconscious desires to be in. Hamlet calls these events "Excitements of my reason and my blood," and they are exciting, but not in a way that he consciously recognizes. He finds at some deeper level himself excited and unable to be enraged at Claudius for carrying out his own deep-seated wish.

At this point, I think I have a rough plan for an essay:

The problem: How can this passage be used to help readers understand Hamlet's hesitation?

The answer: We see him using some classic strategies to avoid two realities: (1) Killing Claudius will probably involve getting himself killed, and he just can't justify that, and (2) killing Claudius will involve killing himself in a symbolic sense because Claudius has done what he wanted to do, unconsciously (kill his father and sleep with his mother).

Drafting

And here's a draft, worked out from this plan.

The Psychology of Hamlet's Hesitation: A Reading of 4.4.32–66

> Introduces the problem: why does Hamlet hesitate?

Shakespeare's *Hamlet* would be a simple case of king-killing and revenge except for one thing: Hamlet hesitates. Like Mona Lisa's smile, Hamlet's delay in carrying out his revenge is puzzling because we do not know his motivation. Some possible reasons are obvious. Perhaps he is not sure that the ghost is telling the truth. Perhaps he is waiting for the perfect revenge, when Claudius is doing something evil rather than praying, thus increasing the near-certainty that he will go to hell. Perhaps he wants to survive his revenge-taking. Perhaps he just wants to be sure he can succeed.

> Possible explanations.

> But Hamlet himself doesn't agree with these.

Any or all of these reasons might well be sufficient to explain Hamlet's delay, but Hamlet does not himself accept these reasons. In Act IV, scene iv, after repeated efforts at self-analysis, Hamlet can still say:

> I do not know
> Why yet I live to say, "This
>   thing's to do,"
> Sith I have cause, and will, and
>   strength, and means
> To do't.   (43–46)

> Oedipus complex extended to hesitation.

If Hamlet does not know by this time why he is waiting, then perhaps the cause of his delay is not conscious or rational.

Hamlet's psychology has often been examined. The idea that Hamlet's attitude toward his mother is motivated by an Oedipus complex is well known. But Hamlet's hesitation to revenge his father's death can also be profitably connected to his unconscious psychology as an examination of his soliloquy in Act IV, scene iv will show. Hamlet is unable to admit to himself that "honor" is not a sufficient reason for self-sacrifice; nor is he able to understand that he identifies with Claudius, despite his detestation of him.

> A problem: revenge equals the bestial.

After observing Fortinbras and his army advancing to fight and die for a small piece of worthless ground, Hamlet exclaims: "How all occasions do inform against me, / And spur my dull revenge!" (32–33). When Hamlet says that all occasions "spur" his revenge, he compares his mind to a horse being spurred. But the next few lines clash with this metaphor: "What is a man, / If his chief good and market of his time / Be but to sleep and feed? a beast, no more" (33–35). Hamlet wants his revenge to be bestial, yet he censures those who act like beasts. He's caught in a dilemma: how to be "spurred" without becoming less than human?

Hamlet's denial of the realm of Freud's id, the realm of bestial desires, is expanded upon in the next few lines:

> Sure He that made us with such
>   large discourse,
> Looking before and after, gave
>   us not
> That capability and godlike
>   reason
> To fust in us unus'd.   (36–39)

In saying that we are made "with such large discourse," Hamlet is pointing out the vastness of man's reasoning ability, which makes him, Hamlet believes, "godlike." Unlike the id, man's ego is able to look to the future and the past, "Looking before and after." We should use that reason. But using our reason does not promote violent action, as Hamlet's next few lines indicate:

> Now whether it be
> Bestial oblivion, or some craven
>   scruple
> Of thinking too precisely on
>   th' event—
> A thought which quarter'd hath
>   but one part wisdom
> And ever three parts coward—I do
>   not know
> Why yet I live to say, "This
>   thing's to do,"
> Sith I have cause, and will, and
>   strength, and means
> To do't.   (39–46)

Humankind ought not be bestial.

Neither bestial oblivion nor the rational mind seem conducive to revenge. After asserting that he should use his reason, rather than letting it get moldy, Hamlet says that reasoning blocks decisive action. To kill Claudius, Hamlet must assume a "godlike" role, handing out justice; yet his godlike faculty does not support such dangerous action any more than his bestial instincts support it.

<table>
<tr><td>Reasoning works against revenge.</td></tr>
</table>

Consciously unaware of this conflict, Hamlet continues to berate himself, saying "Examples gross as earth exhort me." That is precisely the problem: His reason obstructs his action, and the examples exhorting him are "gross as earth." The kind of primitive, bestial violence required of Hamlet is foreign to him. He has suppressed his bestial self even as he recognizes on one level that it needs spurring. Hamlet seems to think he is exhorting himself to action when he points to the massive army, which is "Exposing what is mortal and unsure / To all that fortune, death, and danger dare, / Even for an egg-shell" (51–53). But the logi-

<table>
<tr><td>Further support.</td></tr>
</table>

cal absurdity of the example actually works against Hamlet's desire: Anyone who thinks about it at all will realize that it is stupid for men to die for an eggshell.

Hamlet's cause is not an eggshell, and the next few lines indicate further just how deluded Hamlet is in his comparisons:

> Rightly to be great
> Is not to stir without great
>   argument,
> But greatly to find quarrel in a
>   straw
> When honor's at the stake.   (53–56)

His case is not a straw, and the idea that one should not stir "without great argument" actually justifies his delay, even though Hamlet consciously believes he is talking himself into taking action. What is perhaps most intriguing here, however, is the question of how Hamlet's "honor" is involved. The play would seem to be about murder, regicide, and justice. Compared to these, honor would seem to be a minor concern.

<table>
<tr><td>Honor and revenge.</td></tr>
</table>

But the relevance of honor emerges in the next lines:

> How stand I then,
> That have a father kill'd, a
>   mother stain'd,
> Excitements of my reason and
>   my blood,
> And let all sleep, while to my
>   shame I see
> The imminent death of twenty
>   thousand men,
> That for a fantasy and trick of
>   fame
> Go to their graves like beds,

fight for a plot
Whereon the numbers cannot try
the cause,
Which is not tomb enough and
continent
To hide the slain?   (56–65)

Honor and the
Oedipal urge.

Hamlet feels that his mother is "stain'd," even though it is unclear that she knows anything about Claudius' murder. But Hamlet has already shown himself to be obsessed with his mother's sexuality, especially in the bedroom scene. And the lines following the mention of his mother's stain demonstrate Hamlet's subconscious expression of his own desire. He refers to the "Excitements of … my blood," and to "sleep," to "fantasy" and a "trick," and to "beds." While Hamlet is consciously focused on burying the dead in an insufficient tomb, his bestial self is concerned with his mother's womb and dying in a sexual sense.

Conclusion:
Hamlet's
psychological
conflicts account
for his hesitation.

Thus we can see that Hamlet fails to take action because his rational ego and his bestial id block his revenge and because his own Oedipal desire to do what Claudius has done—kill his father and possess his stained mother—tends to defuse his resolve. We may notice that the conclusion of his soliloquy does not call for bloody actions. Instead, he says, "O, from this time forth, / My thoughts be bloody, or be nothing worth!" (65–66). Hamlet's psychological conflicts block his action. He cannot actively seek revenge; revenge must come to him, and when it does, his hesitation will be justified by his own doom.

PRACTICING PSYCHOLOGICAL CRITICISM

Freud's theories, as numerous critics have observed, take the male sex as the norm. How does the Oedipus complex apply to young girls? Their first physical pleasure is also contact with the mother; do little girls wish to sleep with their mothers and kill their fathers? If not, why not? Freud was himself mystified by the problem of applying his theories to women, the "dark continent" as he once called them, but he did try to explain how girls passed through the Oedipus complex. Instead of "castration anxiety," which causes the little boy to submit to reality and his father, turning his desires elsewhere, the little girl perceives that she is already "castrated." Is there then no reason that the little girl should turn her affections from her mother? Freud's solution was the notorious concept of "penis envy"—an idea that continues even today to drive people up the wall. The little girl turns to her father, Freud said, because she realizes that her mother also has been "castrated." This envy is hardly as powerful as the fear of castration, it would seem, and Freud did believe that the superego of women was not as powerfully formed as that of men and that women consequently had weaker ideas of justice and authority. The complementary idea of womb envy apparently did not occur to Freud, but it seems equally if not more plausible.

If this all seems too bizarre, let me briefly suggest once more why I'm bringing this up here. Freud's thinking is the foundation of psychological criticism, and the Oedipus complex is central to Freud. Freud's struggles to make this complex work for little girls resulted in his concept of penis envy—a concept that can be interestingly tested, I think, with the following poem and accompanying questions. After Dickinson's poem, you'll find two other poems with questions to guide you in practicing psychological criticism, plus an invitation to practice on your own psychology.

A Narrow Fellow in the Grass
Emily Dickinson

A narrow fellow in the grass
Occasionally rides;
You may have met him,—did you not,
His notice sudden is.

The grass divides as with a comb,   5
A spotted shaft is seen;
And then it closes at your feet
And opens further on.

He likes a boggy acre.
A floor too cool for corn.   10
Yet when a child, and barefoot,
I more than once, at morn,

Have passed, I thought, a whip-lash
Unbraiding in the Sun, —
When, stooping to secure it,   15
It wrinkled, and was gone.

Several of nature's people
I know, and they know me;
I feel for them a transport
Of cordiality;   20

But never met this fellow,
Attended or alone,
Without a tighter breathing,
And zero at the bone.

(1866)

Questions

1. This poem was one of the few poems published while Dickinson was alive. It appeared under the title "The Snake," which was not Dickinson's title, but the addition of an editor. Dickinson, in fact, rarely gave titles to her poems. How does adding that title affect a reader's experience of this poem?

2. Which words in the poem seem odd in the context of a snake?

3. From a Freudian perspective, paraphrase the poem; that is, narrate what happens.

4. Dickinson's handwritten versions of this poem say "boy" instead of "child" in line 11. What difference does this alternative make? Why might an editor change "boy" to "child"?

5. What might "zero at the bone" mean? What fear or desire might be expressed by this phrase?

6. Dickinson's manuscript versions of her poems (two copies of this poem exist) famously do not follow the normal conventions of punctuation, using dashes where readers would usually expect a comma, semicolon, or period. The dashes vary in size, with some appearing almost to be dots. This poem, for instance, ends with a dash in Dickinson's handwritten version. Should editors print whatever a writer left behind, or should they correct what appear to be distracting errors or eccentricities?

7. Why would Dickinson write almost 1,800 poems and publish none of them (although at least ten were made public in her lifetime)? Might her use of dashes instead of conventional punctuation be somehow related to this production-versus-publication paradox?   ∎

O to Be a Dragon
Marianne Moore

If I, like Solomon, ...
could have my wish—
my wish ... O to be a dragon,
a symbol of the power of Heaven—of silkworm
size or immense; at times invisible.   5
Felicitous phenomenon.

(1951)

Questions

1. Can this poem be related to Dickinson's "Narrow Fellow" poem?
2. In what way does a psychological perspective alter your reaction to this poem? ■

Dover Beach
Matthew Arnold

The sea is calm tonight.
The tide is full, the moon lies fair
Upon the straits;—on the French coast the light
Gleams and is gone; the cliffs of England stand,
Glimmering and vast, out in the tranquil bay.   5
Come to the window, sweet is the night-air!
Only, from the long line of spray
Where the sea meets the moon-blanched land,
Listen! you hear the grating roar
Of pebbles which the waves draw back, and fling,   10
At their return, up the high strand,
Begin, and cease, and then again begin,
With tremulous cadence slow, and bring
The eternal note of sadness in.

Sophocles long ago   15
Heard it on the Aegean, and it brought
Into his mind the turbid ebb and flow
Of human misery; we
Find also in the sound a thought,
Hearing it by this distant northern sea.   20
The Sea of Faith
Was once, too, at the full, and round earth's shore
Lay like the folds of a bright girdle furled.
But now I only hear
Its melancholy, long, withdrawing roar,   25
Retreating, to the breath
Of the night-wind, down the vast edges drear
And naked shingles of the world

Ah, love, let us be true
To one another! for the world, which seems   30
To lie before us like a land of dreams,
So various, so beautiful, so new,
Hath really neither joy, nor love, nor light,
Nor certitude, nor peace, nor help for pain;
And we are here as on a darkling plain   35

Swept with confused alarms of struggle and flight,
Where ignorant armies clash by night.

(1867)

Question

Nancy Chodorow (in, for example, *Feminism and Psychoanalytic Theory*) notes that girls are able to identify with the adult they spend the most time with; but boys, who cannot identify with the mother, must separate and withdraw themselves from the mother. Thus girls, according to Chodorow, feel more connected to the world and to their caregiver. Girls typically engage in *cooperative* play, while boys typically engage in *competitive* play, Chodorow says. Girls think in terms of relationships, and boys think in terms of rules and rights. Girls cultivate intimacy; boys may find it uncomfortable.

How might Chodorow's work be related to "Dover Beach"?   ■

Your Dream Here

Keep a pen and paper beside your bed (and a flashlight if you share a bed or bedroom), and see if you can capture one of your dreams. If you wake and remember a dream, write it down immediately. It's striking how quickly dreams recede. If you're unable to remember any of your dreams (and everyone does dream), then see if you can "borrow" a dream from a friend. Using your dreams as your text, see if you can interpret them using Freud's ideas. If dreams are the symbolic fulfillments of desires that cannot in reality be fulfilled, as Freud asserted, what desires are you disguising? For fun, you may want to invent a dream to interpret, and then see if your readers can tell whether your dream is real or manufactured.

USEFUL TERMS FOR PSYCHOLOGICAL CRITICISM

As you're employing psychological criticism, the following list of commonly used terms may be convenient for you to review. The illustrations refer to Shakespeare's *Hamlet* and specifically to the passage discussed.

Denial: Refusing to acknowledge what one knows. Hamlet says he doesn't know why he fails to act, but the answer is right in front of him: He doesn't want to end up like the 20,000 men marching to their meaningless deaths.

Displacement: Shifting one's emotions from a threatening target to a less threatening one. Hamlet, rather than getting mad at Claudius, gets mad at himself.

Intellectualization: Explaining away emotions rather than feeling them. Hamlet acknowledges the possibility that he is "thinking too precisely on th' event."

Isolation: Not feeling what one ordinarily would be feeling. Hamlet should be feeling rage, yet his revenge is "dull."

Projection: Assigning one's own emotions to another person. Hamlet thinks Fortinbras feels the same injury he does, yet Fortinbras takes action. In reality, Hamlet doesn't know what Fortinbras is thinking or feeling.

Repression: Submerging an idea or emotion, putting it out of the conscious mind. Hamlet should at least consider the possibility that he is delaying because he fears losing his own life. He doesn't—a major repression.

Reversal: Turning a situation around; saying the opposite of what is the case. Hamlet says the 20,000 men march to their meaningless deaths to his shame, but isn't the shame really their own?

✔ Checklist for Psychological Criticism

1. Assume that some wish or fear is being disguised and expressed in the work.

2. Look for clues that suggest what is underlying the work's "surface"—details that don't quite fit or seem unusual.

3. Connect those clues to some common developmental pattern or (if you know the author's or reader's or character's biography) to some trauma or event.

Works Cited

Adler, Alfred. *The Individual Psychology of Alfred Adler*. Ed. Heinz and Rowena R. Ansbacher. New York: Anchor Books, 1978. Print.

Coleridge, Samuel Taylor. *Collected Letters*. Ed. Earl Leslie Griggs. 6 vols. Oxford: Clarendon, 1956–1971. Print.

Eagleton, Terry. "Psychoanalysis." *Literary Theory: An Introduction*. Minneapolis: U of Minnesota P, 1983. 151–193. Print.

Freud, Sigmund. "The Ego and the Id." *The Freud Reader*. Ed. Peter Gay. New York: Norton, 1966. 628–658. Print.

—. *New Introductory Lectures on Psychoanalysis*. Vol. 22 of *The Standard Edition of the Complete Psychological Works*. London: Hogarth, 1933. Print.

—. *The Psychopathology of Everyday Life*. New York: Macmillan, 1915. Print.

Recommended Further Reading

Freud, Sigmund. *The Interpretation of Dreams.* 1900. Oxford: Oxford UP, 1999. stimulating work, fairly accessible, enormously influential.

Holland, Norman. *Literature and the Brain.* Gainesville, FL: PsyArt Foundation, 2009. A stimulating discussion of how the human brain processes literature and creates fiction.

—. Holland, Norman. *Norman Holland's Homepage.* May 18, 2015. A wealth of resources at this website, including much that is related to Holland's teaching; accessible for students. Available online, linked to this site: *Holland's Guide to Psychoanalytic Psychology and Literature-and-Psychology* (1990).

Meltzer, Francoise. "Unconscious." *Critical Terms for Literary Study.* 2nd ed. Ed. Frank Lentricchia and Thomas McLaughlin. Chicago: U of Chicago P, 1995. 147–162. A stimulating discussion of this fundamental idea.

Noel-Smith, Kelly. "Harry Potter's Oedipal Issues." *Psychoanalytic Studies.* 2001; 3: 199–207. Print. Available online at http://human-nature.com/free-associations/harrypotter.html. An entertaining and suggestive application of Freud's theory to the popular series.

Surprenant, Celine. "Freud and Psychoanalysis." *Literary Theory and Criticism: An Oxford Guide.* Ed. Patricia Waugh. Oxford: Oxford UP, 2006. 199–211. A lively introduction to applying psychoanalysis to literary works.

Willbern, David. "Reading After Freud." *Contemporary Literary Theory.* Ed. G. Douglas Atkins and Laura Morrow. Amherst: U of Massachusetts P, 1989. 158–179. An excellent introduction to Freud's impact on literary study.

Zizek, Slavoj. *How to Read Lacan.* New York: Norton, 2007. A wickedly clever introductory guide to a difficult French psychoanalytical thinker, Jacques Lacan.

Gendering the Text

Feminist Criticism, Postfeminism, and Queer Theory

I am already performing a feminine critical act, namely refusing to speak from a position of supposed neutrality and pseudoscientific objectivity.

—Naomi Schor (263)

What you'll learn in this chapter:

- To identify opportunities to use political approaches, such as feminist, postfeminist, and queer theories.
- To develop ideas about texts using political theory.
- To write and revise essays, step by step, about literary texts, using political criticism.
- To apply political theories in a variety of contexts.

It may seem silly at first glance to think that the study of literature is going to have any real-world effects on anything. Ecocriticism, or environmental literary criticism, or green cultural studies may be harmless enough, occupying the time of people who are worried about climate change and pollution and the loss of habitat, but the Chinese leaders who are building coal-fired power plants, the loggers who are decimating the Brazilian rainforest, the industrial farmers who are pouring herbicides on their crops— these people are not likely to be reading literary criticism. And yet, culture matters. As Christopher Hitchens puts it in *Unacknowledged Legislators* "there are things that pens can do, and swords cannot" (xiv). Hitchens' title refers to Percy Bysshe Shelley's famous claim that "Poets are the unacknowledged legislators of the world," and a good example of literature's legislative power for Hitchens is the twentieth-century collapse of the Soviet Union's empire, the consequence in large part, especially in Eastern Europe, of "a civil opposition led by satirical playwrights, ironic essayists, Bohemian jazz players and rock musicians, and subversive poets" (x).

Literary critics have sometimes naïvely imagined or at least pretended that their work has no political implications, as if the reading of literature and culture were somehow beyond the shaping and wielding of power and influence. But among those strategies that have been openly and avowedly political, feminist criticism has been one of the most visible and influential over the past few decades. Indeed, key figures in the struggle for women's equality have been academic scholars of literature: Germaine Greer, for instance, who published a classic bestseller in 1970, *The Female Eunuch*, wrote her doctoral dissertation on Shakespeare's early comedies; Kate Millett, whose 1969 *Sexual Politics* is another classic of the women's liberation movement, deals extensively with literature in her work.

This chapter aims to illustrate the creative power of politically self-conscious reading by focusing on feminist criticism, postfeminism, and queer theory—with the understanding that race, ethnicity, the environment, economics, class, and many other political concerns provide fertile interpretive grounds. These approaches, like politics itself, are unavoidably grounded in history, in how we interpret and make sense of what has happened, and what we are going to do about it. This chapter should therefore

© *The New Yorker Collection* 1991 Peter Steiner from Cartoonbank.com.
All Rights Reserved.

be seen as a companion to the earlier chapter on biography and history. Political criticism in all its varieties is concerned with identifying and opposing the ways that individuals and groups of people within a culture are excluded, suppressed, and exploited. Feminist criticism, like feminism itself, is concerned, of course, with the status of women. Jonathan Culler, in fact, argues that "feminist criticism" is "the name that should be applied to all criticism alert to the critical ramifications of sexual oppression, just as in politics 'women's issues' is the name now applied to many fundamental questions of personal freedom and social justice" (56). In this expansive sense, interestingly enough, the examination of masculine roles and stereotypes, men's (or masculinist) studies, would be considered a branch of feminist criticism—which seems nicely appropriate.

Postfeminism, as you might imagine, also grows out of the feminist movement. The term has sometimes been used to describe a reactionary stance, occupied by such figures as Naomi Wolf, Camille Paglia, and Rene Denfield, who reject the idea that women today are inevitably victims oppressed by men—an assumption that they attribute to mainstream feminism. In this sense, postfeminism is akin to "antifeminism." But another way of thinking about "postfeminism" is that the term refers to what comes *after* feminism, suggesting that feminism has substantially done its work, and men and women have pretty much become equals—in the most important respects, in modern cultures anyway. From this "postfeminist" perspective, the main goal of what is sometimes called the "first wave" of feminism—equality—has been achieved, at least in the sense that women have the freedom to determine their lives. They can vote, own businesses, defer childbearing, be elected to office, pursue any career they're physically and mentally capable of. Sure, prejudice against women still exists (and in many parts of the world is regnant), but it is pervasively dying out in first-world countries as quickly as its adherents can pass away—or evolve. (Hold this thought.)

Postfeminism can also be seen as an extension of feminism in the sense that poststructuralism is an extension of structuralism, or postmodernism pushes beyond modernism. If the first wave of feminism sought equality for women, then the "second wave" of feminism (it's generally agreed) focused on the distinctive needs of women. Equal opportunity is good, but if women are still primarily responsible for childrearing, housekeeping, socializing, and so forth, then equal opportunity is not really equal. Therefore, some second-wave feminists (Mary Daly and Andrea Dworkin, for instance) have argued that we should reverse the established patriarchy. Such a reversal does not lead, of course, to the end of prejudice and oppression; an elephant upside-down is still an elephant. Thus, getting beyond such a reversal, postfeminism becomes the next step in feminism: a liberating deconstruction of the whole business of gender and sexuality. The historical progression here does fit the classic structure of deconstruction: First, notice the binary relationship (men and women) and which element is privileged (the first wave); second, expose the arbitrariness of this privileging by reversing it, advocating matriarchal values (the second wave); and third, deconstruct the binary, dismantling the very oppositional structure that makes oppression and prejudice possible (postfeminism, which has sometimes been called the third wave).

What does such a deconstructive move amount to in practice? A commitment to disrupting comfortable patterns of thinking leads inevitably, it seems, to a pluralistic outlook. For instance, by rejecting the idea of women as victims, and at the same time embracing the self-determination of women, postfeminists (in this third wave incarnation, anyway) might well be reluctant to condemn pornography. Whereas first- and second-wave feminists have typically seen pornography as a dramatic instance of the exploitation of women, a postfeminist theorist might ask what happens when women are involved in the writing, directing, and producing of pornography. If women enjoy watching pornography, are they still being exploited? (In the same way?) Or, if pornography is inherently exploitative, is there any intrinsic reason why women are exploited more gravely than men? As Ann Brooks argues in *Postfeminisms: Feminism, Cultural Theory, and Cultural Forms* (1997), the opposition of man versus woman is just too simple, and too unhealthy: Postfeminism therefore replaces dualism with diversity, and consensus with variety. It sets aside assumptions. One might well decide that pornography is singularly exploitative of women, or that men are equally exploited, or that no one is exploited; that pornography actually serves a useful purpose, or that it is profoundly evil. The point of postfeminism, or of feminism's third wave, is that our comfortable assumptions ought to be destabilized, opening up our thinking.

Such a rethinking of traditional cultural values has been the goal of a related critical effort—gay and lesbian studies—which has expanded to include bisexual and transgendered perspectives (commonly abbreviated as "LGBT"), and even "questioning." This expanding field has much in common with feminist criticism, striving to identify, recover, and appreciate work by LGBTQ authors, as well as expose the means by which LGBTQ people have been culturally represented. Homosexuals have certainly suffered discrimination and oppression; gay and lesbian studies works to reverse that prejudice. "Queer theory," for instance, has transformed a harshly insulting word into an academic descriptor. The progress from gay and lesbian studies to queer theory parallels the development from feminism to postfeminism: Just as postfeminism seeks to deconstruct the oppositional thinking of feminism (male versus female), so does queer theory seek to destabilize the binary of heterosexuality versus homosexuality.

Specifically, queer theory challenges the idea that there is a gay identity (just as postfeminism questions the notion of a feminist identity). There
is no one way to be gay or lesbian. In fact, finally, queer theory undermines
the very idea of stable sexual oppositions. Things are just much more complicated than the categories we have inherited. And the shared political aim
of these stances—feminism, postfeminism, and queer theory—is to break
down our preconceptions and prejudices. If you are thinking "hmmm, that
sounds a lot like deconstruction," then you're right. Deconstruction has
clearly opened up the field for any number of approaches by undermining
whatever status quo is in place.

It is possible, most obviously by denying the historical reality of sexual oppression, to resist the premises of feminist criticism. One can argue,
for instance, that Western society has actually been structured to protect
women from the brutalities of war and commerce, allowing them to be
nurturers, mothers, and homemakers. Rather than exploiting or suppressing women, this line of thinking goes, Western society has celebrated and
cherished them. While I have no doubt this idea may be sincerely held, and
even to some degree supported, it will not stand up to analysis. It is at best
too simple; and at worst, flat-out wrong.

It overlooks the way that insulation and honor are themselves a kind
of suppression and exclusion. (If a woman is put on a pedestal, she can't *do*
much of anything up there.) And it assumes that women are the weaker
sex (emotional, unstable, passive, irrational), needing protection, unable to
compete with men. But all women are not weaker than all men in any way.
Many women are taller, stronger, smarter, and more aggressive than many
men. But more importantly perhaps, these qualities are the yardsticks of
a man-oriented, or patriarchal, culture. Even by those values, which certainly may be questioned, generalizations about "men" and "women" are
troublesome.

It can be eye-opening to view movies from the 1940s to 1960s and
think about how women are portrayed. Molly Haskell, in *From Reverence
to Rape* (1974), argues convincingly that women overwhelmingly have
been presented as either evil vixens or innocent virgins. Women either
need the help and protection of men to survive, or they must deceive
and corrupt men to succeed. Some films, to be sure, have been challenging these stereotypes for many years—think of Sarah Connor in the
Terminator series, *Xena: Warrior Princess* or *Buffy the Vampire Slayer* on TV,
or the amazing Artemisia I of Caria as portrayed by Eva Green in *300:
Rise of an Empire*.

In fact, as queer theory in particular emphasizes, even dividing
humankind into stereotypical men and women can be problematic since
there is no simple genetic or hormonal or physiological test that will clearly
divide all humans into "male" and "female." Determining clear *psychological*

differences between the sexes appears to be even more complex and elusive. Although we can articulate certain stereotypical ideas of "masculine" or "feminine," hetero or gay thinking, we could not use these features to sort males and females, straight or gay perfectly—any more than we could use height, or weight, or muscle mass.

A particular individual may have the external appearance of a female and the biochemistry of a male, or vice versa, or an infinity of in-between states. We can, of course, like the Olympic authorities, impose a definition of "male" and "female," prescribing, for example, a certain maximum level of testosterone for a "female" body, but such limits are ultimately arbitrary and subject to tampering. Racial categories are similarly subject to arbitrary definition. Even if there were some essence of "Indian" or "Negro" blood (the biological consensus is that there isn't and that the concept of "race" is inherently problematic), where should one draw the line? Is a "Native American" someone who has two Native American parents, or is one sufficient, or is one grandparent enough, or even a great-grandparent? Historically, in various cultures, individuals have been assigned to a particular racial minority with as little as one-twentieth of their genetic material purportedly coming from that race. But if "race" is itself a biologically suspect category, then how can we determine whether someone is in a particular group or not? Is it enough for someone simply to declare membership in a particular group?

Political criticism of every variety has struggled with such essential questions of identity: What is an "African American"? (Is someone with a Caucasian mother and a black father still in the category of "black"?) What is a "woman"? (Is this a biological category, set at birth, or is it a flexible marker, subject to surgical or social or psychological forces?) What is the "working class"? (Must one have a certain kind of job, or a certain level of income, or a certain social outlook?) What is a "bisexual" person? (Is it desire-based or performance-based or what?) Such difficulties have led to the idea that it would be more useful, for starters, to think in terms of a continuum rather than two totally distinct opposites. This insight allows us to distinguish "sex" (the biological status of male and female) from "gender" (our conceptions of "man" and "woman"). As Simone de Beauvoir puts it, "One is not born a woman, one becomes one" (301). An individual, in other words, may be born female (sex), but that status does not entail the attributes of "woman" as our culture has defined them (gender). Our conceptions of femininity (and masculinity), Beauvoir is saying, are social constructions that are imposed on individuals. Or as Thomas Laqueur puts it in his detailed history of the ways we have invented our ideas of gender, sex "is situational; it is explicable only within the context of battles over gender and power" (11); and "two sexes are not the necessary, natural consequence of corporeal difference" (243). Or as Barbara Johnson says, "The question of gender is a question of language" (37). Or as Judith Butler argues in *Gender Trouble,* gender is "a performance" (25) created by what one does, not what one is.

In fact, the more one considers the sexual diversity of human beings and the way that biological "sex" is fashioned into social "gender," the more inadequate seems the idea of a continuum stretching from "male" to "female." Such a continuum still depends upon the idea of "male-ness" and "female-ness," categories from which particular individuals may differ to one degree or another. And a male-to-female continuum also ignores questions of sexual preference, which suggest another continuum ranging from heterosexual to bisexual to homosexual. Unsettling our various sexual categories has provided a rich opportunity in the arena of literary criticism for all kinds of redefinition and debate, about what it means to be a man or a woman, about how one becomes such an entity (or not), about what such processes reveal about our culture. The changes in attitudes toward women and sexuality, in the Western world at least, have been both dramatic and breath-taking in their speed. The Pew Research Center has noted, for instance, that support for gay marriage in the United States went from 35 percent in 2001 to 52 percent in 2014—with 67 percent of people born after 1981 in support.

It is, of course, always possible that you just don't agree that women have been oppressed and that generalizations based on sexual orientation or gender are dumb. What would be the purpose of feminist criticism for such a person? Can such a nonfeminist even do feminist criticism? For that matter, is it even possible for a man to do feminist criticism? At the risk of irritating or even outraging some of my readers, I think the answer is that *anyone*—a male, even a male chauvinist, even Rush Limbaugh—can do feminist criticism and do it "honestly" in a sense. One of the wonderful things about words is that we can use them to try out ideas, to speculate, to put on roles and explore. We construct arguments and conduct analyses not only to persuade others but also to investigate things for ourselves—if we have an open, critical mind, that is. Writing is a process of learning.

If you already inhabit a feminist outlook, then applying it to literature may help you understand both the work and your outlook better. And if this way of thinking isn't where you find yourself today, it won't hurt you to visit and try to think like a native for a while. You'll enlarge your vision. At the least you'll have a better understanding of feminist thinking. Your performance as a feminist critic (or any other sort of critic) may be an act, a role you've taken on, but it need not (and ought not) be an *insincere* performance. One can *pretend* to play Macbeth or Willie Loman, or one can sincerely *play* or *inhabit* these characters. Your job is to immerse yourself in feminist criticism, genuinely attempting to appreciate its insights, regardless of whether you finally accept them.

And when is some form of feminist criticism appropriate? It's always a possibility, an available option. The way to see if a feminist approach is appropriate is to try it out. Even if the text isn't obviously dealing with feminist concerns, a feminist approach may be revealing. In fact, the absence of women or their concerns may be quite significant. For some texts, admittedly, a feminist reading may require considerable care and imagination. But, again, the pervasiveness of sexual bias in our society ensures, I would argue, that most texts will readily provide ample materials for a feminist response. Just as we expose the presence of a virus by assuming its existence and then running tests to establish its effects, we might likewise assume the existence of bias and prejudice and make efforts to expose its effects. When feminist criticism can find nothing to talk about, when all its tests come out negative, then its work will be done. Then we can assume that traditional literary studies will sufficiently include issues of sex and gender; then we can neglect to consider the implications of our actions in the context of such issues. Then we will live in a very different world.

HOW TO DO FEMINIST CRITICISM, POSTFEMINISM, AND QUEER THEORY

According to Cheryl Torsney, feminist criticism is not a single method, but rather a patchwork or "a quilt" of different methods stitched together with a common conviction: "that one can read, write, and interpret as a woman" (180). This plurality of approaches is one reason that Robert Con Davis has suggested "that the future of literary studies is being decided in current feminist theory and criticism" (161), as various ways of reading are woven together, blended, contrasted, and questioned. My survey of critical approaches ends with feminist criticism—as an example of political criticism—because it can draw on each of the theories described here, as well as on others. Any act of criticism, to be sure, is likely to draw on various strategies, blending together complementary and sometimes even contradictory assumptions and practices. But feminist criticism, postfeminism, and queer theory are perhaps uniquely positioned to benefit, and benefit from, other approaches.

I'll focus here then on two illustrative concerns of feminist criticism: how women have written and how women have been written. The first of these concerns deals significantly with the status of women writers, and its most influential formulation is probably Virginia Woolf's *A Room of One's Own*, published in 1929. Woolf's impetus can be seen in her revealing thought experiment: What if, Woolf asks, Shakespeare had a sister, equally as brilliant and talented as Shakespeare himself? What would have become of her? She would not have had the same educational opportunities, the same financial independence, the same social freedom or professional access. Obviously, her career would have been strikingly different from Shakespeare's. In fact, Woolf doubts that she would have had a career at all. In "Professions for Women," Woolf explains how her own career had been obstructed by narrow conceptions of womanhood, which offered virtually no role for serious women writers. In calling for "a room of one's own," Woolf is asking for the freedom and the space for all Shakespeare's sisters to speak honestly out of their own experiences, without assuming male pseudonyms or adopting masculine voices.

Some extraordinary women, as Woolf makes clear, somehow did manage to write, and this tradition of women's writing is extremely important because "we think back through our mothers if we are women" (*Room* 79). Without some sense of these "mothers," the woman writer will be unable to make a creative room of her own, being forced instead to suppress her unique voice and attempt to fit into the mansions of the male tradition. Literary history—a *new* literary history that includes women—thus becomes a vital action, making it possible for women to write *as women*, whatever that means. (For Woolf it appears to have included the freedom to transcend gender.)

The effects of the effort to recover women's writing have been dramatic: Most obviously, the canon of honored, "serious" literature has been enlarged to include more works by women, and an alternative canon of women's writing has also arisen. Certain genres long considered minor or secondary have received serious attention. Women did write in the major genres (fiction, drama, poetry), but their creative energies also found outlets in letters, journals, diaries, and other long-neglected forms. In recovering this work of their "mothers," feminist critics have often invoked Woolf, attempting to describe this nearly lost tradition of women's writing. Elaine Showalter in her influential *A Literature of Their Own* (1977) uses the term "gynocriticism" to refer to this study of women by women.

The second concern has to do with the way women have been written—that is, with the image of women in literature. The most influential work here, without question, is Simone de Beauvoir's *The Second Sex*, published in French in 1949. Beauvoir's point is simple but powerful: Females have been depicted in literature and culture as either Mary or Eve, the angelic mother or the evil seductress. Such a representation of women, especially in works by men, serves to make women unreal, other, the absence of maleness, rather than anything positively female or mutually human. This vision is especially pernicious when it is unnoticed and is perceived to be "natural" or "realistic." The work of the reader, then, is to expose this opposition—misogyny (woman seen as monster) or idealization (woman seen as saint)—thereby undermining its power by exposing its artifice. Notable followers of Beauvoir's tradition include Mary Ellman, whose *Thinking About Women* (1968) argued that gender stereotypes in literature are applied not only to characters but to *everything*, and Sandra Gilbert and Susan Gubar, whose *Madwoman in the Attic* (1979) argued that women writers both accept and reject the angel versus seductress stereotypes, thereby creating their own distinctive vision.

These two concerns—woman as writer, woman as written—can be illustrated by looking briefly at Mary Astell's *A Serious Proposal to the Ladies*, published in 1692. We should note first that merely reading Astell's work verges on a feminist act. Her *Proposal* certainly has not held a secure place in the traditional canon. In Tillotson, Fussell, and Waingrow's popular *Eighteenth-Century Literature* textbook, published in 1969, Astell's work does not appear (the volume covers 1660–1800). Representative works of some ninety men do appear, spread over 1,538 pages. Women writers are virtually ignored: Three are represented, occupying less than two pages. Let's recap that score: men—1,538; women—one and a fraction. In John Mahoney's anthology for the same period, *The Enlightenment and English Literature*, published about eleven years later (in 1980), we might expect to see more women writers, especially given the surge of interest in feminist criticism in the 1970s. But there are, in fact, no women at all in Mahoney's anthology.

Such neglect points to the need for alternative collections, such as Gilbert and Gubar's *Norton Anthology of Literature by Women*, which covers the middle ages (fourteenth century) to the present, and presents fifteen women writers (including Astell) in its eighteenth-century section; or Roger Lonsdale's *Eighteenth-Century Women Poets*, which offers the work of over one hundred women; or Robert Uphaus and Gretchen Foster's *The "Other" Eighteenth Century: English Women of Letters*, which presents in some depth the work of twenty-two women, including Astell. But merely offering alternatives to the traditional surveys seems to many people entirely inadequate, leaving the writing of women in a secondary, supplementary position. It is no longer plausible, after the advent of feminist criticism, to argue that women writers are justifiably omitted from the standard anthologies ("the canon") because their writing is inferior to the writing of men. For one thing, women's writing has gone largely unread, even in graduate survey courses, so that even "experts" in eighteenth-century literature may know little about Astell or any other female writer. One cannot say that the writing of men is better without having read the writing of women. For another thing, the standards used to construct "the canon" are the invention of mostly male critics and scholars, who are themselves the product of the exclusion of women: Women aren't included now because they haven't been included in the past, and the cycle perpetuates itself. Feminist criticism therefore may show how some works by women meet the traditional standards of excellence, but it may also challenge the arbitrariness of those same patriarchal notions of excellence.

So, let's consider the following two passages from Mary Astell's *Serious Proposal*. In the first Astell announces precisely what her proposal is; in the second she summarizes her plan. As you read these two excerpts (labeled A and B) pay attention to how women are presented. What images of "woman" do the passages convey? (I have numbered the sentences for easy reference.)

(A)

(1) Now as to the proposal, it is to erect a monastery, or if you will (to avoid giving offence to the scrupulous and injudicious, by names which though innocent in themselves, have been abused by superstitious practices), we will call it a religious retirement, and such as shall have a double aspect, being not only a retreat from the world for those who desire that advantage, but likewise, an institution and previous discipline to fit us to do the greatest good in it; such an institution as this (if I do not mightily deceive myself) would be the most probable method to amend the present, and improve the future age. . . .

(2) You are therefore ladies, invited into a place, where you shall suffer no other confinement, but to be kept out of the road of sin: You shall not be deprived of your grandeur, but only exchange the vain pomps and pageantry of the world, empty titles and forms of state, for the true and solid greatness of being able to despise *them*. . . .

(3) Happy retreat! which will be the introducing you into such a paradise as your mother Eve forfeited, where you shall feast on pleasures, that do not, like those of the world, disappoint your expectations, pall your appetites, and by the disgust they give you put you on the fruitless search after new delights, which when obtained are as empty as the former; but such as will make you truly happy now, and prepare you to be perfectly so hereafter. (4) Here are no serpents to deceive you, whilst you entertain yourselves in these delicious gardens. (5) No provocations will be given in this amicable society, but to love and good works, which will afford such an entertaining employment, that you'll have as little inclination as leisure to pursue those follies, which in the time of your ignorance passed with you under the name of love, although there is not in nature two more different things, than true love and that brutish passion, which pretends to ape it. (6) Here will be no rivalling but for the love of God, no ambition but to procure his favour, to which nothing will more effectually recommend you, than a great and dear affection to each other.

(B)

> (7) The ladies, I'm sure, have no reason to dislike this proposal, but I know not how the men will resent it to have their enclosure broke down, and women invited to taste of that tree of knowledge they have so long unjustly monopolized. (8) But they must excuse me, if I be as partial to my own sex as they are to theirs, and think women as capable of learning as men are, and that it becomes them as well.
> (9) For I cannot imagine wherein the hurt lies, if instead of doing mischief to one another, by an uncharitable and vain conversation, women be enabled to inform and instruct those of their own sex at least; the holy ghost having left it on record, that Priscilla as well as her husband, catechized the eloquent Apollos and the great Apostle found no fault with her. (10) It will therefore be very proper for our ladies to spend part of their time in this retirement, in adorning their minds with useful knowledge.

Since Astell's *Proposal* is considered a feminist classic, it is interesting to note how she appears to reinforce the idea of women as weak sensualists, daughters of Eve, tending toward sin. Astell tells "the ladies" that their "confinement" will allow them to "be kept out of the road of sin," as if women can resist temptation only if they are removed from it (2). Further, she explicitly links all women to Eve, asserting that this "Happy retreat" will introduce them "into such a paradise as your mother Eve forfeited" (3). Astell's ladies will be able to reenter or recreate paradise not because they are any stronger or smarter than Eve, the epitome of feminine susceptibility, but because there will be "no serpents to deceive you" in Astell's "Happy retreat" (4).

In addition, the inducements Astell offers "the ladies" are themselves sensual, as if she can tempt them into a second paradise only by promising pleasure—in fact, the same pleasure for which women originally were ejected: In the garden of Eden, it was, of course, the forbidden fruit from the tree of knowledge that Eve could not resist; in Astell's retreat, women will get to enjoy such fruit once more, being able to "*feast* on pleasures" more durable than those of the world, avoiding "*the fruitless* search after new delights," entertaining themselves in these "*delicious* gardens" of learning (3, emphasis added). Astell seems here to be reinforcing the stereotype that women are controlled by their appetites: To entice them to learn, she discusses knowledge as if it were food—a "delicious" and fruitful "feast." Astell further seems to accept the conventional sexism of depicting women as aesthetic objects, concluding that it is proper for women to be "adorning their minds with useful knowledge" (10)—as if knowledge were valuable as an adornment, an intellectual sort of ribbon or bow to make women more attractive. In consecutive sentences, Astell promises ladies that the retreat will "entertain" (4), providing "entertaining employment" (5), as if women seek only diversion, avoiding diligence.

This reading of Astell's *Proposal* deals admittedly with only a portion of her text, but it could be extended easily, and it illustrates sufficiently, I think, one activity of feminist criticism: exposing stereotypes of women. Although this exposure is often at the expense of male authors, we should not be surprised to find such sexism in Astell's text, despite her place as an early feminist: How could she entirely evade the assumptions of her time? As Janet Todd puts it:

> If "feminism," in a 1970s sense, claims absolute equality of the sexes and complex identification of roles, then no women in eighteenth-century England advocated it; if it implies equal opportunity, then probably only Mary Wollstonecraft, who hinted at female politicians while extolling motherhood, might qualify. But if a feminist is one who is aware of female problems and is angry or irritated at the female predicament, then almost every woman writer and many men could claim the title. (qtd. in Ruthven, p. 17)

We are all products of our culture, our language, our myths, and our history; therefore, attempting to identify the negative or stereotypical images in Astell's work does not constitute an attack on her. The vision of educated women in *A Proposal to the Ladies* is indeed extraordinary.

In addition to this negative strategy of unmasking prejudices, feminist criticism also undertakes the positive business of reading women's writings with a particular attentiveness to their difference either from male texts or from the dominant discourse, supposed to be controlled by men, and therefore "patriarchal." Such a recuperative reading of these passages from Astell's *Proposal*, rather than targeting the depiction of women, might look more closely at what Astell was attempting to do with these images. How does Astell's own gender affect her discourse and its aim? As a woman, writing in the late seventeenth century, proposing a kind of "monastery" to educate women, Astell addresses her text as *A Serious Proposal **to the Ladies***, but any reflection at all must acknowledge that her audience had to include men. It would have been impossible, after all, in her day, to create the sort of institution Astell proposes without the approval and even the active support of men. Astell depicts herself as speaking "to the ladies," but she surely intends to be overheard by those holding the power. How does this dual audience affect her writing?

The most obvious critical strategy would be to look for contradictions, or for assertions that can be taken two ways, or for two different phrasings of the same assertion, as Astell speaks different things to different audiences with the same text. It seems reasonable to assume that Astell's position is hardly unique, that other women writers also confronted a divided audience. Indeed, for Gilbert and Gubar, a strategy of both conforming to and undermining patriarchal cultural conventions has distinguished women's writing since Jane Austen. Although Astell's work appeared over a century before Austen's, much the same (if not worse) conditions applied. What examples of a double-voiced discourse do you find in Astell's passages? For a start, we might notice that Astell first says her proposal is to "erect a monastery" for single women, but she quickly alters "monastery" to "religious retirement" (1). Astell says she makes this change to avoid the prejudice against the term "monastery," which would have linked her project to Catholic monks, who had a reputation in Astell's day, among some anti-Papists anyway, for dabbling in the supernatural ("superstitious practices," as Astell says). But Astell might have used "nunnery" or "priory" instead of "monastery"; so, why did she first offer the term associated with monks, then withdraw it? Because, I would argue, "monastery" makes clear to one part of her audience that she is offering them a chance to move into a domain heretofore jealously controlled by men. By saying she wants "to *erect* a monastery," Astell subtly underscores the masculine privilege she wants to usurp. Lest some male readers be threatened by women assuming such erections, Astell immediately portrays her project as a "retreat," a "confinement," a withdrawal into a feminine space, not a masculine intrusion. But the empowering potential of the retreat's "delicious gardens" has already been indicated to Astell's discerning reader.

Having glimpsed this potential power, the ladies, Astell says in the second passage, will "have no reason to dislike this proposal." But, she continues, "I know not how the men will resent it to have their enclosure broke down, and women invited to taste of that tree of knowledge they have so long unjustly monopolized" (7). Earlier, Astell has taken pains to make sure her proposal is not seen as an invasion, but rather a retirement. And in the body of her proposal, Astell has repeatedly limited the ambition of her idea, making it less threatening to men: She does not believe a woman needs to study "languages" as diligently as men, but only as "are necessary to acquaint her with useful authors"; she does not desire "that women should teach in the church, or usurp authority where it is not allowed them," but only that they be allowed "to understand our duty, and not be forced to take it upon trust for others" (116). But this subsequent image reverses the earlier one of "retreat": Instead of the women confining themselves, they will be *breaking down* the "enclosure" of the men. If this proposal describes a retreat, it is a retreat into the intellectual space already occupied by men.

Likewise, although Astell has repeatedly alluded to Eve's weakness, confirming the patriarchal myth of mankind's fall, and thus reassuring part of her readers that she understands the dangerous and sinful nature of women, her concluding reference to the Genesis story also reverses the implications of the earlier allusions. Somehow Eve's disastrous deed, tasting the fruit from the forbidden tree of knowledge, has become precisely the activity that men have "so long unjustly monopolized" (7). Although Astell has appeared to reinforce the male-oriented view of the fall of "man," this version of the story now becomes problematic: Men have been zealously indulging in the same activity for which Eve has been unceasingly castigated. How can "tasting" of the tree of knowledge be considered evil? Isn't knowledge good? Why have men monopolized it?

Astell thus shrewdly intimates that men—with Godlike presumption— have built their own paradise or "enclosure," eating from the tree of knowledge themselves, while forbidding women to partake. Despite her earlier concessions to the limited ambition of women's learning, Astell's position in the later passage is much bolder, asserting that women are "as capable of learning as men are, and that it becomes them as well" (8). This radical position is balanced, but not obscured, by Astell's more modest stances earlier. But even these earlier references to the weakness of women can be played two ways.

For instance, when Astell points out to the ladies that her "Happy retreat" will be "introducing you into such a paradise as your mother Eve forfeited" (3), she appears to be acknowledging woman's sinful nature and offering a chance to undo the fall of mankind. But there is a dramatic difference between the first and the second paradise: No Adam will inhabit Astell's, for it will include single women only. This lack of men does not appear in the least to be a deterrent to the ladies' happiness; on the contrary, Astell's retreat will allow women to avoid "that brutish passion, which pretends to ape" true love (5). Instead of the love of men, which Astell suggests is animalistic, simian even, she holds out the promise of the ladies' "great and dear affection to each other" (6). The positive significance of this male absence is rather subtly conveyed by what must be seen as the most appealing aspect of this second paradise: "Here are no serpents to deceive you, whilst you entertain your selves in these delicious gardens." A single serpent ruined the first paradise for Eve (and the rest of us); but in pointing to this crucial difference, Astell uses the plural "serpents." Given the phallic symbolism of serpents, we can easily conclude that Astell is talking about bipedal serpents—the same ones who have now enclosed the tree of knowledge (which women had the courage to eat from!), keeping women out.

In this case, as I have read these passages, the negative view of women that emerges in one sort of feminist criticism (woman as written) becomes part of a positive strategy in the other kind (woman as writer).

THE WRITING PROCESS: A SAMPLE ESSAY

Let's see what opportunities a feminist approach affords a reader of the following poem, written by Samuel Johnson in 1746, about 50 years after Astell's proposal. Although he was struggling to make his reputation in 1746, Johnson would go on to become arguably the eighteenth century's greatest and most versatile writer, the second-most-quoted author in our language, after only Shakespeare.

Before you read the poem, it may be helpful to know (if you don't already) that "Stella" was often used in eighteenth-century poetry as a kind of generic name for a beautiful, youthful, charming woman. Likewise, "nymph" in this period also usually refers to such a woman, although the word literally means, in Greek and Roman mythology, a female spirit that inhabits and somehow embodies a feature of nature. (For instance, there might be a nymph of the Ohio River, who would be the spirit of the river, standing for it and living somehow "in" it.) So, a nymph or a Stella would be a beautiful woman that one could imagine being part of a lovely rural setting. "Stella" and "nymph" in this poem refer, it seems clear, to the "Miss _____" of the title. And this person seems, at some point anyway, to have been a real person: When the poem first appeared, its title was "To the Honble [short for "Honorable"] Miss Carpenter," who was Alicia Maria Carpenter, daughter of Lord Carpenter. But Anna Williams reprinted the poem in her *Miscellanies* with the current title; and since Johnson presumably assisted Williams with her collection of poems (Williams was a blind poet, given lodging and support by Johnson), it seems likely he made or approved of the change.

Now read the poem several times, noting your reactions and questions on paper.

To Miss _____ On Her Playing Upon the Harpsichord in a Room Hung With Some Flower-Pieces of Her Own Painting
Samuel Johnson

When Stella strikes the tuneful string
In scenes of imitated spring,
Where beauty lavishes her pow'rs
On beds of never-fading flow'rs,
And pleasure propagates around   5
Each charm of modulated sound,
Ah! think not, in the dang'rous hour,
The nymph fictitious, as the flow'r,

But shun, rash youth, the gay alcove,
Nor tempt the snares of wily love.   10
    When charms thus press on ev'ry sense,
What thought of flight, or of defence?
Deceitful Hope, and vain Desire,
For ever flutter o'er her lyre,
Delighting, as the youth draws nigh,   15
To point the glances of her eye,
And forming, with unerring art,
New chains to hold the captive heart.
    But on these regions of delight,
Might Truth intrude with daring flight,   20
Could Stella, sprightly, fair and young,
One moment hear the moral song,
Instruction with her flow'rs might spring,
And wisdom warble from her string.
    Mark, when from the thousand mingled dyes   25
Thou see'st one pleasing form arise,
How active light, and thoughtful shade,
In greater scenes each other aid;
Mark, when the diff'rent notes agree
In friendly contrariety,   30
How passion's well-accorded strife
Gives all the harmony of life.
Thy pictures shall thy conduct frame,
Consistent still, though not the same;
Thy musick teach the nobler art   35
To tune the regulated heart.
           (1746)

Preparing to Respond

After you've invested some effort in the poem, becoming familiar with it, compare the results of your reading to my own, printed below.

Reading Notes on "To Miss _____ "

    Line 1: "strikes the tuneful string"? I suppose this means her playing upon the harpsichord.
    Line 2: "In scenes of imitated spring"? What does this mean? It must refer to her paintings of "some flower-pieces," which would be an "imitated" spring.

Line 4: "never-fading flow'rs"—because they're painted, not real.

Lines 7–8: The warning here seems odd: "think not . . . / The nymph fictitious, as the flow'r," as if someone couldn't tell the difference between a girl playing the harpsichord and a painting! There must be something else going on here.

And why is this hour dangerous? Because of "the snares of wily love" (10). The speaker is afraid he will fall for the nymph if he doesn't watch out. Or, rather, he's afraid the "rash youth" (9) will fall. Is he the rash youth?

Lines 11–18: This section makes clear that the speaker fears the effect of Stella upon the youth. Her artistry will capture him if he is not careful, creating "New chains to hold the captive heart."

Lines 19–24: In this section the speaker points out that the tremendous power Stella has to take prisoners might also be used for good: "Instruction" might come from her painting (23); "wisdom" might come from her music (24). To get these benefits, "Truth" will have to "intrude with daring flight" (20) into "these regions of delight" (19). What does this mean? That her art and music will have to do more than just give pleasure or seduce the affections of rash youths. Stella herself will have to "hear the moral song" (22) if her charms are to have some useful purpose.

Lines 25–34: We're told to "mark," or take note of, the way painting works, and then the way music works. Specifically, we're told to notice how all the different "mingled" colors come together to make "one pleasing form," and how all the "diff'rent notes" come together in "friendly contrariety."

Lines 35–36: I think these lines make clear why we are instructed to "mark" how conflicting dyes and notes come together in harmony. The speaker is most concerned earlier in the poem by the charms of Stella's music and painting, which could make a "captive" of the "rash youth." These charms could be the forces for good, however, as the third section asserts. This fourth section then explains how harmony comes from contrariety. So, what is the "contrariety" here? The speaker wants Stella's pleasure to be opposed, or complemented, or completed by instruction. The sensual indulgence of her art will serve some higher purpose if her painting could "thy conduct frame" (33) and her music could "tune the regulated heart" (36).

Who is "thy" in these closing lines? Stella? The youth? The speaker? The reader? My guess would be all of the above. Stella is being addressed—the poem is "To" her after all, which might mean "in honor of" or "to be sent to." But other readers clearly are meant to overhear, or "oversee," the advice, especially the rash youth, perhaps Johnson himself.

Now we want to evolve a feminist reading of the poem.

Johnson is not, I think it's safe to say, a neglected woman writer, and so the feminist approach that seems most promising here would focus on the following questions:

- What role does sex or gender play in this work?
- What image of women is conveyed by the poem?
- How is the relationship between men and women depicted?

Some material toward answering these questions is already beginning to appear, I think, in my notes above: The speaker of the poem clearly sees Stella, or her charms, or the charms of her music and painting, as "dang'rous" (7); and Stella is encouraged to add "Truth" (20) and "Instruction" (23) to the pleasures of her charming arts. The next step will be to identify materials that will allow me to address the questions above and then to think about the audience I'm trying to reach and what I'm trying to accomplish. Feminist criticism characteristically tries to intervene in the ongoing traditional discussion. How can a feminist perspective on this poem affect our thinking?

Before you look at my annotations here, I encourage you to look at the poem again yourself, then compare my notes to your own.

Shaping

My first impression had been that the poem celebrated Stella's (or Alicia Carpenter's) artistic and musical talents and encouraged her to add instruction and virtue to those charms. Focusing on a feminist stance altered my own view, and what emerged here for me was the speaker's unrelenting vision of Stella as a threat. As I continued to reread the poem, I was surprised by the intensity of the speaker's fear: What is so threatening about a young lady playing a harpsichord in a room with some of her paintings? The declared danger is her effect on the youth—love, or infatuation, or lust, which becomes some sort of loss of independence and autonomy. Everything I saw as I annotated seemed aimed at one thing: neutralizing, controlling, managing somehow the tremendous feminine power that Stella's charms represent—the power to enchain the heart of any rash youth, which certainly must include the speaker, who (I can't help suspecting) may be Johnson himself.

My goal at this point is beginning to emerge, as I realize that I want my audience to see that Johnson's overt morality may be something more oppressive: The poem aims to control "Stella" or get her to control herself, and the reason for this effort is precisely that the speaker fears he cannot control himself. It is not imperative to bring Adam and Eve into the discussion, but the poem does seem to replay that enduring story: woman as temptation, who causes man to fall. In other words, the poem seems to demonstrate once more Simone de Beauvoir's thesis that women tend to be presented as Eve or Mary, evil temptress or virginal saint. I imagined an audience that might think I'm making too much out of this—seeing something sinister when it's just a poem about self-control; so I planned to try to anticipate this reaction and provide careful, balanced support.

I jotted down my supporting ideas and played around with them until some logical progression began to emerge. Here is the order I came up with (the items may make more sense when you see them in my draft essay):

1. Erasing Miss _____'s name: the title
2. Thesis: Johnson aims to blank out women's sensuality and danger
3. Johnson's audience: Miss _____ ostensibly, but really a warning to the youth; to the reader; ultimately to Johnson himself
4. Surface message to "Stella": include instruction/wisdom
5. Restrictive actions become clearer in the end: to tune and to frame
6. Stella as danger: sensual enslavement ("Chains")
7. Sensual disorientation—what is real?
8. Promiscuity (woman as potentially uncontrollable desire):
     painting "lavishes" on "beds"
     music "propagates"
9. Stella is not real—a fiction: the speaker as confused as the youth
10. "Truth" called in: regulate Stella's art
11. Add instruction to pleasure
12. Morality for the youth's benefit, not hers
13. Identity: Limit hers to save his

Drafting

The next step was to transform my individual ideas and annotated poem into a rough draft, which I could then revise and polish. I also did a little more research on the poem, reading the notes to the poem in the standard *Yale Edition of the Works of Samuel Johnson*. This step, as always, takes some time and patience; but if you're sufficiently prepared and you have adequate time, it has its substantial satisfactions. You may want to sketch out your own essay before you look at mine.

Beware of Women with Harpsichords and Paintings: On Samuel Johnson's Misogyny

Introduces the poem and the problem: the erasure of "Miss Carpenter."

The title to one of Samuel Johnson's occasional poems is perhaps most revealing in what it leaves out: "To Miss _____ On Her Playing Upon the Harpsichord in a Room Hung With Some Flower-Pieces of Her Own Painting." Why has the woman's name become a blank, especially since "Stella" appears in the first line, and since the poem was originally addressed "To the Honble Miss Carpenter" (the "honourable" Alicia Maria Carpenter, daughter of the second Lord Carpenter)? Why has Johnson erased Miss Carpenter and ignored "Stella," presumably his pseudonym for her? (The poem appeared first in Dodsley's *Museum* in November of 1746; it was reprinted with the altered title in a collection "edited" by Johnson's friend Anna Williams, who was blind, and who relied heavily on Johnson's assistance. I am assuming Johnson is responsible for the title change.)

Thesis: the poem is about the threat of women (women as Eve).

This paper argues that Johnson has removed Miss Carpenter's name because the poem really is about the threat that women pose and the need to blank them out, erase them, neutralize them, render them less dangerous. Although the poem is addressed "To Miss _____," its more urgent message is directed at another audience, the unnamed "rash youth" in the poem, who stands for anyone like the speaker, like Johnson, who is foolish enough to go near a woman with a harpsichord and some paintings—or any other props for that matter.

The surface reading: set-up for what follows.

The poem, to be sure, may appear on a superficial reading to be nothing more than advice to a young artist and musician, encouraging her to include instruction in her performances, adding morality, virtue, "Truth," to the pleasures of her forms and harmonies. The poem's conclusion summarizes this surface message:

> Thy pictures shall thy conduct frame,
> Consistent still, though not the same;
> Thy musick teach the nobler art
> To tune the regulated heart.
>
> (33–36)

The frame as containment.

But why, we must ask, does Johnson (or the speaker) believe that Stella's "conduct" needs a "frame"? Why does her heart need to be tuned and "regulated"? Although framing and tuning are laudable when applied to music or art, Stella is not a painting or a song, and Johnson's conclusion makes her an object and expresses a criticism: Stella needs to be closed in, limited, set apart (framed); she needs to be standardized, fixed, corrected (tuned). And the reason for this discipline and confinement is, quite simply, she is "dang'rous" (7).

> Sexuality is dangerous.

The danger, specifically, is that Stella threatens to enslave any "rash youth" with her art, both aural and visual, forming "New chains to hold the captive heart" (18). Her "unerring" art, Johnson says, is so powerful that the poor youth is totally disoriented in the poem's first section, unable to tell what is real and what isn't: The flowers, Johnson feels compelled to tell the youth, are not real; the woman is. The point seems absurd (imagine telling someone this) until we realize exactly what the threat of "the dang'rous hour" is: It is sexuality, sensuousness, passion, "wily love"; and these entities are so powerful that they make truth and fiction run together.

> Imagination is dangerous.

But the distinction between the woman and her art is crucial. Her art is promiscuous and enduring: her painting "lavishes her pow'rs / On beds of never-fading flow'rs"; "pleasure propagates around" with her music, indiscriminately pleasing all. But the youth should not confuse the painted beds or melodious propagation with real beds, real propagation: The woman is not a fiction or a fantasy, receptive to his "Hope" or "Desire" (13)—his "Deceitful Hope, and vain Desire." But the speaker, like the rash youth, is having trouble seeing what is real: "Stella," after all, is not the woman's name. She is the speaker's creation. The reality is that her "charms," which "press on ev'ry sense" at the moment, cannot be totally framed or regulated because the speaker and the youth participate in their creation. And because Stella, the "real" Stella, cannot be possessed, the overwhelming hope and desire that she stirs up become dangerous, threatening to engulf the identity of the youth, who will become simply the one who hopes and desires, the victim of his own imagination.

> Conclusion: Miss Carpenter must be contained and blanked out by the poem; women are dangerous.

Rather than give in to the illusory "regions of delight," Johnson calls in the pleasure police—"Truth," who will supposedly rein in "Stella, sprightly, fair, and young" by exposing the artificiality of her charms. Sensual indulgence, Johnson asserts, should be neutralized by "friendly contrariety," as reason cancels out passion. The act of removing

"Miss Carpenter" from the poem, then, leaving an empty
space, is simply the logical extension of Johnson's effort
to frame, regulate, abstract, and oppose the passion of
women. Since the youth cannot control his imagination
and desire, losing his ability to tell truth from art, then
Stella must restrain her art. To save his identity, the poem
takes away hers.

Revision: Gay and Lesbian Criticism

Earlier I referred to Jonathan Culler's assertion that "feminist criticism"
is "the name that should be applied to all criticism alert to the critical
ramifications of sexual oppression" (56). Certainly, the forms of "sexual
oppression" and gender expression in our society are more varied than this
chapter has acknowledged so far, and we might expand our consideration
here to include gay and lesbian studies and queer theory, which have made
impressive contributions to the study of literature in the past few decades.

If we consider my own draft above, it seems clear that I have made a
revealing and unwarranted assumption: The "rash youth," I have taken for
granted, is a male. Specifically, I have assumed that the youth is a heterosexual male enamored of the presumably heterosexual Stella. But the sex
of the youth, as you may have noticed, is actually nowhere indicated in the
poem. If it is sexist to use "he" to refer to men *and* women (and it clearly
is), then it's similarly heterosexist to assume that undesignated romantic or
sexual relationships always refer to heterosexual couples, isn't it? Johnson
doesn't make the sex of the rash youth clear, and he therefore opens up
various other readings. Consider for a moment how the possibility that the
youth is female might alter or further expand our reading of the poem.

For instance: The poem's caution against "pleasure" might immediately take on a different hue, for the "dang'rous hour" might be the one
in which the youth is tempted to fall in love with another woman. And
the odd injunction, "think not . . . / The nymph fictitious, as the flow'r"
makes considerable sense, as the speaker warns the youth not to imagine
that the nymph would be receptive to a lesbian encounter; or (alternatively)
the speaker warns the youth not to imagine that the nymph is actually a
man. The nymph is not "fictitious"; she is only what she appears to be, and
falling in love with her would be disastrous for the female "youth," lesbian
or not. Even though "charms thus press on ev'ry sense," the youth is being
advised to resist these "New chains."

More specific is the warning to "shun, rash youth, the gay alcove, /
Nor tempt the snares of wily love." An alcove is "a small, recessed section of a
room, a nook" (*Webster's*)—or in other words, a closet. If "gay" had meant
"homosexual" in Johnson's day (it apparently did not), then avoid "the gay

alcove" would mean shun "the gay closet"—avoid being a hidden homosexual. For modern readers, "gay alcove" does suggest such a meaning, which it is difficult (for some readers anyway) to erase from the poem. Further, it would be difficult to say with certainty that "gay alcove" could not possibly have suggested to Johnson, extremely sensitive to connotations, the great lexicographer, something of its future meaning. Douglas Atkins, in fact, provides such an anachronistic reading of "gay" in Alexander Pope's poetry (see Atkins, p. 124). This kind of emphasis upon the reader's response, rather than the author's assumed or even stated intention, enables gay and lesbian critics to construct illuminating and controversial readings. Barbara Smith, for instance, has argued in a pioneering essay that Toni Morrison's *Sula* (1973) champions the same-sex relationship between Nel and Sula and denigrates heterosexual marriage—a reading that Morrison herself has rejected. By its very name, queer theory strives to upset the sexual status quo, with critics such as Judith Butler, Alan Sinfield, and Eve Kosofsky Sedgwick challenging the simple division of human beings into homosexual and heterosexual, and thereby promoting a multifaceted attack on homophobia.

Returning to Johnson's poem, such an antihomophobic stance might suggest that "wily love" covertly refers to the danger of the "snares" of lesbianism, since "wily" has the same root word, *wigle* (Old English), as "witch." At least, we can now see better the point of the poem's conclusion, advocating "diff'rent notes," "friendly contrariety," and "well-accorded strife": Johnson's heterosexism urges us to endorse "difference" in love, attacking (in rather cloaked terms) same-sex love, which belongs in a closet we shouldn't enter. This reading I have sketched here is obviously only one possibility—a rather daring one, I think, in fact. I can also see an entirely different reading in which the youth is a gay man, and "shun the gay alcove" means "stay out of the closet; accept your sexuality."

Feminist, postfeminist, and queer theory approaches have much in common, as I have suggested. Their shared aim is to expose stereotypes and fight prejudice, dismantling oppressive ideas of two natural sexes or genders, uniformly opposed and attracted. The question of whether homosexuality represents a choice or a destiny, a matter of preference or biology, becomes finally irrelevant to the more fundamental question of freedom and tolerance.

PRACTICING FEMINIST, POSTFEMINIST, AND QUEER THEORY CRITICISM

I hope at this point you have some idea of the way these approaches can make writing about literature more interesting and revealing. More important, I hope you can see how doing this kind of criticism involves you in an important exploration of our culture and your own principles. After this political criticism, it is especially difficult to say that the study of literature has no real relation to our lives. Literature is a particularly revealing and influential part of the myriad of culture that surrounds and shapes (with or without our compliance or resistance) you and me. Literary criticism can help us see that and perhaps do something about it.

As I've suggested above, feminist criticism can be applied (at least in theory) to any work—including not just "great" novels or poems or plays, but also television shows, movies, detective stories, science fiction, advertisements, greeting card verse, bumper stickers, whatever. To get you started, I've provided below two well-known poems, a short story, and some comments on a movie director that I hope will stimulate your thinking.

Shall I Compare Thee to a Summer's Day?
William Shakespeare

Shall I compare thee to a summer's day?
Thou art more lovely and more temperate.
Rough winds do shake the darling buds of May,
And summer's lease hath all too short a date.
Sometimes too hot the eye of heaven shines,   5
And often is his gold complexion dimmed;
And every fair from fair sometimes declines,
By chance, or nature's changing course, untrimmed.
But thy eternal summer shall not fade,
Nor lose possession of that fair thou ow'st;   10
Nor shall death brag thou wand'rest in his shade,
When in eternal lines to time thou grow'st.
    So long as men can breathe or eyes can see,
    So long lives this, and this gives life to thee.

(1609)

Questions

1. The poem aims to be flattering, it seems clear, but what is the basis of its flattery? That is, what does the speaker value?
2. It is usually assumed that this poem is addressed to a woman. Is there any support for this supposition in the poem itself? What is the sex of the speaker of the poem? Do these questions alter your perception of the poem or open up alternative readings?
3. If the loved one is a woman, how does this poem reinforce conventional ideas about aging and beauty? How is a person not like a summer's day?

4. How comforting would the final couplet be to the person addressed? What is the source of the loved one's immortality? Who has the power? How does the poem reinforce this power?   ■

My Life had stood—a Loaded Gun
Emily Dickinson

My Life had stood—a Loaded Gun—
In Corners—till a Day
The Owner passed—identified—
And carried Me away—

And now We roam in Sovreign Woods—   5
And now We hunt the Doe—
And every time I speak for Him—
The Mountains straight reply—

And do I smile, such cordial light
[Upon] Opon the Valley glow—   10
It is as a Vesuvian face
Had let its pleasure through—

And when at Night—Our good Day done—
I guard My Master's Head—
'Tis better than the Eider Duck's   15
Deep Pillow—to have shared—

To foe of His—I'm deadly foe—
None stir the second time—
On whom I lay a Yellow Eye—
Or an emphatic Thumb—   20

Though I than He—may longer live
He longer must—than I—
For I have but the power to kill,
Without—the power to die—

                                                        (1863)

Questions _____

1. What is "Vesuvian"? (You'll find a dictionary helpful.) What is an "Eider Duck"? What is the "Yellow Eye"? What do you think the "emphatic Thumb" might be?

2. Assuming the speaker is female, what is the significance of comparing her life to a loaded gun? How does she view herself? Does the speaker have any autonomy or independence?

3. What is implied about the relationship of men to women? Who has the power? What kind of power?

4. What is the source of the speaker's pleasure, do you think?

5. How would the poem change if the speaker were assumed to be male? How would the central metaphor, for instance, be affected?

6. How does the final stanza reinforce conventional or archaic ideas about women and their relationship to men?

7. Does the speaker have any autonomy or independence?   ∎

Say Yes
Tobias Wolff

They were doing the dishes, his wife washing while he dried. He'd washed the night before. Unlike most men he knew, he really pitched in on the housework. A few months earlier he'd overheard a friend of his wife's congratulate her on having such a considerate husband, and he thought, *I try*. Helping out with the dishes was a way he had of showing how considerate he was.

They talked about different things and somehow got on the subject of whether white people should marry black people. He said that all things considered, he thought it was a bad idea.

"Why?" she asked.

Sometimes his wife got this look where she pinched her brows together and bit her lower lip and stared down at something. When he saw her like this he knew he should keep his mouth shut, but he never did. Actually it made him talk more. She had that look now.

"Why?" she asked again, and stood there with her hand inside a bowl, not washing it but just holding it above the water.

"Listen," he said, "I went to school with blacks, and I've worked with blacks and lived on the same street with blacks, and we've always gotten along just fine. I don't need you coming along now and implying that I'm a racist."

"I didn't imply anything," she said, and began washing the bowl again, turning it around in her hand as though she were shaping it. "I just don't see what's wrong with a white person marrying a black person, that's all."

"They don't come from the same culture as we do. Listen to them sometime—they even have their own language. That's okay with me, I *like* hearing them talk"—he did; for some reason it always made him feel happy—"but it's different. A person from their culture and a person from our culture could never really *know* each other."

"Like you know me?" his wife asked.

"Yes. Like I know you."

"But if they love each other," she said. She was washing faster now, not looking at him.

Oh boy, he thought. He said, "Don't take my word for it. Look at the statistics. Most of those marriages break up."

"Statistics." She was piling dishes on the drainboard at a terrific rate, just swiping at them with the cloth. Many of them were greasy, and there were flecks of food between the tines of the forks. "All right," she said, "what about foreigners? I suppose you think the same thing about two foreigners getting married."

"Yes," he said, "as a matter of fact I do. How can you understand someone who comes from a completely different background?"

"Different," said his wife. "Not the same, like us."

"Yes, different," he snapped, angry with her for resorting to this trick of repeating his words so that they sounded crass, or hypocritical. "These are dirty," he said, and dumped all the silverware back into the sink.

The water had gone flat and gray. She stared down at it, her lips pressed tight together, then plunged her hands under the surface. "Oh!" she cried, and jumped back. She took her right hand by the wrist and held it up. Her thumb was bleeding.

"Ann, don't move," he said. "Stay right there." He ran upstairs to the bathroom and rummaged in the medicine chest for alcohol, cotton, and a Band-Aid. When he came back down she was leaning against the refrigerator with her eyes closed, still holding her hand. He took the hand and dabbed at her thumb with the cotton. The bleeding had stopped. He squeezed it to see how deep the wound was and a single drop of blood welled up, trembling and bright, and fell to the floor. Over the thumb she stared at him accusingly. "It's shallow," he said. "Tomorrow you won't even know it's there." He hoped that she appreciated how quickly he had come to her aid. He'd acted out of concern for her, with no thought of getting anything in return, but now the thought occurred to him that it would be a nice gesture on her part not to start up that conversation again, as he was tired of it. "I'll finish up here," he said. "You go and relax."

"That's okay," she said. "I'll dry."

He began to wash the silverware again, giving a lot of attention to the forks.

"So," she said, "you wouldn't have married me if I'd been black."

"For Christ's sake, Ann!"

"Well, that's what you said, didn't you?"

"No, I did not. The whole question is ridiculous. If you had been black we probably wouldn't even have met. You would have had your friends and I would have had mine. The only black girl I ever really knew was my partner in the debating club, and I was already going out with you by then."

"But if we had met, and I'd been black?"

"Then you probably would have been going out with a black guy." He picked up the rinsing nozzle and sprayed the silverware. The water was so hot that the metal darkened to pale blue, then turned silver again.

"Let's say I wasn't," she said. "Let's say I am black and unattached and we meet and fall in love."

He glanced over at her. She was watching him and her eyes were bright. "Look," he said, taking a reasonable tone, "this is stupid. If you were black you wouldn't be you." As he said this he realized it was absolutely true. There was no possible way of arguing with the fact that she would not be herself if she were black. So he said it again: "If you were black you wouldn't be you."

"I know," she said, "but let's just say."

He took a deep breath. He had won the argument but he still felt cornered. "Say what?" he asked.

"That I'm black, but still me, and we fall in love. Will you marry me?"

He thought about it.

"Well?" she said, and stepped close to him. Her eyes were even brighter. "Will you marry me?"

"I'm thinking," he said.

"You won't, I can tell. You're going to say no."

"Let's not move too fast on this," he said. "There are lots of things to consider. We don't want to do something we would regret for the rest of our lives."

"No more considering. Yes or no."

"Since you put it that way—"

"Yes or no."

"Jesus, Ann. All right. No."

She said, "Thank you," and walked from the kitchen into the living room. A moment later he heard her turning the pages of a magazine. He knew that she was too angry to be actually reading it, but she didn't snap through the pages the way he would have done. She turned them slowly, as if she were studying every word. She was demonstrating her indifference to him, and it had the effect he knew she wanted it to have. It hurt him.

He had no choice but to demonstrate his indifference to her. Quietly, thoroughly, he washed the rest of the dishes. Then he dried them and put them away. He wiped the counters and the stove and scoured the linoleum where the drop of blood had fallen. While he was at it, he decided, he might as well mop the whole floor. When he was done the kitchen looked new, the way it looked when they were first shown the house, before they had ever lived here.

He picked up the garbage pail and went outside. The night was clear and he could see a few stars to the west, where the lights of the town didn't blur them out. On El Camino the traffic was steady and light, peaceful as a river. He felt ashamed that he had let his wife get him into a fight. In another thirty years or so they would both be dead. What would all that stuff matter then? He thought of the years they had spent together, and how close they were, and how well they knew each other, and his throat tightened so that he could hardly breathe. His face and neck began to tingle. Warmth flooded his chest. He stood there for a while, enjoying these sensations, then picked up the pail and went out the back gate.

The two mutts from down the street had pulled over the garbage can again. One of them was rolling around on his back and the other had something in her mouth. Growling, she tossed it into the air, leaped up and caught it, growled again and whipped her head from side to side. When they saw him coming they trotted away with short, mincing steps. Normally he would heave rocks at them, but this time he let them go.

The house was dark when he came back inside. She was in the bathroom. He stood outside the door and called her name. He heard bottles clinking, but she didn't answer him. "Ann, I'm really sorry," he said. "I'll make it up to you, I promise."

"How?" she asked.

He wasn't expecting this. But from a sound in her voice, a level and definite note that was strange to him, he knew that he had to come up with the right answer. He leaned against the door. "I'll marry you," he whispered.

"We'll see," she said. "Go on to bed. I'll be out in a minute."

He undressed and got under the covers. Finally he heard the bathroom door open and close.

"Turn off the light," she said from the hallway.

"What?"

"Turn off the light."

He reached over and pulled the chain on the bedside lamp. The room went dark. "All right," he said. He lay there, but nothing happened. "All right," he said again. Then he heard a movement across the room. He sat up, but he couldn't see a thing. The room was silent. His heart pounded the way it had on their first night together, the way it still did when he woke at a noise in the darkness and waited to hear it again—the sound of someone moving through the house, a stranger.

(1985)

Questions

1. Explain the story's last sentence. Why does it end with the word "stranger"?

2. Why does Ann pursue this question? Did the husband come up with the right answer? Explain. Why does Ann ask her husband to turn off the light?

3. Is the husband a sexist? A racist? How would you describe him? How does Wolff want us to see him? How might this story affect a reader opposed to interracial marriage?

4. How do the small details of washing the dishes contribute to the story? Consider, for instance, the still-greasy dishes, the color of the washing water, the injury to Ann. Consider especially the husband's decision to mop, and the way he describes the floor.   ■

Gender in the Movies

Howard Hawks was a successful American filmmaker whose later works included *Sergeant York* (1941), *The Big Sleep* (1946), *Red River* (1948), *Gentlemen Prefer Blondes* (1953), and *Rio Bravo* (1959). According to Peter Wollen, a British film critic, Hawks portrayed men as the "prey" of women: "Women are admitted to the male group only after much disquiet, and a long ritual courtship, phased round the offering, lighting, and exchange of cigarettes, during which they prove themselves worthy of entry" (86). Is Wollen correct? Watch some of Hawks' work and see if men are depicted as the prey of women, and if there is a cigarette ritual allowing women to bond with men. Another idea: Compare the portrayal of women and men in a Hawks movie to their depiction in a current movie. Are there gender-based rituals displayed in contemporary films?

Useful Terms for Political Criticism

Canon: The group of works that are usually reprinted, read, assigned, written about, and taken most seriously. Feminist criticism has been particularly effective in arguing that some works are included and others ignored on largely political grounds. Historically, women as a rule have had few opportunities to write; and when they have somehow managed to produce works of merit, these often have not been appreciated or understood (some women writers have adopted male pseudonyms in order to get a fair reading). Critics have similarly pressed to open the canon to African American, American Indian, and other neglected writers.

Constructed: This term is particularly powerful because it reminds us that any representation of a particular ethnic or racial or sexual group is something that is made up. It is not inevitable, nor does it fully (or even partially) depict reality. Our notions, in other words, of women, or African Americans, or American Indians, or gay men, or any other segment of society are just that: our notions.

Double-voiced: A member of an oppressed group, attempting to speak to and through the dominant culture, faces a tricky situation: how to speak one's mind without being silenced. One strategy is to write with two voices, saying what can be taken on the surface in a nonthreatening way, and on a deeper level in a subversive or challenging way.

Exclusion: What we value as great literature depends on what values we bring to our reading. Since white European males have dominated the worlds of publishing and criticism, it is not surprising that white European males have dominated the canon of literature. Some works may have been excluded from study because of the status of their authors; others may have been excluded because their virtues are not appreciated by established literary values.

Gender: "Gender" refers to the cultural aspects of sexuality. In other words, gender includes not just biological factors, but also psychological and social factors as well. We are still trying to discover just how much of "maleness" and "femaleness" can be attributed to biology, and how much to other factors. It seems clear that gender is not entirely constructed by cultural influences, that there are some differences between the sexes (surprise!). But the wide range of variation within "male" and "female" makes it difficult to say definitively what those differences always are, and thus how "gender" (the construction of male and female) relates to "sex" (the biological status).

Marxist: Because Karl Marx considered issues of economy and class to be fundamental, shaping everything, literary criticism that focuses on economy and class is often termed "Marxist," even when the critic does not embrace the same principles as Marx. This way of reading, attaching primary importance to the material sources of a work in class and money, is also sometimes called "materialist," especially when the physical conditions and circumstances are the focus.

Materialist: *See* Marxist.

Patriarchy: Literally, "father-ruled," the term points to the superior status of men within a culture. The opposite term, "matriarchy," refers to a culture in which women are superior.

Sex: *See* Gender.

Sexist: Assuming that someone has certain characteristics because of his or her sex is sexist. Usually, the term is used to describe pejorative characterizations of women as a group, or of individual women as representative types of that group.

✔ Checklist for Political Criticism

1. Consider how the writer's sex, race, class, or other identity has influenced the work.

2. Look for stereotypes based on sex, gender, race, class, or other convention.

3. Imagine how the work might be read differently by a reader of a particular sex, class, race, or other identity.

Works Cited

Astell, Mary. *A Serious Proposal to the Ladies*. London, 1692. Excerpt (with omissions) rpt. in *The Norton Anthology of Literature by Women*. Ed. Sandra Gilbert and Susan Gubar. New York: Norton, 1985. 113–117. Print.

Atkins, Douglas. *Reading Deconstruction, Deconstructive Reading*. Lexington: UP of Kentucky, 1983. Print.

Brooks, Ann. *Postfeminisms: Feminism, Cultural Theory, and Cultural Forms*. London: Routledge, 1997. Print.

Butler, Judith. *Bodies That Matter: On the Discursive Limits of Sex*. London: Routledge, 1993. Print.

— . *Gender Trouble*. London: Routledge, 1990. Print.

Culler, Jonathan. "Reading as a Woman." *On Deconstruction: Theory and Criticism after Structuralism*. Ithaca, NY: Cornell UP, 1982. 43–64. Print.

Davis, Robert Con. "The Sexual Dialectic." *Contemporary Literary Criticism*. Ed. Robert Con Davis. New York: Longman, 1986. 161–165. Print.

de Beauvoir, Simone. *The Second Sex*. Trans. H. M. Parshley. New York: Vintage, 1974. Trans. of *Le deuxieme sexe*. 2 vols. Paris: Gallimard, 1949. Print.

Ellman, Mary. *Thinking About Women*. New York: Harcourt, 1968. Print.

Gilbert, Sandra, and Susan Gubar. *The Madwoman in the Attic*. New Haven, CT: Yale UP, 1979. Print.

Haskell, Molly. *From Reverence to Rape: The Treatment of Women in the Movies*. New York: Holt, 1974. Print.

Hitchens, Christopher. *Unacknowledged Legislators: Writers in the Public Sphere*. New York: Verso, 2002. Print.

Johnson, Barbara. *A World of Difference*. Baltimore: Johns Hopkins UP, 1987.

Laquer, Thomas. *Making Sex: Body and Gender from the Greeks to Freud*. Cambridge, MA: Harvard UP, 1992. Print.

Ruthven, K. K. *Feminist Literary Studies: An Introduction*. Cambridge: Cambridge UP, 1984. Print.

254 Gendering the Text

Schor, Naomi. "Feminist and Gender Studies." *Introduction to Scholarship in Modern Languages and Literatures.* 2nd ed. Ed. Joseph Gibaldi. New York: MLA, 1992. 262–287. Print.

Sedgwick, Eve Kosofsky. *Tendencies.* Durham, NC: Duke UP, 1993. Print.

Showalter, Elaine. *A Literature of Their Own: British Women Novelists from Brontë to Lessing.* Princeton, NJ: Princeton UP, 1977. Print.

Sinfield, Alan. *Cultural Politics: Queer Reading.* Philadelphia: U of Pennsylvania P, 1994. Print.

Smith, Barbara. *Toward a Black Feminist Criticism.* New York: Out and Out P, 1977. Print.

Torsney, Cheryl. "The Critical Quilt: Alternative Authority in Feminist Criticism." *Contemporary Literary Theory.* Ed. G. Douglas Atkins and Laura Morrow. Amherst: U of Massachusetts P, 1989. 180–199. Print.

Wollen, Peter. *Signs and Meaning in the Cinema.* Bloomington: Indiana UP, 1972. Print.

Woolf, Virginia. *A Room of One's Own.* 1929. New York: Harcourt, 1981. Print.

—. "Professions for Women." In *The Death of the Moth and Other Essays.* New York: Harcourt, 1942. 235–242. Print.

Recommended Further Reading

Crewe, Louie, and Rictor Norton. "The Homophobic Imagination: An Editorial." *College English.* 1974; 36: 272–290. Print. A pioneering essay, helping to open the door for gay and lesbian studies.

Eagleton, Mary, ed. *Feminist Literary Criticism.* London: Longman, 1991. Print. An appealing collection for further study because essays offering opposing views are paired.

Freedman, Estelle. *The Essential Feminist Reader.* Boston: Modern Library, 2007. Print. This thoughtfully chosen collection spans five centuries, offering a rich introduction to primary sources.

Gamble, Sarah. *The Routledge Companion to Feminism and Postfeminism.* London: Routledge, 2002. Print. Fifteen authoritative essays by various experts on everything from "Second Wave Feminism" to "Feminism and Film."

Gilbert, Sandra M., and Susan Gubar, eds. *Feminist Literary Theory and Criticism: A Norton Reader.* New York: Norton, 2007. Print. An outstanding selection of essays and excerpts.

Jehlen, Myra. "Gender." *Critical Terms for Literary Study.* Ed. Frank Lentricchia and Thomas McLaughlin. Chicago: Chicago UP, 1990. Print. An excellent far-ranging essay, unfolding usefully the relationships between "gender" and "sex."

Phoca, Sophia, and Rebecca Wright. *Introducing Postfeminism.* New York: Totem Books, 1999. Print. An entertaining and engaging illustrated introduction.

Rooney, Ellen, ed. *The Cambridge Companion to Feminist Literary Theory.* Cambridge: Cambridge UP, 2006. Print. A masterful collection of informative essays.

Sedgwick, Eve Kosovsky. *Epistemology of the Closet.* London: Harvester, 1991. Print. An engaging book, important in establishing gay and lesbian criticism.

Smith, Barbara. "Toward Black Feminist Criticism." *New Feminist Criticism.* Ed. Elaine Showalter. New York: Pantheon, 1985. Print. An important perspective, lucidly presented.

Woods, Gregory. *A History of Gay Literature: The Male Tradition.* New Haven, CT: Yale, 1999. Print. A fascinating history.

Appendix I

John Donne
(1572–1631)

The Canonization

For God's sake hold your tongue, and let me love,
    Or chide my palsy, or my gout,
My five gray hairs, or ruined fortune flout,
      With wealth your state, your mind with arts improve,
        Take you a course, get you a place,   5
        Observe His Honor, or His Grace,
    Or the king's real, or his stampèd face
      Contèmplate; what you will, approve,
      So you will let me love.

Alas, alas, who's injured by my love?   10
    What merchant's ships have my sighs drowned?
Who says my tears have overflowed his ground?
      When did my colds a forward spring remove?
        When did the heats which my veins fill
        Add one more to the plaguy bill?   15
    Soldiers find wars, and lawyers find out still
      Litigious men, which quarrels move,
      Though she and I do love.

Call us what you will, we are made such by love;
    Call her one, me another fly,   20

We're tapers too, and at our own cost die,
    And we in us find the eagle and the dove.
        The phoenix riddle hath more wit
        By us; we two being one, are it.
So, to one neutral thing both sexes fit.   25
    We die and rise the same, and prove
    Mysterious by this love.

We can die by it, if not live by love,
    And if unfit for tomb and hearse
Our legend be, it will be fit for verse;   30
    And if no piece of chronicle we prove,
        We'll build in sonnets pretty rooms,
        As well a well-wrought urn becomes
The greatest ashes, as half-acre tombs,
    And by these hymns, all shall approve   35
    Us canonized for Love.

And thus invoke us: "You, whom reverend love
    Made one another's hermitage;
You, to whom love was peace, that now is rage;
    Who did the whole world's soul contract, and drove   40
        Into the glasses of your eyes
        (So made such mirrors, and such spies,
That they did all to you epitomize)
    Countries, towns, courts: beg from above
    A pattern of your love!"   45

(1633)

Appendix 2

A Note on How Theories Relate

One way to think about how the different theories relate to one another would be in terms of the elements involved in any act of communicating. Most people would agree that communication requires an author, a work, an audience, and a world.

M. H. Abrams uses these four elements in his famous study of the critical tradition, *The Mirror and the Lamp* (1953), noting that different kinds of criticism emphasize different elements. The rhetorical theorist James Kinneavy, in his *Theory of Discourse* (1981), relates these four elements to the dominant goals or aims of writing: expressive (author), persuasive (audience), referential (world), and literary (work).

World

Work

Author   Audience

When readers view literature *as a mirror of the world*, appreciating how accurately and usefully it captures or imitates the world, then they are employing, Abrams says, a "mimetic" theory of literature. These readers may well be interested also in the author, the audience, or the work itself, but their most important concern is with the work's relationship to the world. When readers focus on *the effects of the work on its audience*, then their approach, in

258

Abrams' terms, is "didactic." *Emphasis on the author* leads to an "expressive" critical stance, and a "formalist" stance highlights *the features of the work itself.*

The work itself is, of course, the focus of New Criticism, which seeks to celebrate those formal features that define great artistic works. New Criticism assumes that the work creates its own world; that what we need to know of the author is captured in the work; and that our own peculiar reactions are irrelevant to the enduring monument of the work itself.

The audience is emphasized by reader-response criticism, which embraces the idea that meaning is something we make. Although a book certainly may exist in a library even if no one reads it, it is not a literary work—it has no meaning—unless there is a reader and a reading.

The author moves to center stage in some biographical criticism, as the work becomes an expression of a particular genius or inspiration; the world provides insight into the author's life and times; and the reader's task is to recover as much as possible of the great mind that created it.

For some historical criticism, the world is ultimately what an individual literary work is about, shedding light on events, ideas, people, and places. Because an author uses his or her own experience, the work may well help readers to understand history in especially vivid ways.

World ➔ Historical Criticism

Work ➔ New Criticism

Author ➔ Biographical Criticism   Audience ➔ Reader–Response Criticism

---

Structuralism seeks to understand those patterns or structures in a work that allow readers to make sense. Structuralism is thus concerned with certain aspects of the relationship between the work and the audience. Poststructuralism is also concerned with this relationship, but it exposes the reversibility, the instability, the arbitrariness of the meanings that playful readers create with the text. Deconstruction might be seen as New Criticism pushed to the point that it becomes its opposite, as a compulsive attention to the text's unity reveals its gaps and differences. Or, deconstruction might be seen as an extreme extension of reader-response criticism, affirming that the reader constructs the meaning of a text by offering the most singular and unexpected readings. Perhaps, in a way, deconstruction is where New Criticism and reader-response criticism, apparently opposites, come together on some other side of the critical globe.

But what is the emphasis of, say, feminist criticism? Which element in the communication model does feminist criticism highlight? The author? Certainly many women writers have been reassessed and recovered. The audience? Yes, the significance of reading as a woman has been an important idea in feminist criticism. The work? Much has been said about whether there is a distinctively feminine style, and if there is, how a text written by a woman differs from a masculine text. We wonder, for instance, whether women authors have tended to gravitate to some genres and not others for social and political reasons, or because of some biological difference? And the world is surely the focus of much feminist criticism, as scholars have explored what literature can tell us about women's history. Perhaps this model's usefulness for feminist criticism lies in sorting out its variety, assessing which element is being privileged in any particular instance of feminist criticism; but there is also a sense in which all feminist criticism is about the world and its relationship to the audience: Feminist critics, I would argue, ultimately read literature in order to reveal bias and to change the world. Thus, feminist criticism, like other kinds of political criticism—Marxist, postcolonial, African American, Latino, Native American, queer theory, and others—focuses on the relationship between the reader and the world.

Psychological or psychoanalytical criticism can stress the mental processes of the author, the reader, or characters in the work. I suppose that psychologists might even use literary works for referential purposes, studying texts empirically to learn about the world of mental processes. So, psychological criticism can fit into Abrams' model at any point except "the work." Criticism that is centered on the relationship between the author's consciousness and the world is usually called "phenomenology," which might be seen as a kind of psychological criticism. Rhetorical criticism, which seems to overlap with psychology in a slightly different way, concentrates on the relationship between the author's persuasive goals and the manipulation of audiences, and so I have mentioned it in the chapter on reader-response criticism.

There are many other things to do with literature that haven't been mentioned here. Bibliographical and textual studies, for instance, look at the work within the context of history. But rather than complicate the model further, let's settle for what we have at this point. I wouldn't want to insist on the accuracy of this model. Someone else might configure things differently. The goal here is simply to give you a way to begin to think about how different approaches relate to one another:

World ➜ Historical Criticism

Phenomenology   Political Criticism

Work ➜ New Criticism

Psychological Criticism   Structuralism, Deconstruction

Author ➜ Biographical Criticism   Audience ➜ Reader–Response Criticism

Rhetorical Criticism

Text Credits

and renewed 1975 by Cleanth Brooks. Reprinted by permission of Houghton Mifflin Harcourt Publishing Company. All rights reserved.; Clampitt, Amy. "Discovery" from A SILENCE OPENS by Amy Clampitt, copyright © 1993 by Amy Clampitt. Used by permission of Alfred A. Knopf, an imprint of the Knopf Doubleday Publishing Group, a division of Penguin Random House LLC. All rights reserved.; Lipking, Lawrence. "The Practice of Theory." *Literary Theories in Praxis*. Ed. Shirley Staton. Philadelphia: University of Pennsylvania Press, 1987, p. 426–40.; Paston, Linda. "Ethics" from WAITING FOR MY LIFE by Linda Pastan. Copyright © 1981 by Linda Pastan. Used by permission of W. W. Norton and Company, Inc. Used by permission of Linda Pastan in care of the Jean V. Naggar Literary Agency, Inc. (permissions@jvnla.com); Yeats, William Butler. "Sailing to Byzantium." Reprinted with the permission of Scribner, a Division of Simon & Schuster, Inc., from THE COLLECTED WORKS OF W. B. YEATS, VOLUME 1: THE POEMS, REVISED by W. B. Yeats, edited by Richard J. Finneran. Copyright © 1928 by The Macmillan Company, renewed 1956 by George Yeats. All rights reserved. **Chapter Six:** Cheever, Benjamin. From "The Letters of John Cheever," edited by Cheever's son, Benjamin. New York: Simon and Schuster, 1988.; Cheever, John. "Reunion" from THE STORIES OF JOHN CHEEVER by John Cheever, copyright © 1978 by John Cheever. Used by permission of Alfred A. Knopf, an imprint of the Knopf Doubleday Publishing Group, a division of Penguin Random House LLC. And used by permission of The Wylie Agency LLC. All rights reserved.; Cheever, John. Excerpts from THE JOURNALS OF JOHN CHEEVER by John Cheever, edited by Robert Gottlieb, copyright © 1990 by Mary Cheever, Susan Cheever, Benjamin Cheever and Federico Cheever. Used by permission of Alfred A. Knopf, an imprint of the Knopf Doubleday Publishing Group, a division of Penguin Random House LLC. And used by permission of The Wylie Agency LLC. All rights reserved.; Cheever, Susan. "Home Before Dark," Boston: Houghton Mifflin Harcourt, 1984.; Donaldson, Scott. "John Cheever: A Biography," New York: Random House, 1988.; Tillyard, E. M. W. "The Elizabethan World Picture," New York: MacMillan, 1944. **Chapter Seven:** Dickinson, Emily, "A Narrow Fellow in the Grass," edited by Mabel Loomis Todd and T.W. Higginson. Published by Roberts Brothers of Boston, 1890.; Moore, Marianne. "O to Be a Dragon," from THE POEMS OF MARIANNE MOORE by Marianne Moore, edited by Grace Schulman, copyright © 2003 by Marianne Craig Moore, Executor of the Estate of Marianne Moore. Used by permission of Viking Books, an imprint of Penguin Publishing Group, a division of Penguin Random House, LLC. **Chapter Eight:** Astell, Mary. "A Serious Proposal to the Ladies," London, 1692. Excerpt reprinted in The Norton Anthology of Literature by Women. Ed. Sandra Gilbert and Susan Gubar. New York: Norton, 1985, p. 113–17.; Emily Dickinson, Emily. "My Life had stood—a Loaded Gun." from THE POEMS OF EMILY DICKINSON: READING EDITION, edited by Ralph W. Franklin, Copyright © 1998, 1999 by the President and Fellows of Harvard College. Copyright © 1951, 1955 by the President and Fellows of Harvard College. Copyright © renewed 1979, 1983 by the President and Fellows of Harvard College. Copyright © 1914, 1918, 1919, 1924, 1929, 1930, 1932, 1935, 1937, 1942 by Martha Dickinson Bianchi. Copyright © 1952, 1957, 1958, 1963, 1965 by Mary L. Hampson.; Schor, Naomi. "Feminist and Gender Studies - Humanities" from *Introduction to Scholarship in Modern Languages and Literatures*, 2nd edition. Modern Languages Association of America, 1992.; Todd, Janet quoted. in Ruthven 17. Ruthven, K. K. "Feminist Literary Studies: An Introduction," Cambridge: Cambridge University Press, 1984.; Wolff, Tobias. "Say Yes" from *Back in the World*, © 1996 Tobias Wolff. Used by Permission. All rights reserved.

Index

Overview of Critical Strategies

Approach	Assumptions
New Criticism (See pages 21–23 and Chapter 3)	1. The work itself should be your focus—not the author's intention, not the reader's response. 2. The purpose of your focus is to explain the work's organic unity—how every feature, large and small, contributes to its meaning. 3. Great literary works are marked by some kind of complexity, as levels of meaning, oppositions, tensions, ironies, and ambiguities are unified.
Reader-Response Criticism (See pages 24–26 and Chapter 4)	1. The reader's response is what counts. We can't know for sure what an author intended, and the text itself is meaningless unless a reader responds. 2. Readers actively create (rather than passively discover) meanings in texts, guided by certain goals and rules that may be personal, or shared with other members of a community. 3. Responding to a text is a process. Descriptions of that process are valuable as one person's response may enrich another's response.
Structuralist and Deconstructive Criticism (See pages 26–28 and Chapter 5)	1. Meaning is made by binary oppositions (happy/sad, man/woman, black/white); and in every binary relationship, one item is favored over the other one. 2. This favoring can be reversed and questioned by imaginative and playful reading. 3. Such reversals and questionings undermine dogmatic thinking, opening up new ideas, suggesting that meaning is ultimately unstable and open-ended.
Historical, Postcolonial, and Cultural Studies (See pages 29–33 and Chapter 6)	1. It matters when and where something was written, and by whom. 2. These important considerations include facts about the author's life and status, the larger history around the author and the work, and he intellectual paradigms available to the author and the readers. 3. Although you must be careful to distinguish literature and "real" life, each can illuminate the other powerfully.
Psychological Criticism (See pages 33–36 and Chapter 7)	1. Creative writing—like dreaming—represents the disguised fulfillment of a repressed wish or fear. 2. Everyone's formative history is different in particulars, but there are basic recurrent patterns of development for most people. These patterns and particulars have lasting effects. 3. In reading literature, we can make educated guesses about what has been repressed and transformed.
Feminist Criticism, Postfeminism, and Queer Theory (See pages 36–39 and Chapter 8)	1. Your interpretation is influenced by your own status, including gender, class, race, sexual preference, religion, and much else. 2. In the production and reception of literature, all people have not had equal access to writing, publishing, and reading. People of color, women, working-class people have often been excluded. 3. Literature is an arena for influencing social change.